"Alice Combs undertook a journey into the world women know little about—the hidden world of products that allow the economy to thrive. In her memoir, Alice is revealed as a creative, courageous and prescient woman and mother who remains humble and honest about her life efforts. The title is aptly drawn from the man's world in which she competed and excelled."

—Dr. Linda Lambert, author of *The Justine Trilogy* and eight books on leadership

"The Lady with Balls, Alice Combs's memoir about her struggles to create a good career for herself in a male-dominated business world, is a page-turner. Alice is such a vivid character! I came to admire her courage and her determination to do what was right for herself and her two girls. The book is very worth reading, a clear reminder of how exceptionally strong women have in recent times made real headway for younger women in the workplace."

—Ida Rae Egli, author,
No Rooms of their Own: Women Writers of Early California, 1848–1869

"In *The Lady With Balls* Alice Combs certainly manages to keep plenty of balls in the air: she launches a successful woman-owned company, lands on her feet after a difficult divorce, finds a happy second marriage after thirteen years of love affairs that weren't, fights off predatory competitors, and deals with difficult employees and the stresses of the life she has chosen. Combs is a tough and determined woman, and this is a very candid book about her life."

—Michael Lipsey Author of *I Thought So – A Book of Epigrams* and
I Thought So Volume 2 – More Original Epigrams

"Alice Combs provides a refreshing and unabashed tale of business-building success that's an endless source of motivation and practical wisdom for any entrepreneur who wants to succeed in the face of over-whelming odds. *The Lady with Balls* is a rip-roaring, can't-put-it-down, roller-coaster ride!"

—John C. Robinson, best-selling author of *Webinars That Sell:
How to Turn Your Online Presentations into Virtual Cash Machines*

May you enjoy Vulcan's success story.
Alice

THE LADY WITH BALLS
A SINGLE MOTHER'S TRIUMPHANT BATTLE IN A MAN'S WORLD

ALICE COMBS

Cypress House

The Lady with Balls: A Single Mother's Triumphant Battle in a Man's World
© 2019 Alice Combs

Cypress House
155 Cypress Street
Fort Bragg CA 95437
www.cypresshouse.com
800-773-7782
Author site: https://ladywithballs.com/

Cover design by Cypress House / Kiersten Hanna
Cover photograph © Michael Combs

Publisher's Cataloging-in-Publication Data

Names:	Combs, Alice, author.
Title:	The lady with balls : a single mother's triumphant battle in a man's world / Alice Combs.
Description:	First edition.	Fort Bragg CA : Cypress House, [2019]
Identifiers:	ISBN: 9780998785417	LCCN: 2019937549
Subjects:	LCSH: Businesswomen–United States–Biography.	Vulcan Wire–History.	Women-owned business enterprises–California–Biography.	Single mothers–United States–Biography.	Recycling industry–California–Biography.	Steel wire industry–California--Biography.	BISAC: BIOGRAPHY & AUTOBIOGRAPHY / Women.	BIOGRAPHY & AUTOBIOGRAPHY / Business.
Classification:	LCC: HD6054.4.U6 C66 2019	DDC: 338/.04092--dc23

Printed in the United States of America

2 4 6 8 9 7 5 3 1

First edition

DEDICATION

To my most enthusiastic cheerleader
and darling husband,
Michael Combs.

And to those of my current and
future offspring who want to learn
about their family tree.

TABLE OF CONTENTS

Part II: Mates of All Kinds, 1979–1989

Part III: Treacherous Waters, 1992–1997

Part IV: Poseidon, 1997–2018

PREFACE

If you really look closely, most overnight successes
took a long time.
—Steve Jobs, founder of Apple Inc.

I penetrated the man's world of 1974, a bastion far stronger then than now. Reality hadn't caught up with Title VII of the Civil Rights Act of 1964, the federal law that prohibits employers from discriminating on the basis of gender, race, color, national origin, and religion.

Forty-three years ago there was no such thing as a laptop, a cell phone, standard email usage, the World Wide Web, Google, or Wikipedia, and most of us had never heard of the embryonic cut-copy-paste options. In those times, the primary form of official communication was through the US Postal Service; even fax and copy machines weren't yet affordable for individuals, let alone small businesses. Above all, crowd funding wasn't an option to obtain working capital.

I was a divorced mother of two young girls, on food stamps, and waitressing but determined to become a college graduate. Upon earning my BA, I was hired by Mervyn's Department Store[1] for their buyers' program, and shortly thereafter fired—because I wasn't "corporate material." My self-esteem took a nosedive, and I never wanted to give another person the power to terminate me, so from my home in the San Francisco Bay Area, I built my own business, selling wire used to bind recyclable waste that formerly was burned or dumped into landfills.

Back then I knew nothing about the recycling process or about the industry's wire needs. I didn't know where discards went; I didn't know that many of them had monetary value. I knew that schools collected used newspapers, and I presumed the only reason was to eliminate the smog that would have been created if they'd been burned in the back-yard incinerators of the '50s. I certainly didn't know that newspapers and other products, besides hay, were baled with wire.

Today, Vulcan, the company I founded, sells $10 million of wire per year.

PART I: THE LAUNCH

1974–1979

CHAPTER 1
DOWN THE HATCH

We hold ourselves back in ways both big and small, by lacking self-confidence, by not raising our hands, and by pulling back when we should be leaning in.
—Sheryl Sandberg, technology executive, activist, author, and billionaire

San Francisco Bay Area, 1978

I hate the way that man holds so much power over me. If he doesn't pay up, it could mean bankruptcy, losing my house, and getting locked up in jail—making my life pointless. If I can't even take care of my kids, what good am I?

I'm so sick of the routine, my having to call "Mr. Important" *after* business hours, so his damn secretary can't shield him from me, and getting him to agree to have the check ready by 11:00 a.m. two days later. This will be my fourth personal collection. I resent the necessity of making the hour-long round-trip from my Dublin home to his Oakland office. Why can't he just send me payment in the mail like everyone else? But the huge loads of wire I sell to Osgood Recycling every couple of months make this miser valuable enough to put up with his shit.

Owning a small business is like playing Russian roulette. Three years ago I had no fear of being one of those four out of five small businesses that, statistics say, implode in the first three to five years. I thought selling this industrial baler wire would be a lucrative piece of cake. I even broke the law to get the working capital I needed to start my business. If I fail and can't pay back my seed money, my life will fall apart like a sandcastle in a tsunami.

I had no idea of the crap I'd have to put up with to support my little girls and myself. It's not an easy balancing act to buy just the right amount of greasy black wire (not too much, not too little); keep after my two fabricating companies (not too lax, not too pushy); calculate pricing above my costs (not too high, not too low); and finally, collect my due from slow-paying customers like Mr. Important. I try to be firm yet genteel.

Thinking positively, after I collect from Osgood today, I'll kill two birds with one stone. With the check in my purse, I'll be meeting a potentially dreamy blind date nearby. Maybe this mystery luncheon will lead to a happily-ever-after life. I'm banking on my dating service to eventually make a good match for me. Fritz and I have been legally separated for five years; it's time I settled down.

I feel attractive in my new pink polyester dress. The skirt is full, but the slinky, shiny fabric enhances my figure, and I've always felt pretty in pink. Once I get my promised check, I should be in a relaxed mood for my hoped-for Prince Charming. I'll stop worrying about paying my bills and fuming about Osgood, the tightwad.

He's like the Wizard of Oz: I only hear his booming voice on the phone and never get to see him. I begrudge my repetitive trek up to his elegant reception room. He's disguised the yellow brick road in his office building with a beautiful, shiny wood stairway. His munchkins will probably be hiding behind all the closed doors when the beautiful Good Witch behind the glass partition smilingly hands me the envelope containing my $5,000.[2]

I'm disgusted that the skinflint is comfortably and expensively cocooned in such opulence. What a contrast to my office, a ten-foot-square former guest bedroom that I share with my part-time helper, Mary, a high school student. *Yet, I'm never late paying my debts.*

"The check isn't ready for me?"

My high-pitched, panicked voice erupts at the perfectly groomed, soft-spoken, emotionless receptionist. How could Osgood renege on the agreement we made only two days ago? I need this five grand to stay in business. It's bad enough that Fritz's meager child support checks are unpredictable. People are counting on my money, and I'm counting on this stingy beast's payment.

I can't wait around. It's nearly noon, and I've got to meet my date at Jack London Square. Who knows, this guy might be *The One.* He sounded so nice over the phone.

"Would you please find Walt Osgood and remind him he promised to have it ready by now?" I say firmly.

The receptionist shakes her head. "I'm sorry. He's in a meeting."

"I don't *care* if he's in a meeting. He promised me his payment would be waiting by eleven o'clock. Now it's a quarter past."

"I can't just interrupt the meeting."

"Well, *I* can't leave without my check." I stomp away. Obsessed with getting my money, I open doors looking for Mr. Jerk. In each office I ask the female occupants, "Do you know where Walt Osgood is?"

By the time I open the third door I'm being followed by a couple of nervous ladies who are saying, "Please come back later. Mr. Osgood is a busy man and mustn't be disturbed."

"Well, *I'm* a busy woman, and *I* don't have time to wait for *my* money," I reply.

Finally I hit pay dirt. I open another door and find about a dozen men, sharply dressed in business suits, seated around the room in horseshoe form. I'll bet these expensive-looking men cost him what would be a fortune to me.

"Who is Walt Osgood?" I demand.

"I'm Walt Osgood," a slight, milquetoast-looking, gray-haired man centered at the far end of the room thunders out as if he's God. He looks too inconsequential to have such a deep, commanding voice.

"Where is my five...thou...zand...doll...*LARS?*" I bark each syllable, and yell the last one.

"It's not here now. You'll get it later."

"You promised me Monday it would be ready at eleven o'clock today."

"That was then, and now is now."

"I want my money *NOW!*" I shout as I hurl my briefcase, purposely just missing him.

All the other men are standing, mouths open. Only my opponent remains seated.

I sit in the nearest newly vacated chair. "Pick that up!" I command Osgood, pointing at my briefcase.

"You pick it up, and get out of here."

"I'm not leaving without my $5,000."

"Then I'm calling the police."

"Good!" I smirk. "Give me your phone, I'll call them for you."

"Not on my dime, you won't." He nods to several henchmen. "Get her out of here."

One man picks up my briefcase and deposits it on my lap. Another two men pick up the chair, with me still in it, and gently carry me out as if I'm a queen on her throne. They carefully put me down at the top of the long, deep, immaculately waxed staircase. Osgood himself, the creepy little man, then lifts me out of the chair. He probably doesn't weigh much more than my 135 pounds.

I don't know if it's deliberate, or he's too weak, or my circle-skirted dress is too slippery, but on the first step, he drops me. I bump down every stair, simultaneously holding my briefcase and keeping my dress over my legs. Upon reaching the ground floor, surprisingly unhurt, I quickly get up and say, with clenched teeth, "See you in court!"

I try to slam the pneumatic door, but it slowly closes as I stomp to the sidewalk.

Determined to sue that despicable jackass, I put a coin in the first pay phone I see and dial my lawyer friend. I'm thankful his secretary puts me right through.

"Hello, Bill. It's Alice Stiller. I think I need you for a lawsuit. I just got tossed down the stairs for refusing to leave the premises of an office until I collected the $5,000 they owe me."

"Are you injured?"

"No, I'm not really hurt—unless I'm too upset to feel anything."

"Alice, you'd be better off spending your time on your business," he says gently. "There wouldn't be much to sue for since you're not injured."

I sigh. "You really think so?"

"Definitely."

"Okay. I guess I'll try to plug away as though nothing happened."

I hope Bill is right. I'll just have to work harder to stay in business now; Mr. Shitbucket will probably try to blackball me. It won't be easy to convince his cohorts that I'm not really a difficult person. My biggest problem, though, is how to get along without that $5,000, which I'm sure he'll never send me. I don't know how I'll manage.

Yikes! I've got just ten minutes to meet my lunch date. I'm not hungry, and now I don't give a damn what this blind date looks like. He could be handsome or ugly, tall or short, skinny or fat—it's all the same to me. He's probably not *The One* anyway.

I wish I could just go home.

Whew! Glad that's over with. I don't remember a word the guy said. I probably bored him by talking nonstop about what just happened to me. Or worse, he probably thinks I'm crazy. I did, after all, interrupt a company meeting and throw a briefcase at the president. I wonder if we'd have had good chemistry if I weren't such a nut case. Unless he's demented, he'll never ask me out again.

I walk into my house feeling glad that Mary's on duty now. She'll be at her desk and, I hope, able to handle the rest of today's business on her own.

She looks up when I come in. "Hi, Alice. Osgood Recycling called about five minutes ago. They said their check is in today's mail, but they never want to do business with us again. I told them I was sorry they felt that way, and there must just be a misunderstanding." Then I said, "I'm sure Alice will clear it up with you when she gets back."

I just nod. Tomorrow I'll tell Mary the whole story; right now I'm emotionally exhausted. I wonder if the secretary was telling the truth about getting the check in the mail. I'm sure she was telling the truth about Osgood Recycling never wanting to do business with me again.

I'm unable to think straight enough to do any work, so I change my clothes and go for a bike ride till Jeanette and Julie get home from school.

Bing! Bing! Bing! Bing!

Damn that alarm! It seems like I *just* feel asleep. I was awake, fretting, into the wee hours. For three years I've worked so hard to build up my company, and only in the last year have I earned a decent living. Now I'll never live down the scene I created in that boardroom. I haven't had a temper tantrum like that since I was seven.

If only I could just peacefully doze for the next thirty hours and then find Osgood's $5,000 in my mailbox. I don't want to face the day, and I've got one of those not-enough-sleep headaches. I feel so out of sorts that I must look like hell. Clearly, I won't be able to concentrate on acting charming and listening to what people say when all I can think about is whether I'm going to have big-time financial worries—let alone how Osgood will sully my reputation with all his acquaintances. I think today I'll hide from everyone except Mary and my Tiny Girls. If I can avoid it, I won't even talk to anyone on the phone.

I'm not up to creating a backup plan about what monetary sacrifices I'll make if "the check is in the mail" is just another lie. Even if I really do get my money, I'll need to find three or four good customers to make up for losing Osgood Recycling. I'll target non-recycling markets—people there will never hear about my crazy outburst.

Until the mail arrives tomorrow or the day after, I won't know if that lowlife really did send a check. I can't afford to goof off like I did yesterday afternoon. Hopefully, paperwork and organizing projects will tamp down all my woeful thoughts, and tomorrow I'll be productive. No more hiding in my shell and doing busywork. I must think positively—*the check will come; the check will come; the check will come*—and work hard to find new customers to fill the slot Mr. Scumbag vacated.

I'm still terrified. It's been some time since I've worried about going to jail. To fill the cash-flow gap, I'll have to cut back on absolutely everything: shoes and clothes, eating out, even fresh meat, fruits, and vegetables. We'll just have to live out of discounted dented cans for a while—half a year at least.

I'll have to adjust my inventory-to-sales with pinpoint accuracy, find only customers who actually pay their bills on time, and, for the first time in my life, I'm going to have to wait to pay all my bills till the very day before I'm slapped with a late penalty. If I do all this, with luck and hard work, I just might be able to remain in business.

My future is like a standing row of dominoes: one wrong move and everything tumbles. For more than a year I've been able to ignore the fact that I obtained my working capital illegally. If I fall behind paying off my ill-gotten second-mortgage debt to Crocker Bank, I'll lose Vulcan and my house, and worst of all, my reputation for being honest.

To think that three years ago I thought baler wire could bring me "easy" money. I thought getting into this business was as good as stumbling into an unclaimed goldmine. *Ha and double ha!* If I can't manage my money problems, I'll feel like the mine contained nothing but fool's gold.

CHAPTER 2
BEFORE BALER WIRE

A successful man is one who can lay a firm founda-
tion with the bricks that others throw at him.
—David Brinkley, journalist, newscaster

Joe Sears peers down at me as I sit stiffly on the austere chair facing him. He's comfortably seated in an executive chair behind an
imposing, uncluttered desk. I can almost hear my heart's rapid beats as
I disbelievingly concentrate on every word of his monologue, which
ends, "So, Alice, I have to conclude that you just aren't management
material, nor are you corporate material. We can't continue paying you
$2.70 an hour[3] as a pre-trainee, but beginning Monday we can keep you
on as a regular sales clerk at $2.35 an hour."

"Then as far as I'm concerned, you're firing me. I certainly didn't
acquire a college degree to work for Mervyn's as a sales clerk paid
barely over minimum wage.[3] Even $2.70 an hour isn't enough to cover
my family living expenses, but I took your ninety-day pre-trainee position because I counted on getting my promised $3.30-an-hour trainee
promotion beginning next week."

"Does that mean you're quitting?" Sears asks matter-of-factly, his
expression deadpan.

"It certainly does!" I reply with a firm nod, immediately rise from
my chair, and turn my back to him. With as much dignity as possible
I take the few steps to his office door, which I'm careful not to slam.
I speed-walk through the store, out the door, and to my car. I shakily
fumble in my purse for the keys, get in quickly, and remain poised.

Not till I reach the privacy of my (fortunately empty) house do I take a deep breath and burst out, "I'm fired!" Copious tears and heaving spasms follow. I wallow in the disappointment of falling off the road that was supposed to lead me to an exciting professional position.

I keep hearing my ex say, in his booming baritone, "You're going to be a loser, just like your mother!" He resented my decision to forgo pink-collar work and continue my college education. I planned on going to law school after completing my BA. He compared my educational efforts to my mother's when, at age forty-three, she attended USC to get her postgraduate Library Science degree, then worked as a librarian for only three years before quitting. Mommy ended up hating her librarian job, but I know I'd have loved being a children's advocate attorney. Later, however, due to financial restraints, I switched tracks and traded my law school plans for work in women's affordable fashion. My objective was to be a buyer.

That dream is now smashed.

Until this fateful Friday the 13th, I'd envisioned a quick run along the path to my goal. I've loved clothes ever since I can remember. After completing my seventh-grade sewing class, one of my favorite pastimes became shopping in fabric stores for patterns and materials to make stylish outfits. When my daughters came along, I made some memorable numbers for them, too. Over the years, I've received many compliments and noticed admiring glances at our attire. My favorite thing about musicals has never been the music but the costumes. I even hoped to become a costume designer, until I realized my drawing skills were inadequate to the task.

I wonder if I'd still be in line to become a Mervyn's clothes buyer if my flat feet, like Daddy's military-exempt feet, didn't ache so much all the time. Too often I purchase new shoes that I really can't afford, always hoping that a different pair of high heels will leave my tootsies in less pain. Eight and a half years ago, the doctor told me to avoid standing for any length of time and delivered the bad news: "Your flat feet will never get better, only worse."

For these past three months I've been standing eight hours a day on Mervyn's far-from-plush carpeting, which hides an unforgiving cement slab. I've stood and folded and refolded clothes. I've stood and talked with shoppers. I've stood and worked the cash register. I've stood and spoken with management. I've stood with my brains in my feet, thinking not much more than *ouch, ouch. Ouch!*

Even though I've felt excruciating pain upon awakening, I've always looked forward to beginning another workday. By the end of the day, however, I'm counting the minutes till quitting time. I'm sure I've smiled a lot less and haven't been as clever as I would've been if those eight hours had been pain-free.

Nonetheless, every agonizing day I've envisioned future success. I've fantasized sitting in an ergonomically designed swivel chair behind an imposing desk and placing stylish clothing orders from my phone. Other times I've pictured myself driving or jetting (first class, of course) to clothing factories and fashion shows where solicitous salespeople greet me. What a glamorous and exciting career I've anticipated.

Done! Over! Forget it!

Fortunately, the girls are still playing at their friends' houses. It's nearly time for Bob to be here to take us all out to dinner, as he does every Friday. I want to be able to cry on his shoulder without upsetting my daughters. Bob will be the perfect person to help me regain my lost self-esteem.

When he arrives, all I can manage is a "Hi, Bob" before tearfully reaching out to him. He holds me, and I tell him the whole story between sobs. He continues to hold me as I vent. Then we sit on the living room couch, cuddling.

"A.M. [short for Alice Marie], that Joe Sears is a very stupid ass not to realize what a valuable contribution you could have made to Mervyn's," he says. "I know what an asset you could be to any business. I'm not an idiot like that imbecile, and I have a great idea that'll be good for you and me both."

Sniffling, I look up. Bob nods his dark, curly-haired head. "Tell you what, A.M. You can help me rebuild my business, Vulcan Metal Joining Consultants. You remember how I told you that Vulcan was formerly a thriving concern for me and my two partners? And the reason that it fell apart was that vindictive ex-wife of mine? She turned my partners against me, and then we three went our separate ways. Because I was the leader, I kept the name and made Vulcan a sole proprietorship, but the business required more work than I could handle alone, so it went downhill. With your help, we can make it a going concern again."

I totally believed Bob's story till two and a half years later, when I inadvertently came across his past tax statements. I then realized there hadn't ever been partners—or a profit. I never confronted Bob about that, however, because by then I felt very grateful to him for having directed me toward what was becoming a profitable venture. Had I known Vulcan's true history beforehand, I never would've attempted to build it back up. I'd probably have taken some low-paid, boring job.

Bob never made my heart go pitter-patter as Fritz and a couple of my high school heartthrobs had. For one, he wasn't tall like all the guys I'd previously fallen for (Fritz was six foot two, so Bob, at five eight, was way too short). Instead of Fritz's lankiness, Bob had a firm, muscular body—at least before he started to add pounds right after he moved in. He had small, beady, dark brown eyes to Fritz's big, round, appealing bluish green. His freckled skin was too light for my taste; I had preferred Fritz's unblemished skin with just a hint of olive tone. And where Fritz's hair was a straight, nondescript brown, Bob's tightly cropped, curly, almost kinky hair was a blackish brown. (I'll always wonder what Bob's hair would've looked like if he hadn't had his ridiculous permanent every three to six months. He sure looked silly sitting under the beauty parlor dryer with curlers all over his head.)

But Bob adored me like no one before—and that counted for a lot. He was my elder by seven years, whereas Fritz was only half a year older than I. Fritz had made me feel like an inept, worthless, over-the-hill thirty-year-old, whereas Bob made me feel like a clever, accomplished young siren. Fritz had no interest in sexually pleasing me, whereas Bob treated me like a princess in bed.

Bob and I met at the Hayward chapter of Toastmasters International in October 1973. (Only the previous month had women been officially admitted. Bob had confided to me that prior to my entrance, another woman had hoped to join, but the men had voted to keep their Hayward chapter a male-only group.) There were about twenty men there, and perhaps because Bob didn't fit my stereotype of a good-looking man, I didn't even notice him at first. Toastmasters was good fun, in part because there was very little homework. In fact, only a couple of people each week were expected to have prepared speeches, meaning that I'd have to invest preparation time in only one out of ten weekly assemblages. The majority of our meeting was spent on two-minute extemporaneous speeches on whatever subject we were given immediately before we had to walk to the podium.

In early January of '74 we were encouraged to bring our children and give them a chance to join in the two-minute speeches. The only children who attended were two boys and my two girls. One youth declined, and the other, after having been coaxed up, stared, terrified, at the audience, and blubbered. The father walked up, lovingly put his arm around the boy, and walked him back to his seat. His son was eight and a half, and my Jeanette was five days short of her eighth birthday.

Nonetheless, Jeanette was gung-ho to have her turn. Her given subject was *Snoopy,* and she appeared very composed as she spoke seriously about the cute little cartoon character. I was very proud of her and felt sorry for her male counterpart. (Little Julie, my youngest, not yet six, wanted no part of speechmaking.)

Shortly after that, I began to notice Bob Brown. He didn't particularly intrigue me, but none of the other men did either—a good thing, because they were all married. Bob's marital separation had begun only a couple of months before mine, so we had in common the fact that we'd both recently become single. During our ten-minute social breaks, I found Bob always standing beside me. Then he began finding excuses to keep me talking in the parking lot after the meeting ended at 8:30 PM, even as I sat in my car with the key in the ignition, sometimes with the motor running.

Usually I tried to rush home because I had to pay my babysitter fifty cents an hour, but on the meeting night that fell during Easter vacation, both my daughters had an overnight at a friend's house, so Bob and I talked in the parking lot till after ten o'clock. Fortunately, I too was on school break—no pressure to complete homework or get up early for class.

The following week, despite the babysitting expense, I let the clock continue ticking long after the meeting ended. When I finally decided I couldn't afford any more time away from home, I courteously tried to end our discussion, but Bob was skillful at prolonging it. Just as I was pleading a final goodbye, he kissed me passionately and started to shake. I was moved by his emotions and held him tightly. Many kisses followed before we finally parted. Bob and I began to date on the weekends, and I was soon sharing my bed with him. One contributing factor was his enthusiasm for my impending college graduation. He kept saying how proud he was of me—such a contrast to Fritz's discouraging and hurtful words. I was also impressed that Bob insisted I go through with the ceremony on June 14 so he could applaud me. With Bob's doctorate in metallurgy, he obviously wasn't intimidated by my mere Bachelor of Arts degree, as I suspected Fritz was, even though he too had a BA.

Bob knows a lot about the strictly enforced OSHA (Occupational Safety and Health Administration)[4] laws. Because these federal regulations are only four years old, and because I'd completed my primary business classes in the sixties, I know nothing about them. Bob, however, has the idea that I should sell consulting services to educate businesspeople about these rulings.

"That sounds way too hard, Bob. I've never sold an intangible—just cookies, candy, and Christmas cards."

"A.M., you're an attractive, intelligent, and personable woman," he replies. "You can sell anything in the world. I know you'll be successful selling my consulting services. I *know* you can do it!" He looks me in the eye. "You sell them via fear, and fear is stronger than a desire for cookies and candy, and definitely Christmas cards. The first part of your sales pitch comes when you tell them the Library of Congress estimates the papers of the OSHA act and related references, if stacked up, would be over thirty feet high.[5] Then you emphasize the impossibility of their reading that while adequately managing their businesses. In the second part of your spiel you tell them about businesses that were ruined due to lack of knowledge of OSHA's complicated laws. Finally, you tell them Dr. Brown can impart what they need to know in far less time than it would take them to study the rules."

"Okay," I say, still a bit doubtful. "I'll give it a try. But how do I start? Where will I go?"

"I have appointments in San Leandro on Tuesday. I'll take you with me and drop you off at some of the nearby small businesses."

I think Bob and I will make a great team. He spends countless hours training me to be a professional salesperson. I've never greeted people with the standard "Hi, how are you?" Bob makes that mandatory for strangers as well as people I've previously met. I'm so fearful of flubbing that I actually write, "Hi, how are you?" as part of my canned script. I add, "Fine, thank you" "My name is Alice Stiller. What's your name?" a phrase I've been using ever since I long ago saw Daddy introduce himself to a next-door neighbor.

Bob also makes a handshake requisite. I've never felt comfortable shaking hands because people often laughingly remark, "Cold hands, warm heart." I hate exposing the clammy coldness of my hands.

For my starting sales pitch I write an overview of what OSHA is, as well as what it can do to businesses ("surprise you with a nasty visit and end up fining you, and sometimes even closing down your business").[6] In order to frighten people who've heretofore been unconcerned, I follow up with documented hardship cases I've carefully memorized.

It's easy to emphasize the lack of time business owners have to learn about all these complicated new laws. It's even easier to recite the various stories about businesses that have been shut down because of OSHA nonadherence. The hard part is getting the right person to listen to my speech.

Often I encounter imperious women protecting their male decision-makers from people who might waste the boss's valuable time. I suspect some are jealous wives and some are jealous mistresses. When I approach one front-desk man, he tells me he's sure the owner won't be interested in any Avon products. Even after I explain my mission, he still refuses to take me seriously and practically shoos me out the door.

Another man, who says he's the manager, tells me that the owner of the business almost never comes in because he's old and sickly; but he suggests I tell him what I'm selling so he can later inform the owner. This is my first chance to give my complete talk. I have so little confidence that I overly thank the fatherly gentleman for listening to me. I don't care that he's negative about his boss's wanting to follow through. I'm just happy he's willing to give me his undivided attention with no interruptions.

With each following full speech, my nervousness decreases. After half a dozen my timidity is replaced with the desire to interest someone enough to make an appointment for Bob's free presentation. My seventh try is rewarded. On a Friday I get Mr. Johnson to make an appointment for the following Tuesday. He and his three partners will attend.

Fritz has the girls this weekend, so Bob spends each of the next two days working nine to ten hours at my house, preparing. Observing Bob poring over his formidable heap of OSHA information, and still reveling in Mr. Johnson's interest, I have high hopes, even expectations, that my efforts will be profitable enough that I'll never again have to work for an employer. Bob persuades me that his free presentation will motivate the owners to employ him for three to five days of workshops at $300 a day.

During Bob's speech, I'm very proud to be connected with him, as he proves extremely well versed and organized, just like he's always been at Toastmasters. He speaks for over two hours and allows a half hour for questions. All four men seem satisfied with his answers.

As the three partners exit the meeting room, Bob hands Mr. Johnson an invoice for $350. I'm as shocked as Mr. Johnson is, because I'd assured him that this first presentation was to be free. Mr. Johnson explains this to Bob who, looking mystified, turns to me and says, "How could you have said that?"

"That's what you told me to say, Bob!" I reply indignantly.

Bob regards me gently but gravely. "I've invested too much work to consider this a free service." Turning back to Mr. Johnson, he says, "I apologize for Alice's misunderstanding."

Embarrassed, I repeat in a high-pitched and louder-than-before tone, "*That's what you told me to say, Bob!*"

"Calm down, Alice," Bob says dismissively. He looks at Mr. Johnson. "Alice is a new salesperson for Vulcan Metal Joining Consultants, and I apologize for her overzealousness." Hardly taking another breath, he follows up with, "Mr. Johnson, you must admit that you and your team learned a lot about the preventive measures you need to take and got satisfactory answers to your many questions, didn't you?"

"Yes, I'll admit that, but this $350 bill comes as a shock," Mr. Johnson says.

"Will you also admit that you'll save thousands of dollars of fines for an investment of only hundreds of dollars of improvements that you now know about thanks to today's dissertation?" Bob presses.

Mr. Johnson sighs. "I'll admit that also," he says resignedly. "We'll write you a check, but I don't want further classes because we'll be too busy and too broke implementing everything we've learned today."

With the check in his hand, after we're out of earshot, Bob exclaims what a great salesperson I am and says he's bursting with pride over my accomplishment. I simultaneously feel horrible and wonderful. Also, I realize for the first time that Bob is dishonest.

I'm too hungry for the confidence buildup I constantly receive from Bob to call him a liar and a cheat and dump him, but I tell him I no longer want to sell consulting services, for three reasons: 1) with my 50 percent share of the $350, and calculating that I've spent about seventy-two hours before I hit pay dirt, I've made only $2.43 an hour, which isn't as much as I can make elsewhere; 2) I don't think I could even have made the $175 had Mr. Johnson realized he would be billed; and 3) I consider the bait-and-switch tactic Bob employed to be immoral. Bob doesn't refute any of my three reasons.

When I tell Bob it's time for me to seriously go job hunting, he quickly says he has another idea: I can sell welding rod—the more standard, everyday kind, not the highly technical stuff he sells. I agree to give that a try. Over lunch, Bob gives me some very elementary lessons about this product, which I've never heard of before.

Now I feel like we're a couple of scam artists, and I had thought we would make a great team. I shouldn't say *team,* though, because although Bob assured me we would split our earnings, I don't receive my share of Mr. Johnson's payment. Instead of giving me my half of the $350, Bob gives me two-dozen roses and effusive praise.

"Honey, to show you how very, *very* proud I am of you, I want to present you with these roses," he says, beaming and holding the flowers toward me.

"Thank you for the pretty roses, Bob. Now may I have my $175?"

"Oh, honey, you know how hard I worked for this $350. Surely you admit I wowed them, didn't I? Now that you don't want to continue the OSHA sales, all the time I invested in it won't be further applied. For all that knowledge I imparted and won't make future money on, it doesn't seem right that I earn only $175."

I swallow my anger and don't bug him further about it. I *do* value his presentation over and above my sales efforts, and besides, between the new clothes he's bought for me and the handful of very expensive meals he's treated both the girls and me to, he's spent far more than $175. Inwardly, however, I fume: *A deal should be a deal. Period!*

I tell Bob that the only way I'll try selling welding rod is if I'm entitled to 100 percent of the profits made from any sales, at least till I average $3 per hour. Then we can renegotiate. Bob agrees, and I'm sure he won't renege because I'm the one who'll make the deliveries and collect the checks.

Bob knows where to buy welding rod at the lowest price, so he makes the purchases. Later, after I cash the checks for my sales, I'll reimburse him only for the amount on his receipts. I wonder if the welding-rod manufacturing company he works for, Wall Colmonoy, sells to this local distributor. If so, I realize that indirectly, via his set salary and/or his commissions, Bob eventually receives a profit from our arrangement.

In the weeks that follow, as he'd done while I made my consulting-service sales attempts, Bob leads me to businesses near his work appointments, where we separate till lunch—which Bob always treats me to, sometimes in conjunction with one of his customers. I become more relaxed in business encounters, and find myself building a great rapport with nearly everyone. Even the women protecting their bosses from time-wasters begin to seem more like friends than obstacles. With my new warm, confident grip, I even enjoy shaking hands.

Despite my 30 percent gross profit, my sales aren't worth my time investment if the quantities I sell are too low. I don't dare raise my prices, especially after one man explains that because he can't justify overpaying for my welding rod from company funds, he has to absorb these purchases out of the petty cash fund. I begin to suspect I receive these low-dollar orders for only two possible reasons: 1) buying from me is more economical than sending even their lowest-paid employee to pick up what I could quickly get for them; or 2) they just enjoy my visits. But the bottom line is that I earn less than the minimum wage of $2 an hour, and I don't anticipate much increase in the near future. *I'll bet the Avon ladies make more than that!*

For the second time I tell Bob I can't make enough money with Vulcan, so I'd better hurry up and make a concerted effort to find a *real* job. At that, Bob comes up with his last new idea: "Ask people what they need that they can't get. Then find it for them."

This baffles me, but I decide to give it a try in conjunction with my welding-rod sales. What harm could it do?

On my seventeenth day of asking people what they can't get, one woman explains that her company needs four very strange gadgets, the description of which is so complicated and foreign to me that I only vaguely understand what I need to find. I carefully write out the detailed requirements and spend more than a full workweek combing through the *Yellow Pages* and calling around. After more than sixty calls, I'm finally able to coordinate the efforts of two small manufacturers. One company says they can fabricate the main part of these gizmos, and the second says they can complete them.

I add together quotes from these two establishments, which roughly total $350 plus tax. Then I add $10 for my driving expense, and double my costs, after which I phone and quote $720 plus tax to the lady who has presented this challenge (the first woman I ever negotiated with via Vulcan). I explain I'll need 50 percent up front. She agrees, and before I place my initial order, I collect the check.

I figure it took me 120 hours to find that customer, get her requirements, research, drive here and there, and handle the paperwork—a significant investment, but this time I ended up making $3 per hour, almost a sufficient wage. I decide to hang in there.

It's been a month since I sold my gizmos, and I'm relieved that my coordination with those two manufacturers worked well enough that I haven't received any complaints, but I also haven't received any more remunerative requests. I decide that for the next five weekdays I'll concentrate on the places where I've at least sold welding rod. All I accomplish are a few paltry sales. I tell Bob that if nothing lucrative happens during the next week, I'll have to delve into alternate employment possibilities.

CHAPTER 3
DISCOVERING BALER WIRE

Keep on going, and the chances are that you will stumble on something, perhaps when you are least expecting it. I never heard of anyone ever stumbling on something sitting down.
—Charles F. Kettering, inventor, engineer, businessman

"Karl, I'd like to sell you more than just welding rod. What do you need that you can't get?"

"Honey, I need baler wire. Even the farmers can't get it."

"C'mon—only farmers use baling wire. What do you really need?"

"Look, sweetie, I'm not kidding. We need baler wire for our scrap. Put on these earplugs and safety glasses, and one of these face masks if you want, and I'll take you into our plant and show you what I mean."

My God! This noisy place smells weird, almost like a giant bakery, but not delicious or like anything is burning, either. "Karl, what is this strange odor?"

"That's the warm paper pulp that makes up our corrugated cardboard, honey. It smells sort of pleasant—almost makes you hungry, doesn't it?"

I've never seen so much activity in my life: All sorts of pounding machines, rows and rows of them. As they drive here and there, little elevated vehicles beep while they almost sweep the floor with steel arms as long as I am tall. Some carry neat stacks of unused cardboard, while others transport enormous bales of torn-up cardboard. The drivers are seated above eye level.

Overhead throughout are sturdy, transparent plastic tubes the diameter of doorways; they contain what look like hundreds of thousands of gargantuan beige moths frantically colliding with each other. This factory reminds me of a bad drug experience I had while anesthetized for a tubal ligation. It's so big and confusing I'd be lost without Karl.

"Look, dear. Here's what I'm talking about."

He shows me an automobile-sized contraption, on each side of which are five black wire spools, dinner-plate size in diameter and the width of a hand; each feeds wire into a horizontal steel channel flanking an enormous block of corrugated cardboard scraps.

Rat-a-tat-tat-tat-tat! I flinch as this sudden racket overpowers all the other earsplitting noises. Karl explains this sound is from two successive operations. First, all five pairs of wire are cut simultaneously, leaving just enough to join on the outer side. An instant later, wheels turn, enabling each wire pair to be twisted tightly together. The wires remain in place on what is now a completed bale, which is released to follow the finished bale ahead of it.

The new bale, twice the size of a hay bale, ends up on a slow-moving conveyor belt. When it reaches the end it falls onto a loosely slatted, square wooden platform atop a huge scale. A man checks the digital weight indicator, which shows 1,003 pounds when I look at it. Then he marks that number on a tag and he attaches it to the bale.

Almost immediately, another man steers the tines of one of the steel-pronged vehicles into the six-inch space between the two levels of the wooden platform, lifts the bale, and maneuvers it outside to join its mates in the backyard.

"Once we accumulate a truckload's worth of bales," Karl says, "they'll be driven to a pulp plant. There the scraps will be mixed with water to become pulp so they can eventually be formed back into cardboard. Just one big circle, doll!"

I look up again, and notice tan cardboard particles flutter down like colossal flakes of dirty snow out of the opening of the clear plastic pipe. Overhead, similar pipes come from other locations before they join the bigger tube and drop into the steel-skirted chamber that produces a future bale.

"So, Karl, in addition to making cardboard sheets, do you take in old, cut-up boxes?"

"Oh, no, dear! We only make the sheets for new boxes. Follow me."

Farther down are conveyor belts with various widths of cardboard, all with rough edges. Thin steel instruments slice off the ragged sides, like trimming excess pie dough, and these cuttings swiftly rise up into those translucent overhead tubes.

"So, if you can get me the wire I need, hon, it'll make your welding-rod sales look microscopic. Also, I'll give you several personal referrals and tell you where another half-dozen similar plants are. We usually order 10,800 pounds, but let's start off with just 3,600. Just be sure it's 12-gage annealed."

"Okay, Karl, I'll start my research on this project so I can get you some wire as fast as possible."

This is going to be quite a project. Well, if I was able to eventually get those weird gizmos for that other company, I guess I'll be able to get this wire for Karl; but if even the farmers can't get baler wire, how will I? I must get it, because this is a hot-ticket item. Onward to my friendly Yellow Pages. *I wish I knew what "12-gage annealed" means.*

I can't believe how easy this is! I find a wire company only five miles from Karl's company, and they'll have my wire ready in two weeks. I still don't know what 12-gage annealed is, but this company has it. *Why doesn't Karl know he can get this stuff in his own backyard?*

All I have to do is rent a truck to pick up the wire and deliver it. Bob will tag along to drive the truck because I've never driven one. What's scary, though, is that I have to front the money for the wire, and neither of us has $1,200 in our checking accounts. Bob has convinced me that it will be okay to pay with a check anyway, if I rush to the bank and deposit my payment as soon as I receive it. He says this procedure even has a name: kiting. *I'll bet it's illegal, but no one will ever find out, so what do I care?*

CHAPTER 4
DESPERATE FOR WORKING CAPITAL

*The ladder of success is best climbed by
stepping on the rungs of opportunity.*
                              —Ayn Rand, writer and philosopher

3:00 PM

"Well, Karl, here's the solution to your problem, and it'll cost you only $1,860.23, including freight and tax."

"Sweetie pie, you impress me, but you need to know we don't pay sales tax on our baler wire."

"But *I* had to pay sales tax. Why can't I pass it on to you?"

"We have a resale license, honey, and you should too if you plan to sell more baler wire to us and the other sheet plants. It's a certificate that exempts us from sales tax because we resell the wire along with our baled corrugated scrap, so there's no way I can pay you sales tax. I'd get in trouble."

I shoot Bob a worried look as he waits in the truck. *Well, thanks to this weird rule, I'm losing more than $100 profit. Now I'll make less than $400 instead of over $500.*

I sigh. "Okay, then you owe only $1,716.65."

"Just send us the bill, honey."

"Oh… I need the money *now*. I had to pay for it today, and—"

"Doll, the only way we can pay COD—cash on delivery—is when we take money out of petty cash, like for the welding rod I've bought from you. We don't even have 500 bucks in our petty cash fund. You need to wait thirty days, actually a little longer."

"That would be catastrophic for me, Karl. Can't you please, please pay me now?"

"I don't know how we can do that, hon."

"Please try to work something out. You can't imagine the problems I'd have if I had to wait thirty days." *Like going to jail for writing a humongous check without available funds!* "If you can't pay me, I probably should take back the wire and return it."

"Okay, sweetie, you win. I'll go to the office and try to get permission from headquarters. Just wait here."

3:43 PM

I never dreamed I wouldn't be paid immediately. I'm going crazy waiting. Karl's been gone over half an hour.

Oh, Karl, please hurry up and show me your smiling face with a big fat check in your hand. If you can't get me a check I'll have to try to return the wire and hope they'll accept it and reimburse me. If they refuse, I'm doomed. Even if they give me a refund, I'll still be out the $34 for the truck. And if you take much longer, we won't be able to return the truck and get to the bank before it closes. Please, Karl, work this out.

Bob is out of the truck and waits with me.

"This is a real mess, isn't it?" I ask him. "He's taking so long."

"Honey, don't worry, it'll work out. It just takes a while for a lowly plant manager like Karl to get through to the powers that be in their ivory towers. Just calm down, okay?"

"But I'm scared to death that this will all blow up in my face. No money in a few more minutes and my kiting will be detected. I might go to jail. No money at all, and definitely jail, unless I can get my money back from Wire-Up."

"A.M., relax!"

It takes a lot of self-control not to pace back and forth. I hate having to stand still when I'm nervous as all get-out. Insomnia is better than this endless wait.

3:51 PM

"Well, doll, I've got your money, but we can never buy from you like this again. The only reason you're getting a check today is because I'm almost desperate. I should have been doing a lot of other things with my time instead of arguing with corporate for your money. If this stuff works and we want more, you'd better count on not getting paid for at least a month next time. Assuming we like your wire and you won't hold us up for COD again, call me in a week."

And I thought this would be so easy! For now, I don't dare relax till I've deposited Karl's check. After that, I've got some head scratching to do.

No longer smiling, Karl curses. "Now to get a forklift for this god-damned wire. Hey, Joe, over here!"

Oh, so that's what those funny-looking vehicles with the big steel tines are. Forklifts!

Tomorrow I'll need to solve a couple of problems: 1) How to get a resale license (*who in the world can tell me?*); and 2) how to manage future sales without getting paid immediately. Obviously, I won't be able to kite checks again, so what the hell can I do?

I'm more desperate for money now than I've ever been. My unemployment pay has run out. It's just two months short of a year since I graduated college, and when the year is up I'll have to begin paying off my student loan—just as Fritz's alimony is ending. In addition to gifts of clothing for me, Bob pays for all our eating out and some of the groceries my food stamps don't cover, but that's not enough to keep me going.

I'm sure I couldn't get a penny out of Daddy; he doesn't think much of Bob, for one, and even if Bob weren't a factor, Daddy knows most startup businesses fail within a few years. I've heard it takes a lot of time and paperwork to get a government small business loan, and I don't have time for monumental red tape.

Somehow, I've got to make this wire thing work; otherwise I'll have to go job-hunting for some low-wage entry-level position. I've already learned that my Bachelor of Political Science degree doesn't give me significant earning clout. Anyway, I couldn't bear to be fired again.

Enough reveries. If I want to sell wire to Karl and his paper-product friends, I have to get some real money, like thousands of dollars. According to my calculations, a wire career could make me $40,000 a year.[7] If I get a job with my low-monetary-value degree, the most I could ever aspire to would be $18,000 annually, and that would be after many years. *No way!* I'd much rather be my own boss, meet new people, and—best of all—make five times as much money as I could at any other job I could get in the near future.

The value of my house has increased a lot since Fritz and I bought it three and a half years ago, and since Fritz got our Lake Tahoe lot, I owe him only $2,000 on the house. A second mortgage, after costs, should net me $16,000. With that, I could pay off Fritz's equity, pay back my $5,000 in family loans, and use the remaining $9,000 to make this venture fly. Perhaps after a few months of successful wire sales I might even get credit from the supplier. Then I could afford to expand my customer base beyond the contacts Karl gives me.

Unfortunately, given my unemployment and record of poverty since Fritz and I separated a year and a half ago, it's unlikely any bank would give me a second mortgage. Even Bob can't help out. He does, however, have a brilliant idea. *Or is it a very stupid idea?*

Bob says I should create a fake W-2 form for 1974 that shows I have a prestigious job and a good salary. He insists the bank will never know it's phony. He says there are blank forms at the post office, and if not, he can find one for me. Then, if they call Vulcan to verify my employment, Bob will attest to the salary and say I'm a great worker. To make all this more believable, he'll get us a phone-answering service so it won't sound as though I work from home.

Bob sure is clever. Never in a million years could I have thought of such a plan, but all this cunning is so shady. It's not in my nature to be dishonest, but I'm backed to the wall, so how else can I proceed? I don't want to lose this opportunity of a lifetime.

I feel as if I've just escaped a jail term for kiting, and now I'm thinking of committing a far more serious crime. I think it's a felony when someone falsifies anything with the US government. Even if the bank doesn't catch it at first, they will later if the business fails and I can't meet the higher mortgage payments. Bob has planted a sordid seed in my brain that may be the answer to my prayers. *But am I listening to a fallen angel?*

I learn there's a California state agency called the Board of Equalization. It's in Hayward, just a half-hour's drive, and that's where I can get a resale license. I also find out that the BOE is where I should turn in the $84 in sales tax I've collected for the welding rod and other stuff I sold. I discover that businesses must pay sales tax on items they use, such as furniture and office supplies, but not on what they resell. They tell me I've been illegally collecting taxes for the sales I made, but the men there like me and think it's funny. They help me fill out the necessary forms and say they're pleased to see me voluntarily pay the money.

I never considered the $84 mine to spend, so I'm *glad* to part with it. I don't even mind having to dig into my emergency stash for the $100 deposit the BOE guys ask of me. Most of all, I'm thrilled to immediately get a seller's permit, what Karl calls a resale license, because now I no longer have to pay sales tax on goods I purchase to resell.

Bob picks up the W-2 form and I fill it out as an employee of Vulcan Metal Joining Consultants with a $40,000 salary. Tomorrow I'll get second-mortgage forms at Crocker Bank; it would be too risky to deal with Valley Bank, where I've always gotten my food stamps. The people there know me; they'd smell a rat (which I'd truly be) if I showed them any kind of document stating that my income last year was $40,000. I still haven't decided if I dare to actually submit this. I might need a couple of nights to sleep on it.

I feel shifty walking into this bank and explaining that I'm interested in a second mortgage on my home. I know I don't deserve the solicitous respect I'm getting, but of course I act as though I do. As I nonchalantly accept the form the friendly loan officer hands me, I'm outwardly confident. Inwardly, I'm cowering.

Even in the privacy of my house, I can't stop feeling like a goddamned crook. Now that I've entered falsehoods on the questionnaire, I've become a member of the low-life crowd. On the other hand, I won't have committed any crime if I just tear up this possible ticket to the penitentiary.

I'll take the chance. I must. But I'm terrified. I can't do anything till Monday, and I might lose my nerve by then. I wish I were religious, so I could pray over this, but what if God told me to forget it and just find a dumb job? *Probably a slow death for me.*

Even though Jeanette and Julie are seven and nine and no longer believe in the Easter Bunny, I've hidden colorful eggs and artfully arranged Easter treats in their lovely baskets. Ever since the girls were two years old, they've had brand-new dresses every Easter. No matter how poor I am, I always budget for their annual frocks.

Until three years ago I enjoyed sewing the girls' new outfits, but since early '72 I've been too preoccupied with school pressures and trying my best to support us all. The girls and I have always loved my creations; nonetheless, the store-bought dresses are gorgeous. Jeanette and Julie are such pretty, feminine little girls, and the three of us laugh in delight as they twirl happily, their lustrous pastel skirts billowing out.

The girls have to go to Fritz's now—he has his visitation for the rest of the weekend—so I don't get to savor the holiday magic for long. Now alone, I debate what to do. One minute I'm sure I'll give Crocker all that false data, and the next I'm sure I'll rip the forms into a million pieces. I hope Bob can steer me away from all this worry. He always does his best to avoid encountering Fritz, so he's gone when the girls get picked up.

I call him as soon as Fritz drives off. "They've gone," I tell him. "I've thought a lot about the Crocker plan. Maybe it's not such a good idea after all."

"Oh, A.M., stop fretting. It'll work out just fine. Trust me. I hope you're looking forward to that nice Easter brunch I promised you."

"Yes, I am. See you when you get here."

I know Bob found my ruminations very tiresome today. He tried every trick in the book to make me feel better, but nothing worked. My brain was and is bedeviled with conflict. *Should I or shouldn't I? Should I or shouldn't I?*

One thing's for sure: if I don't take the plunge and turn in the loan application by tomorrow, I must seriously begin job-hunting. I'm going to do it. Even though I shouldn't, I'll take the chance. *But I know it's wrong.*

This isn't the first Easter I've gone to bed with a guilty conscience. The other time was when I was married to Fritz. Gosh, that was twelve long years ago!

Before we were married, Fritz's friends wanted to treat him to a Tijuana bachelor party. Fritz went to the sinful city with them but declined their offer to pay for a prostitute. His friends didn't cajole him into it; they were just glad to have their wallets safe in his hands while they had some quick sex. After that, they all watched one of Tijuana's many sordid live sex shows.

When Fritz came back and told me about the trip, I had trouble believing what he described. I wanted to see it for myself. After much pestering, he agreed to take me there.

And there we were! The place he took me to, which stunk like dirty ashtrays, had an audience of mostly young men. A Mexican girl who looked far younger than my twenty-one years danced on a small stage in flimsy, baby blue underwear. Without musical accompaniment, she circled round and made sexually suggestive noises. The men howled lasciviously. She invited one of them to join her.

The girl's antics gradually became so vulgar that it seemed like I was in a live porno den. I felt like an idiot for wanting to see that show. I'd thought it would be fun, but it wasn't one bit fun! I felt dirty watching those disgusting people. I looked at my watch and noted that it was three minutes past midnight. That meant I was watching all this sinful stuff on Easter Sunday. "Fritz, it's Easter," I said tearfully. "I'm so ashamed to be here on such a holy day. I want to go home."

"Oh, Alice, you poor, innocent thing." Fritz put his arm around me. "Okay, love. Let's go."

I'll always feel that I dirtied myself by watching live intercourse on stage, but I survived that night relatively unscathed. I hope one day I'll be able to say the same about my shady dealings with Crocker.

CHAPTER 5
RISKING JAIL

I'm a very strong believer in listening and learning from others.
—Ruth Bader Ginsburg, Associate Justice of the Supreme
Court of the United States

I've just committed a felony! God help me if I get caught! Crocker
Bank now has my phony W-2 and credit application. If they unearth
my fraud and notify the IRS, I'll be prosecuted. I'd never be able to
look my parents in the eye again. I couldn't face my friends, either.
They wouldn't want to face me anyway, since I'd be in jail. It's bad
enough that Mommy and Daddy disapprove of my relationship with
Bob; it would be the death of them if I were incarcerated.

Who would take care of my girls? At age fifty-six, Mommy wouldn't
have the energy. Fritz would be incapable and would probably convince
his sister, Elke, to take them. Jeanette and Julie would be ostracized at
school, and the children would taunt them in mean, singsong voices:
"Ha, ha, your mother's a *jayyylbird!*" Even if some kids wanted to
befriend them, their mothers probably wouldn't let them play with the
daughters of a convicted felon.

When I decided to return to college in December 1971, Fritz bellowed, "Alice, you're going to be worthless, just like your mother.
Don't waste your time going to college when you could be making
money at a job."

Those words shredded my heart, but perhaps they were prophetic. I still don't understand why Fritz so resented my return to school. After all, to help him attend college full time when we were first married, I had taken a pink-collar job and put my remaining year and a half for a BA on hold. I'm incredulous that he wasn't proud to finally be able to support me, that he couldn't appreciate my earlier sacrifice, and had no sympathy for the embarrassment I suffered as the only one of all my childhood friends without a degree or a job of substance.

It always irritated me to listen to Fritz make such a big deal of Mommy attending USC for a Library Science certificate at age forty-three and then working only three years as a librarian. He seemed to think that a woman who doesn't work out of the home had no value. If I'd known he held such insane beliefs, I probably wouldn't have married him in the first place.

Mommy never had a desire to work outside the home. Both my mother and grandmother took pride in the fact that their husbands earned enough to support their families in comfort. In their day, the thinking was that a man was a loser if a second income was needed in his household. My parents thought of a woman's education as a touch of class and an insurance policy in the event her husband died or became disabled. The possibility of a woman, or at least little-old Alice Marie, becoming a divorcee with children to support was unthinkable.

Immediately upon graduating from high school, I was expected to acquire a four-year college degree—but only at an inexpensive institution within commuting distance from home. I was also required to finance half of my education. One semester I paid the tuition and my parents paid for books and other supplies; the following semester my parents paid the tuition and I covered the other necessities.

Mommy had my college career all planned out: I would attend Valley State College[8] for the first two years and spend the last two at UCLA—more prestigious and expensive than Northridge. Her idea was that because UCLA was classier and I would then be close to marriage age, I could land a husband there who'd be superior to one I might meet at Northridge. Even though the UCLA round-trip was two hours, I would have to live at home.

I felt sorry for myself because my closest friends—even those who also enrolled at Northridge, less than half an hour away—got to begin their college years in dorms. I yearned for the *real* college experience of living on campus with roommates, but my parents talked endlessly about the heavy financial woes my braces inflicted upon the family, so I didn't dare complain. I lamented being the poor, underprivileged kid in my crowd, but did so silently.

On the other hand, Mommy was determined that her precious son, Robby, would attend and lodge his full four years at only the best university: Cal Tech, a very costly institution. Even though Daddy's income was very good, it would've been a hardship much greater than my braces to finance Robby through four years there. Consequently, Mommy, for the first and only time in her marriage, found the need to bring home some of the bacon—and when she learned that her earlier undergraduate history diploma from the University of Oklahoma didn't qualify her for any good-paying jobs, she concluded that further education was necessary. Hence she returned to academia.

In September 1964, after Mommy's two years at USC (UCLA had told her she was too old, and the law prohibiting age discrimination in education didn't pass until 1975), she became a high school librarian, planning to apply 100 percent of her income to Robby's Cal Tech expenses. Robby performed so well in his freshman year that he earned a full scholarship for his following three undergraduate years, plus for his master's at UC Berkeley.

Mommy hated her job. The only reason she continued to work for another two years after Robby's scholarship made her income unnecessary was that she wanted some money to call her own. Daddy's earnings had always belonged to the family, but Mommy's were what she called "my money," so even though she wasn't exactly Wonder Woman, it was ridiculous to say she was worthless just because she stopped working.

If I'm incarcerated, Fritz will, of course, be proven right about my worthlessness—in fact, I'll be far below his opinion of me.

Unlike Mommy, I had a strong urge to work. I invested the time and money to take the LSAT (Law School Admission Test), and my scores could've gotten me into all but the most elite schools. My strongest discipline was language: I scored in the upper 10 percent. I wanted to be a lawyer as soon as possible, took the maximum recommended pre-law classes, and made the honors list. I planned to go on to law school immediately after I earned my political science degree.

In the end, however, the considerable costs of law school, my mounting debts to Mommy, Daddy, and Robby, my embarrassment at being only a waitress (with tips, making more per hour than I'd briefly made as a legal secretary), and the humiliation of using food stamps all became too much to bear. Maybe I should have forged on despite the obstacles. I guess I was a quitter.

And now I'm a felon—just one who hasn't been caught.

When I walk into the grocery store today, I immediately run into Gary, the produce guy.

"Hi, Gary. What's the best deal in your produce section today?"

"We just got a load of perfect avocados. Look at that price. You can't afford not to buy them, assuming you like avocados."

"I like them, but my youngest daughter will need some coaxing to eat a bite or two."

Gary grins. "What's new, Alice? You still selling welding rod and things people can't get?"

"Not anymore, but I'm real excited about a new product. It's industrial baling ware. Did you know farmers aren't the only ones who use wire for baling?"

He nods. "Sure. I've known that ever since I worked at Albertsons, because they've got a baler. You know, supermarkets all use baler wire for their old boxes."

"No way! Supermarkets aren't big enough to have that kind of operation. Don't try to April Fool me, Gary." I wag a finger at him jokingly.

"I'm not. Our baler doesn't take up much room, and some balers are outdoors, anyway."

"I can't imagine a supermarket baler, indoors *or* outdoors."

"Well, ours is indoors. I'll show you. Follow me."

I've never been in the back room of a supermarket before. It's not as well lit as the grocery aisles. Also, it's eerily quiet, quite a contrast to the background music and faint squeals of shopping carts. I don't hear any talking, either.

Bang! Crash! Rrrr. Clang! Clang! Rattle! Rattle! I jump as the silence is shattered. Have big trucks collided? I hear an earsplitting cacophony—a high-pitched hum contrasted against the clanking of heavy chains. Then, as suddenly as it started, the sound stops, and there's peace again.

I lower my hands from my ears and look at Gary. "What was that hideous noise?"

"That was our baler making a bale. Just keep on walking."

We stroll by all sorts of produce on various slatted wooden platforms like the ones I saw at Owens-Illinois. Others are piled high with big brown boxes containing who knows what.

"Here you go, Alice." Gary points ahead of us.

This baler is about a fourth the size of the one in Karl's sheet plant. There's neither a conveyor belt nor an overhead tube with flying scraps. Near this small baler are flattened used boxes piled nearly two feet high. I also see boxes still in open-container form, nested into several groupings.

A young man is manually loading the flattened boxes into the baler, which has a cubic cavity that stretches from below his waist to above his head. That done, he gets to work on the nested containers; he breaks them down and folds them flat till they make about a two-foot stack. He now inserts this second batch, and the baler looks crammed. Next he pushes a button, setting off those horrible noises again.

"See, Alice? Looks like there aren't as many boxes in there as before the noise, right?" Gary says when the screeching stops. "That's because an upper steel plate descended and squeezed the air pockets out of the corrugated cardboard. What you heard was these rotating gears and moving chains, like your bicycle gears and chains, but much bigger and more powerful—and probably not as well-oiled."

I crane for a closer look. "But where's the wire?"

As Gary points to the floor, I see the operator bend down and pull out a black wire from hundreds of other wires—all contained in a twelve-foot-long stack. The end nearest the baler seems to have one baby-sized head covered with burlap alongside another head of what looks like oily black curls. These are actually thumb-sized wire loops secured by several even twists, which hold together because the wire is so stiff that the twists can't unravel.

The baler guy inserts the blunt end of the wire into a groove above the opening. He spends less than a minute pushing that wire through a channel. It seems that the wire snakes to the back interior of the baler, and continues down and under the block of box material till the blunt end emerges on the other side. The guy continues to push the wire till it's gone nearly full circle, and the blunt end protrudes about three feet toward him.

The young man grabs this bottom end, inserts it into the loop, pulls downward, and twists the wire around itself several times. He repeats the process with two more wires, one to the right of the first wire and one to the left. With all three loosely tied, there's enough slack for a well-muscled man to easily put his arm between the box material and the wire.

He pushes a second button, and with a thump the bale drops onto an adjacent wooden platform. The packed boxes are now nearly back to the size they were in the baler cavity before that awful noise erupted, so the wires now wrap the bale tightly, with not even enough room for a baby's finger.

"See, Alice?" Gary says, pointing. "Now that the upper steel press is no longer pushing down, the boxes got most of their breath back."

Gary's so nice that I'm willing to expose a little more of my ignorance. "What do you call that wooden platform?" I ask him.

"Oh, that's a pallet. We have loads and loads of them outside. Everything that's delivered here is stacked on pallets. This pallet with the new bale will eventually get transferred outdoors. C'mon, I'll take you out the back way."

I trail after him.

"See all those other pallets stacked with bales? Every Monday afternoon a truck picks them up and delivers them to the Albertsons warehouse. Those same trucks deliver our wire, as well as the wire for all the other San Ramon Valley stores, and even some stores as far away as Sacramento and Modesto."

The wheels in my head are turning. "Thank you so much for teaching me all this. I sure would like to sell this kind of baler wire too, but it's so different from the round coils Owens-Illinois uses. Do you have a term for this kind? And how much do these things weigh?"

"I have no idea what the wire weighs, but we call each grouping a bundle, and each wire is a bale tie. Also, they're 14-gage and twelve and a half feet long, with 250 wires to a bundle—if that's any help."

"Yes, that's a great help. Whom would I contact to sell it?"

"Golly, Alice, I don't know. Jake, here in Dublin, just orders it off of a list of items coming from the warehouse. I have no idea who orders for our warehouse. Maybe Norm, our store manager, knows, but he won't be back till day after tomorrow."

Norm and I are buddies. I sure hope he'll know. I'll come back and find out.

If I get the loan, I should have enough money to sell some of this kind of wire too, but even if I end up with $9,000 after paying off my family and Fritz, it might not be enough to buy lots of bale ties before I get paid for them. I wonder if eventually I might get thirty-day credit terms from a bale-tie manufacturer, like Karl's company gets from everyone they buy from. Probably, manufacturers want to see a good credit record.

Besides home mortgages and cars, the only credit Fritz and I had together were three credit cards, none of which we requested. Two were

from gas companies with no limits; the third, a general credit card is-
sued by our bank, had a $500 limit.

It's a good thing I figured out how to combat Fritz's hand-to-mouth
spending habits early in our marriage. In his opinion any money in our
account was immediately spendable, and he had no interest in securing a rainy-day fund. If I'd hidden our money in a cookie jar or any
other physical location, he might have found it, but he's never known
how to balance a checkbook or understand a bank statement, whereas I
mastered our checking account, so I was able to create a *paper* cookie
jar. I made false check entries for our utility bills, always making sure
they weren't much less than two weeks away from the real payments.
Otherwise, I'd have suffered many sleepless nights.

My biggest challenge in this regard came after we moved to the Bay
Area from Southern California. Fritz's new job as a customer service
representative with Crown Zellerbach included our moving costs. In
tow was more than $7,000 from the sale of our home. Fritz, a musician
at heart, wanted to buy an $800 organ. We had horrible arguments over
that. Because there was no way I could hide $7,000, the best I could do
was remind Fritz that we'd need as much as possible for a down payment on a new home. Regardless, he kept on telling me how ridiculous
it was to say we couldn't afford that organ when we had more than
$7,000 just sitting in the bank.

Before Fritz could badger me to death, we bought our Dublin home.
After the down payment, we were so broke that we bought furnishings
from Goodwill and garage and estate sales. Had we spent that $800, I
don't think we could have swung our home deal.

Two years later, Fritz and I separated. At the time, I was doing
weekend typing jobs, and Fritz, who'd foolishly quit his job four weeks
prior, was unemployed. We were down to our last dollars; only our
secret savings—about $300—was left.

On each of the first three days after Fritz moved out, I cashed a $100
check at our Albertsons supermarket, leaving just forty-eight cents over
the service-charge amount. I then drove to the bank to officially close
the account. I wanted to terminate our credit card too, but was worried

that Fritz had recently used it. When he was angry with me he often threatened to purchase something big with this scary plastic money.

School was still out, so I took my girls with me to the bank. We ended up in an enclosed office space with a rectangular table and chairs where we faced a young man and a matronly sourpuss of a woman who did all the talking for the two of them. She was already aware of the first $100 cashed check, and I explained that I'd recently cashed two others, leaving about $3 in the account.

"Do you have your credit card?" she inquired.

"Yes."

"May I see it?" she asked, her face grim.

I took it out of my purse, and before I could hand it to her she reached across the table and grabbed it out of my hand. Then, with a pair of scissors already on the table, she cut it in half.

She glared and wagged her finger at me. "You shouldn't have cashed those checks. You'd better not write any more checks or try to make any new credit card purchases."

Jeanette and Julie were wide-eyed. They'd never seen anyone other than their father treat me so rudely.

Per Karl's instructions, I call him, but he doesn't answer his extension or call me back. I'm hoping no news is good news. I'll call again tomorrow. In the meantime, I've discovered that selling bale ties to supermarkets won't be as easy as selling wire to paper-product manufacturing plants. I spent most of today visiting fifteen supermarkets, but didn't get to speak to a single person who chooses the bale-tie vendor, or to anyone who knows who the authorized purchaser is.

The chain-store employees are allowed to order from only one designated source, a source decided by someone who works in a corporate office. There are three possibilities: 1) the supermarket's warehouse, as is the case with Albertsons, Alpha Beta, and Safeway; 2) a company named United Grocers, which supplies miscellaneous supermarkets; and 3) a recycling company, as is the case with Lucky.

Now back home, I research the *Yellow Pages* and endure many dead-end phone calls. Eventually, I land the names of two decision-makers. Each has an annoying secretary who tells me, "He's in a meeting." Perhaps it's just as well, because I won't have the means to actually sell wire till I get my big wad of cash—and probably not till I prove myself credit-worthy. At least I know now that the company I bought my other type of baler wire from sells bale ties, and they gave me pricing for the kind Albertsons and Alpha Beta use. Safeway has slightly different specifications, and Lucky uses steel strapping—a sort of steel ribbon—rather than bale ties.

Because the big shots I need to speak with have all sealed themselves in vaults, with secretaries guarding every entrance, I'll put my supermarket efforts on hold awhile and see if it might be easier to get through to the recyclers, some of whom apparently supply supermarkets with bale ties. I'm thinking the grocery volume could be greater than the boxboard manufacturers'. The Crocker loan might not suffice for all that business. My need for funds is getting out of hand.

Maybe I should have gone on to law school and disregarded the debts I was piling up. I didn't mind owing my brother, who was already making good money as an engineer. He was so sweet about not charging interest: he said he'd otherwise spend the money, not bank it, so helping me actually forced him to save. I hated to borrow from my parents. It wasn't that I'd have to pay them interest, but that, unlike with Robby, they expected to have control over me and were obviously resentful that they didn't.

Hell, even when I was twenty years old and on the last date I had with Fritz before our wedding day, I had to do the usual: turn off their 1:15 AM alarm, which was set to alert them to begin looking for me if I missed my 1:00 AM curfew. When I was almost twenty, Fritz and his younger sister, Elke, were angry with me, not with my parents, when I had to cut short our New Year's Eve double date one hour past the New Year so as to be home before that damned alarm went off. I felt lucky my parents had added a half hour to my usual curfew. Fritz and Elke both kept repeating, "What's wrong with you? You're over eighteen and don't legally have to obey your parents."

Nothing was wrong with me; I just knew my parents. Had I disobeyed their rules, I'd have been grounded. Then I would've had to choose between being grounded and leaving home. If I'd left home, I'd have been denied the fancy wedding Mommy and I had just begun to plan. I'd also have had to forgo attending college full time because I'd have had to work all day. To celebrate one additional hour of the New Year at such cost would've been ridiculous. I didn't explain all this to Fritz and Elke, because I was disgusted with their tirade over such a small deal. I was also fuming that Fritz had said he was considering breaking up with me for ruining their party plans.

If he'd actually broken up with me for such a stupid reason, I wouldn't have wanted him for a husband, but would I have been strong enough to remain firm if he'd come to me days later, apologized, and begged to renew our engagement? I was infatuated with his baritone voice even before I knew what he looked like.

I first heard Fritz's low, German-accented voice in Western History class. His every word reverberated, overpowering my fellow students' chatter. The next day I realized the voice belonged to a tall, thin, cute boy. It seemed he was speaking to his girlfriend. I lamented that he was already matched with someone, but on the third day I was happy to note that he and the assumed girlfriend weren't sitting together. On the fourth day, he sat near me and asked me a trite question before class began.

As I answered while looking into his big, round eyes, I felt butterflies in my stomach. After the lecture he walked me to my next class, and his voice magically resonated throughout my body. I found out that his name was Fritz, and that we also had a psychology class together. Best of all, I learned that the girl I'd seen him with was an ex-girlfriend with whom he remained friendly.

Fritz and I became regular walking partners, and I expected him to eventually ask me out. One time in an elevator, a young man made a comment indicating that Fritz and I were a couple. I was embarrassed:

my face burned like it was on fire. Even though Fritz didn't blush, he showed his discomfort by staring straight ahead, as if in a trance.

Six weeks later Fritz still hadn't asked to date me, but he continually sat by me and often walked me to my next class, which I knew was out of his way. Then I saw a campus flyer advertising a Vice Versa dance, and, tired of waiting, I boldly asked him to be my escort.

We had great fun slow dancing, but Fritz chose to sit out the fast numbers. I loved to shake, rattle, and roll, but I was only a little disappointed not to be on the dance floor, because I was entranced with Fritz's every word.

I learned, impressed, that a few years earlier Fritz had donated his paper-route money to his financially strapped parents, who spoke limited English, and that, along with Elke, he had insisted early on that everyone speak English inside the family home. He'd wanted to speak it well enough to be promoted to his age-appropriate grade.

Halfway through the evening, Fritz was holding my hand. On the drive home, he told me about a Mexican restaurant that had great tacos, and asked if he could take me there for dinner the next night. He didn't try to kiss me, but I was okay with that—I was overjoyed that he'd finally asked me out.

We enjoyed the tacos, and at the end of that dinner, I proposed a picnic the following weekend. I brought baked chicken, potato chips, carrot and celery sticks, and my homemade chocolate-chip oatmeal cookies. Fritz supplied the sodas. At the end of that date, I felt let down that we still hadn't kissed—but at least, I told myself, we were holding hands often.

I was sure Fritz would want to make out on our fourth date. (In the 1950s and '60s, "making out" meant only repeated kissing.) We went to the drive-in movie, a classic make-out spot. To my bewilderment, however, he made no such attempt.

Our fifth date was another chicken picnic, this time on the beach. Here, at last, Fritz kissed me. Even though he kept his tongue in his mouth, I'd never felt so passionate and fulfilled. Once home, all I could think of was Fritz, Fritz, Fritz. My feelings for him were deeper and more intense than they'd been for any previous boyfriend.

Though I hadn't made any promises to Fritz about being faithful, I decided to break up with my two alternating boyfriends, one a gentlemanly high school sweetheart who'd chosen the Marine Corps over college, and the other a pushy man of twenty-five who'd persuaded my parents that he was only twenty-one. I was relieved to no longer have to argue with him about my decision to keep my virginity till marriage.

On our sixth date Fritz asked, "Alice, do you know about frenching?"

"Yes," I meekly said, thinking, *of course I do.* From then on, Fritz and I made out every chance we got. Sometimes we'd even skip a class—our grades plummeted as a result.

A month later, Fritz surprised me with a white-gold double-pearl ring and asked me to go steady. I was giddy with joy. In the shower I repeatedly sang, *I Enjoy Being a Girl* and *Que Será, Será.*

Months later, Fritz brought up the idea of marriage. *Marriage?* He was only nineteen, and I was just eighteen. I was in love with him, yes, but marriage seemed so distant. I hadn't planned on even thinking about it till I was at least a college junior. We'd each completed only our freshman year. I'd been brought up to think teenage marriages were strictly for the uneducated. Mommy and Daddy had married when they were twenty-one and twenty-six respectively, and Mommy had been only months away from her bachelor's degree.

After dating Fritz for a year, however, I felt so sexually tempted, filled with desire I'd never known before. I fought a guilty conscience for the sexual delights we partook of. The only rule I insisted on was that no part of Fritz was allowed under my tight-fitting panties. He constantly complained about his sexual frustration, which seemed even greater than my own longings. I began to yearn for marriage as a license to abandon my self-imposed restrictions.

We became formally engaged at ages nineteen and twenty, and three months after my twentieth birthday we had a big, romantic white-gown-white-tux wedding. The after-church reception was in my parents' beautifully landscaped half-acre backyard. In the gazebo— festooned with grapevines ripe with purple grapes, producing a sun-dappled shade—a home movie was made of Fritz and me kissing, full of hunger for each other.

I'm still trying to call Karl, but he doesn't return my calls. I presume my wire is working fine, and he's merely waiting till he's down to a two-week supply. I'll call him tomorrow too.

CHAPTER 6
WIRE BREAKING RIGHT AND LEFT

I failed my way to success.
—Thomas Alva Edison

I f the bank is going to uncover my duplicity and refuse me this new loan, it might as well happen sooner than later. My nighttime tossing and turning can't get any worse—even if I'm caught! Enough of my self-pity and fearmongering; I've got to think positively and work as though I'll soon have the operating capital I need. That means it's essential to move forward and try to sell wire to recyclers. First, though, I'll call Karl again.

"Hi, kiddo. Bad news—your wire is breaking right and left. Also, it was a pain to work with because it's loose, not like the neat, tightly wound hundred-pound spools we're used to getting. Those big, loose thousand-pound coils take up so much room next to the baler they get in everybody's way. That's part of why I didn't use it immediately. I also wanted to wait till at least one of our remaining good spools ran out."

Oh, no! My stomach drops.

"You gave us only five of those big coils," he goes on. "You know the baler has ten places for wire, right? But that's not real important for now, though it would've been a pain to figure out where to cut each coil in two." There's a decided frown in his voice. "Even though there's not much room for a forklift, I decided to locate all five of your damn coils on the wall side so I wouldn't have to worry about people not looking down and accidentally tripping on those monsters. If the goddamned wire had worked, we'd have put up with it, but after too many breaks,

I replaced your crap with some of our last spools. I have a suggestion for you: come over and get samples of what we know works and see if you can duplicate it."

"Oh, Karl. I'm so sorry. I'll be right over."

"Actually, make it Tuesday afternoon. I'm especially busy on Fridays and Mondays. Too many people starting vacations on Fridays and sometimes not returning till Tuesday."

Oh, cripes! Karl might want his money back. If he does, I wonder if Wire-Up will refund me. Either way, Karl will want a replacement as soon as possible. If I do qualify for the Crocker loan, I won't see my money for another seventeen days at the earliest; they said at least three weeks, or no sooner than April 21. Probably longer—maybe even more than two months. Karl won't want to wait till then if he's as desperate as he says he is. *What a mess!*

I wonder whether I might have gotten credit if I'd acted as though I expected it. Crocker money or no, I'm going to try for credit from now on. First things first, however: I've got to find wire that'll work. If I don't, I won't be earning a living selling wire. It won't even matter if I'm granted credit and my financing comes through, but there's not much I can do before I get Karl's samples on Tuesday.

With this bad news it's hard to forge on, but I must wash negative thoughts out of my brain. I'll stick to my plan and research recyclers.

Thanks to the phone and the *Yellow Pages,* I've gathered a ton of information. I'm amazed at the full array of recyclables: paper products (not only boxboard but any paper that ends up in a wastebasket); cloth items, including burlap bags, clothes, and rags; metal items from aluminum cans to used-car parts; used tires; plastic bottles; even glass jars and bottles. There seem to be more businesses in the recycling industry than the paper-product manufacturing industry. And even better, they're great! Most of them aren't blocked by people bent on keeping me from contacting the man in charge. Half the time, the owner himself answers the phone. Everyone I spoke to today was pleasant and even seemed to enjoy our brief friendly chat. It was easy to set up four appointments for Monday.

It's been an interesting and potentially productive day, but now I wonder if I should've invested my time in finding companies that test wire instead. Maybe Wire-Up will be able to conduct the necessary tests. If they don't, I'm sure I can find a company that does, but I'll bet they charge a hefty price for the service. That's a depressing thought, since I no longer receive unemployment checks. Fritz is only gradually catching up from his long unemployment, so I can never count on his measly alimony and child-support checks to arrive on time—let alone in the full amounts due. Bob helps me a little, but never for house payments, utilities, gasoline, or the girls' non-food items. Two months from now, in June, my student loan payments will begin and my alimony checks will end. And did Fritz ever resent that alimony!

Dr. Mimi Wells, my pre-law professor, took a personal interest in me. When I told her that Fritz and I were splitting up, she suggested one of her law partners, Sam Shugart, as my divorce attorney. Sam's private office smelled of a combination of new leather furniture and masculine aftershave. The décor was no-frills and modernist, yet luxurious. Behind his desk was an enormous window overlooking Lake Merritt. The walls on either side of that lovely view were covered with elegantly framed certificates lauding his many achievements. The other walls had relaxing outdoor scenes of lakes encircled by trees and mountains speckled with flowers and wildlife.

Sam was about forty, olive-skinned, hirsute, and moderately handsome. He wore a perfect-fitting suit over his large, well-built frame. He seemed a very nice, avuncular man. He nodded while I spoke, as if understanding my emotional pain, and reached for my hand across his desk. His touch was comforting. He explained that it would be best for Fritz and me to come to an out-of-court agreement, so my next meeting with him should include Fritz. He added that if Fritz and I couldn't come to terms, he would represent only me—Fritz would need his own attorney.

Fritz was still unemployed and living with me, so we drove to the meeting together. We checked in with the receptionist, and Sam came out to usher us into his office. First we covered child custody: The girls would be with me Monday through Friday and spend every other week-end with Fritz. Thanks to Fritz's German custom of celebrating only Christmas Eve, we agreed to split Christmas: Fritz would get the girls before Christmas and bring them home to me by 11:00 PM on December 24. We agreed to divide the daylight hours of Easter. Both Fritz and I shrugged in agreement to Sam's suggestion that I remain in the house till our youngest, Julie, turned eighteen, after which I'd either have to sell the house and split the proceeds with Fritz or pay him half the equity. Fritz agreed to pay a reasonable monthly sum for child support once he again became employed, but when alimony came up, the shit hit the fan.

"It's ridiculous to pay you alimony, Alice!" he said, flushing. "You're perfectly capable of getting a good secretarial job. You had a great job before you quit work, and you could have one again if you'd just try."

I shook my head. "Fritz, I had a stupid job. I only took it as a sac-rifice for you, so you could complete your education. Now it's my turn for college. I'm not even a year away from my bachelor's, and less than four years away from my law degree."

"You're crazy if you think I'm going to finance nearly four years of schooling for you!"

Sam cut in, "I see you two are not in accord on this matter. Unfortunately, it looks like I can't represent you both. As I told you earlier, Fritz, should there not be full agreement between you, I'll only be able to represent Alice." He rose to his feet. "I need to discuss some business in private with Alice now, Fritz. May I ask you to step out for a few moments?"

Fritz didn't argue—he seemed relieved to depart.

Sam didn't talk business. As during our first meeting, he stretched out his hand. Happy to have this sympathetic man reach out to me, I gratefully put my hand in his. After giving me a look of empathy, Sam asked, "Do you still love him?"

"No longer as a husband," I said, my eyes glistening. "Only as the father of my children."

Sam nodded solemnly. "Make an appointment to meet me again next week. I'll walk you to the door." He did—and then embraced me and stuck his tongue in my mouth. I was stunned! I never thought a lawyer would do such a thing. Of course, I resisted his stupid kiss, and my eyes must have been bigger than they'd ever been. This Sam was slippery. I was sure Professor Wells would be as shocked by his behavior as I was. I know she wouldn't have recommended him to me otherwise, law partner or not.

A week or so later, Fritz moved out, and shortly thereafter he chose a lawyer who, in conjunction with Slippery Sam, set up a foursome meeting in the indoor area right outside the divorce courtroom. Approaching Sam and me, accompanied by his attorney, Fritz sent loving looks my way; he still wanted to get back together, but I had moved on. We were, however, united in hopes of a congenial out-of-court agreement.

Instead, Fritz and I became silent witnesses to a bloody battle. Fritz's lawyer said I should get a full-time job instead of wasting my time going to college, to which Sam became indignant and started hurling nasty insults at Fritz, calling him a selfish scumbag and an arrogant good-for-nothing. It suddenly dawned on me that I should have spat out some of those same words long ago. *Why had I been so nice?*

The elevator opened, and Sam, still growling words of disgust, took my elbow to guide me in. He continued his tirade until the instant the doors closed, whereupon he smiled and proudly said, "I sure seemed mad, didn't I?"

Several weeks later, we four met in court. This was one of the most depressing days of my life. In the cold, sterile room of judgment, Fritz and I met as spousal failures, inept at working things out and armed with lawyers because Fritz didn't want to pay me any alimony or as much child support as I expected.

Fritz's attorney told the judge Fritz shouldn't have to pay alimony because I was fully capable of getting a good secretarial job, which I'd had in the past. He also said the child support request was exorbitant because Fritz was currently unemployed, and that no financial obligation should be placed on him before he got a job.

Sam told the judge I had given up college to support Fritz so he could get his degree, and now it was my turn for college. He also pointed out that Fritz was flying to Germany for a two-week vacation the following week, despite his lack of employment. Fritz's lawyer replied that Fritz would be visiting his grandmother, who was financing the trip, and that I had not objected to these travel plans. Sam, in a quiet whisper, asked me if this was true, and I nodded affirmatively.

The judge ruled that Fritz had obligations, and that even though I hadn't objected to the trip, Fritz should be working or at least looking for a job. I was awarded the full amount I'd requested.

Even though I got what I wanted, I didn't feel triumphant, only deflated. It hurt terribly that Fritz didn't appreciate the sacrifices I'd made for him during our marriage, and resented my staying home with our daughters after I'd so lovingly supported him. I thought of how I used to fantasize dancing happily to Glen Campbell's *The Everyday Housewife Who Gave Up the Good Life for Me,* and got a lump in my throat knowing Fritz had never identified with that sentiment.

I'll never understand why Fritz disrespected my original decision to be a full-time homemaker and acted as though I should be bringing in money for our family. All my life I had expected to be a stay-at-home mother till my children would no longer benefit from my continued presence. I was never bored taking care of them. I wanted to be there for the first smiles, the first laughter, the first steps—I savored all of those firsts. I wanted to greet my precious little girls with milk and cookies at the end of each school day, and hear all about their teachers and friends. Even before Fritz and I were married, I had figured I wouldn't resume college till my future children became teenagers. I envisioned myself working again no later than their high school graduation.

Fritz begrudged my return to academia even more than he'd earlier begrudged my being a homemaker. He was convinced that I would follow in Mommy's footsteps, barely making use of my education. It was hard to believe that, having known me for over a decade, he could be so blind to how different I was from my mother.

Granted, it was only recently that I'd gotten fired up to become an attorney; however, for Fritz to insist I was wasting my time studying when I should be earning a living as a clerk or secretary was insulting. I could have killed Fritz the day Jeanette asked him why our family didn't go on away-from-home vacations to fun places like so many of her friends' families did. His response was, "Because Mama doesn't have a job, honey."

I swallowed my anger and said nothing. Later, I was even more infuriated when he came home from work to announce that he'd just received a raise and was going to apply the full amount to sailboat lessons. It disgusted me that he thought of his income not as our joint income but as his and his alone. Again, I seethed quietly.

I felt confused when he looked at me with tenderness, as though he still loved me. For the last year or so he hadn't acted as though he loved me; after all, he'd been constantly putting me down with sarcastic, hurtful remarks. How could he think of me as worthless yet adorable at the same time? I no longer yearned to get inside his head as I once had, but I would forever be curious. My former deep love for him was dead, but I missed it. I'd felt such absolute trust in Fritz, such warm affection. Would I ever have that again?

In a great mood after our win in court, Sam tried to cheer me up, but I was numb. I still can't even remember the transition from the courtroom to being naked in his bed. I lay there like a corpse; finally he stopped thrusting and suggested that we do this another time, "When you feel better." Somehow I got my clothes back on and returned home.

<hr />

This is my weekend with the girls. I got Bob to take us all to Steinhart Aquarium in San Francisco. After a good lunch we burned some energy on a walk around Golden Gate Park. The outing helped me get away from my business worries, and we all had a great time. Jeanette and Julie especially enjoyed the many-colored fishes, and I loved the eating-out part—not only lunch but also dinner. Bob knows where the good restaurants are, and it's a relief to be served rather than have to stand on my feet to prepare food and clean up afterward.

At least my love life is settled now that I'm steadily dating Bob. Because he wishes we were married, Bob keeps pushing me to get my official divorce papers, but I'm not about to initiate more paperwork and be stuck with the bill if Fritz won't pay. Also, I never want to face Sam Shugart again. Bob is a jealous guy; he'd probably go ballistic if he knew about Sam's behavior.

This coming Monday will be exactly one week since I committed my crime. I wonder how many days it could take them to discover I'd fudged my W-2. I wish I knew exactly how second-mortgage applications are reviewed, what procedures are employed and in what order, and why some approvals take as little as three weeks and others sixty days or more. To wait sixty days sounds like hellish torture. If, on the other hand, I'm approved in three weeks, I'll be in heaven—even if I go to the devil later.

Money, money, money! If I have to pay for a wire tester—not only for Karl's wire but for the four recyclers' wire, too—I'm going to dig myself into an even deeper hole. If I were smarter, I'd have spent Friday investigating wire testing instead of going off half-cocked to research and contact recyclers. Since I'm so unimpressed that the wire company gave me the wrong stuff, I'd better expand my search to include other suppliers too. At least I can scan the *Yellow Pages* tomorrow, but I'm sure whatever potentials I find will be closed till Monday. Now, because of my Monday recycler appointments and my Tuesday session with Karl, I can't even devote all Monday or Tuesday to those calls.

Even if I can get my money back from Wire-Up, I'll be in a tough spot, since I've spent nearly all the profit. If I can't get a refund from them, I won't be able to satisfy Karl unless or until I get the Crocker loan. If Crocker smells the rat I am, both they and Karl will pursue legal action against me—and then I *will* end up behind bars.

I can, however, still hope to get a refund from Wire-Up, get thirty-day terms for working wire, and be able to sell bale ties. If it's impossible to sell any kind of wire, I won't be able to earn a living independently. Can I put a stop to the Crocker loan process? Will Crocker expect me to pay a penalty for any work they've already done? My head is spinning. Maybe the best scenario would be that Wire-Up refunds my money, I pay Karl back, my venture ends, and I halt the loan. At least then I won't be incarcerated, but the thought of working for someone else again till I'm sixty-five is unbearable!

Today I let the girls enjoy themselves with their friends while I took a few hours to pore over a pile of phone books. I've assembled a short list of companies that manufacture and test wire. I'll call them Tuesday morning, before my afternoon meeting with Karl. I have only six phone numbers, so I should easily complete my inquiries before I eat lunch and take off for Owens-Illinois.

I may have bitten off more than I can chew with this confounded wire venture. I had no idea the wire had to be just right in order to work. It reminds me of "Goldilocks and the Three Bears." If I can find the perfect wire, though, I might be able to earn a damn good living. *If only I could acquire my start-up money honestly.*

Maybe I should've tried to persuade Mommy and Daddy to lend me seed money for this opportunity of a lifetime. They might have acquiesced—with, of course, some strict stipulations that might have been easier to bear than these restless nights. Probably Daddy would only have wanted to constantly check up on my business dealings, but Mommy would likely have insisted I either marry Bob or stop letting him spend the night. I imagine I would clandestinely continue to have him over but be fearful one of the girls would let the cat out of the bag. Mommy's always had rigid ideas about my relationships with the opposite sex.

When we lived in the country in New York, there were no boys around to play with, but that changed right after my tenth birthday, when we relocated to Southern California. From then on, Mommy always exerted heavy control regarding my interactions with males, beginning with forbidding me to wrestle with boys or expose my tiny, undeveloped breasts. Now that I'm a thirty-three-year-old divorcee, she wants to rule my dating life. To comply with her dictates would be too high a price to pay. I just have to be patient and trust that Crocker will approve my loan.

CHAPTER 7
LEARNING THE ROPES

The reason for most business training is that
employees are too lazy to read.
—Michael Lipsey, author of
I Thought So – A Book of Epigrams

What a relief! I just found out Wire-Up will test both Karl's samples and their own wire for free. They told me they'd do the tests as soon as I brought in the samples, which had to be at least twelve inches long. Nonetheless, because Wire-Up's wire was inadequate, I'll call that other manufacturer in South San Francisco. For now, I'd better scoot to my first recycler's appointment.

The place smells like garbage, but I see no garbage anywhere. It appears that little mobile home is the office. There are only sparse patches of grass on the grounds. I wish there were a walkway to that trailer. A man exits the door and heads my way.

"Hi. You must be the lady who called me last week. I'm Tony," he yells as he strides toward me.

I introduce myself, and Tony walks me to his baler. We dodge a few puddles to get there. I'm thankful I wore black shoes rather than white, but I feel my three-inch heels sink into the slushy parts.

The cardboard, whether loose or baled, doesn't get soiled because it's all kept aboveground on pallets under a corrugated tin roof supported by wooden posts. Mud from recent rains surrounds a cement slab on which I see the baler, a laborer, a pallet, and bale ties. The baler is about the same size as Karl's, though Tony uses bale ties, as most of the supermarkets do. His ties, however, are much longer and thicker than any of the supermarkets have. Tony says the specifications are 18 ft. × 12 gage. He tells me what he pays, and seems agreeable to buying wire from me if I can give him a better price.

There's barely enough room on the concrete block for the toiling guy, who seems to be a one-man band. He busily does all the things that have to be done manually in the supermarkets: thread the wire, twist it, push the buttons, drive the forklift, and fold and insert the cardboard.

Tony is very proud of his operation. He gives me details about negotiating prices to pick up his scrap and sell it in bales. He also informs me that he drives his truck for both the pickups and deliveries. He's in the mood to talk longer than I have time for, and I have to almost be rude to say goodbye.

At my next appointment the garbage smell is even more obnoxious than at Tony's, but I tolerate it cheerfully. I approach a tiny, unpainted cement building with a corrugated tin overhead abutment that protects dozens of bales. At least there's a sidewalk next to the paved parkway.

I notice a closed door alongside an open reception window. The owner's wife remains seated while she talks to me through the window as I stand on the raised concrete step below. She explains that her husband had to take off, but suggests I call the office when I'm ready to give them pricing.

I follow her directions and walk over to check out the nearby baler. It's slightly larger than Karl's and uses super-long silver wire with no loops on the ends. The wire looks thicker than the 12-gage at Tony's or what they use at Owens-Illinois. This wire isn't labeled, but the owner's wife has already informed me it's 21 ft. × 11-gage galvanized, straight-and-cut.

The tall, blue-eyed blond worker looks to be twenty-something. He threads the wires through their six channels, then uses an electric hand tool that wraps the two ends together. He takes the time to tell me he never again wants to work with Japanese wire, because it breaks when the hand tool twists it. I try to assure him I don't sell Japanese wire, but he eyes me skeptically. I hope the owner will be more trusting.

The third place also assaults my nasal passages, and has an office just as unimpressive as the last two had. It too is a cement building, but at least it's painted—hunter green. This structure is larger than the previous one. A wall divides the office from the warehouse, which is stacked with bales. A young man who introduces himself as the general manager invites me inside. He says the owner comes in only about once a week, and would be glad to find good wire at a better price.

"I need some fresh air," he says. "Do you want to see the baler?"

"Oh, yes," I say with a smile.

This baler, also slightly larger than Karl's, uses two spools of wire that operate simultaneously. The spools are huge: they make the ones Karl buys look tiny. Dull silver pipe-like spindles support each spool. Both, as with Karl's ten-spool baler, feed automatically. The spools-in-waiting have handwritten labels that indicate weights between 800 and 1,200 pounds. They're also stamped *12 GA GALV HI-TEN*.

The young man, who seems very intelligent, is quite chatty—my favorite kind of person. He tells me he's working toward a college degree by taking night classes. He likes this job because he can sometimes study indoors while the outside automatic machine is baling away. He just has to supervise the forklift guy, answer the phone, do a little paperwork, and troubleshoot any mechanical problems. He says if anything goes wrong on the baler, it emits a loud warning signal, which he immediately responds to.

"Japan acquires as much recycled paper product as possible for manufacturing paper goods because they don't have enough trees to make everything they need for both their own use and for exports," he tells me.

"That's so interesting," I say. Till recently, the only things I knew got recycled were newspapers—and that's only because of school paper drives. I'd never given much thought to where all that used newspaper went to or what it was used for.

He laughs. "Lots more than newspapers, that's for sure."

"I also had no idea how many recyclable items get baled," I admit. "I wonder what percent of recyclables are shipped overseas versus used here in our good old USA."

"I have no idea," he says. "Let me know if you find out!"

Next, at my last visit, I conclude that all recyclers have stinky operations, but it's a relief that this beige shingle-sided building is larger than the others, and that a friendly woman greets me when I step inside. She suggests I walk out to the baler, which is close to their warehouse.

This baler, about the same size as the previous two, uses only one big spool—identical in size to those of the two-spool baler, except the wire here is black rather than silver. Jeff, the man in charge, exudes aloofness and hostility. He speaks perfect English with me, and fluent Spanish with his worker. I see about a dozen of those pipe-like pedestals, bare of wire coils, stacked in two sets. Jeff refers to them as stands. There are two full stands, their labels stamped *12 GA ANNEALED*, with the individual wire weights noted in pen.

Jeff says the price he pays is proprietary information, and after learning the hard way, he prefers not to switch suppliers. He says he recently had to work with some substandard Japanese wire and won't make that mistake again. I try to assure him I don't represent Japanese-made wire, but just like the guy at the second place, Jeff doesn't seem to trust me. I wonder if he's the proprietor, because he speaks with so much authority, but I'm too intimidated to ask.

Back home, I call the South San Francisco manufacturer, E. H. Edwards Wire Rope,[9] to find out if they test wire. I'm referred to Mr. Price, an apparently knowledgeable man, who asks me a lot of questions about the usage. He then offers to test the wire from all five places I'd like to supply, and says that from what I've told him, he thinks his company can probably match their specifications.

"To get other than stand-wire into workable form, you'll have to use a fabricator—one for the coils and another for the wire lengths," Mr. Price explains. "After we test the samples I'll give you a name and phone number for a coiler and a company that forms bale ties."

"That sounds great," I say.

"Why don't I meet you at your office to pick up the samples?" he suggests.

I nearly choke. I can't let him know I'm a one-woman show who works out of her home. After too long a pause, I say, "My boss, Dr.

Brown, isn't in right now. I'll have to talk to him tomorrow before we can schedule a meeting."

Now what do I do? I'm too exhausted to think. I'm glad Bob isn't coming over tonight. I don't even want to discuss this conundrum with him till tomorrow. Knowing Bob, if I can't drum up anything myself, he'll quickly think of something clever.

I know how to deal with Mr. Price: I'll tell him that Dr. Brown wants to observe his operation before we take another chance on getting substandard wire. I'll say he'll need to assess both of the finishing factories. *Problem solved!*

I didn't tell any of the people I met today that I couldn't sell them anything yet; instead, I acted as though I could. I told them I was selling wire to paper-product companies, period. I didn't mention that I've had only one sale, and an unsuccessful one at that.

Now that I've learned my lesson, I at least asked for samples. I also acted as though I understood the words *gage, annealed, galvanized,* and *high-ten.* When I got home I looked them up in the dictionary, but am still a bit confused.

Gage, also spelled *gauge,* is a measurement unit—in this case probably the wire diameter, but I don't quite get it. By studying the different samples, I've at least gotten far enough to figure out that, crazy as it seems, the higher the gage number the skinnier the wire, and the lower the number the fatter the wire. Now I know that industrial balers only take gages in the 11–14 range.

Annealed has two meanings, both with the commonality of heating and then cooling. One end result is to toughen the wire and reduce brittleness, and the other is to temper, which can mean to harden or to soften. I can't figure out if this term for the wire I want to sell means softened to make it less brittle or to make the wire stronger and tougher—or both.

Galvanized, in reference to baler wire, probably doesn't mean "stimulating with an electric current, especially for stimulating psychologically," so it must be the other meaning, "coated with zinc." I'll bet it's the zinc that makes the wire look silver.

I definitely don't understand *high-ten,* and can't find it in my dictionary. The closest thing I find is *high tension,* which means having a high voltage. I was able to touch the high-ten wire, though, so I know it doesn't have a high voltage.

During today's two o'clock appointment with Karl, I listened sympathetically to his griping about my "lousy wire." Then I took cuttings of both his functional and my nonfunctional wire, along with yesterday's samples, to Wire-Up's plant. After their testing I was very disappointed to hear they couldn't get the appropriate wire coiled and ready till a month from now—too late to make Karl happy. Also, my cost would be higher than what I sold the original wire for. I wonder why.

Then Wire-Up gave me even more bad news: their wire price exactly matches what two of the recyclers are already paying. I hope I hid my frustration. I'll bet the recyclers deal directly with Wire-Up. Unless I can do better with E. H. Edwards, I fear I may have hit a dead end with regard to recyclers—especially since none of these businesses seems as desperate for wire as Karl is. Still, even though they don't seem anxious, a couple of them are open to better pricing.

Because of Wire-Up's long lead-time and high prices, I fervently hope E. H. Edwards can supply my immediate need. I need workable, all-American, excellent-quality wire at a good price. I especially need some of the wire to be coiled and some of it cut with loops on one end. Also, it's vital that the coiled wire be ready in two weeks or less. Can all this be done at a price low enough to enable me to be competitive? If not, then this career dream of mine will immediately morph into a nightmare.

When I phoned Mr. Price to make an appointment, we agreed that Bob and I would meet him at his office tomorrow at 10:00. I wish I didn't feel compelled to involve Bob, but I don't feel confident that people will take me seriously without the façade of a man in charge. Bob definitely looks more impressive in his well-tailored business suits than I do in my pantsuits—all but one of them off-the-rack cheapies. Sadly, a businessman is generally more impressive than a businesswoman. Because he's a man, no one ever thinks *he's* trying to sell Avon products. I'm going to try for credit, and I'm sure having Bob at my side will help sway them.

I wish men would take women more seriously. I remember one time when Bob was mentoring me and I accompanied him as his assistant. His contact insisted I remain in the reception area while the two of them went into the manufacturing plant. That goddamned misogynist insisted it wasn't safe enough for women.

Though I was really steamed, I saved my words of anger for Bob's ears alone. He was as sympathetic as a man could be, and told me not to take it personally. I tried, but was nonetheless indignant at this insult.

CHAPTER 8
MY EARLY GO-NOWHERE CAREER

If your ship doesn't come in, swim out to meet it!
—Jonathan Winters, comedian, actor, author, artist

I n less than four months, I went from being a nineteen-year-old college student and unmarried virgin to a twenty-year-old pink-collar bureaucrat and married woman working to put her hubby through college.

My new employer, Atomics International (AI), was a bewildering place. It had a US government contract to work on Space Nuclear Atomic Power (SNAP), meaning satellites—an exciting new concept. There were five big two-story buildings spread over several acres. Most of the offices and other rooms were windowless. Oversized posters of outdoor scenes decorated the walls. The whole complex looked and smelled new.

AI apparently employed a couple thousand people divided among the campus buildings. Each of us had to get a security clearance. New employees couldn't do any important work till they got a second clearance: SECRET. I'd been told that could take six months. In the meantime, unlike permanent engineers and stenographers, uncleared workers other than the typists reported to what was nicknamed the Bull Pen. Typists reported to a room called the Typing Pool.

We who had passed both the typing and the shorthand tests qualified as stenographers, a higher pay grade than the typists. Shorthand came easily to me; in fact, I could copy up to 120 words per minute, and only 80 wpm was required, but stenographers were required to pass the typing test of 45 wpm with no more than three errors. I squeaked by.

Typing had never been easy for me, and a year earlier I'd failed a similar test for a summer job at Daddy's workplace, Douglass Aircraft. I felt horrible. Daddy had always been so proud of me, and I could tell that the gentleman who tactfully informed me that I didn't cut the mustard was very embarrassed because I was Mr. George Dickinson's *precocious* daughter. In all fairness to me, my parents had forbidden me to use the family typewriter till I took a typing class. All my classmates had typing experience with their parents' typewriters.

AI's typewriters were electric, much easier to use than Mommy and Daddy's manual one. What wasn't easy was that we always had a couple of carbons and tissue sheets to deal with. It was a lot of work to erase our main paper and both tissue papers, so we were very unhappy every time we made a mistake—though Wite-Out was helpful for top-sheet errors.

I guessed that most of the jobs at AI were classified SECRET because the new employees didn't have enough work to keep busy. There was a summer program for undergraduate engineers, but they too had little to do. Most of those young men carried neon-colored squirt guns and had fun aiming and sometimes shooting at us young ladies. The college men also got a kick out of twirling us on our swivel chairs and then sending us skittering along a clear path. Because it helped cut the boredom, we took this in friendly stride.

My new stenographer girlfriends and I were slated to be personal secretaries, assigned to one boss each, but that wouldn't happen till we got our SECRET clearances. In the meantime, our shorthand skills weren't needed.

If we weren't having personal conversations, playing cards, or being harassed by the summer engineers, we did occasional typing jobs and were sent on gopher-type errands, to either fill requisitions for various supplies—typing paper, carbons, erasers, or Wite-Out—or deliver or pick up various missives in big manila envelopes.

After delivering a packet to another building, I needed to use the bathroom. I absentmindedly opened the door and saw dozens of urinals—all in use! I shrieked and raced out as if the men were brandishing their penises at me. I didn't recognize a single man—but had any of them recognized *me?* Before, I'd just been embarrassed to be wearing a wedding ring—a sign to everyone that I was sexually active. Now, I was so self-conscious I couldn't look any male employee in the eye.

When I finally got my SECRET clearance, I was assigned to a mild-mannered, medium-sized Japanese man named Mr. Aki Akimoto. There were five sections like Mr. Akimoto's. Each had a secretary and ten men: five engineers and five technicians. Mr. Akimoto's boss was Carter C. Livingston III, a stern, slender, tall guy with graying hair. While the men called each other and all the women by their first names, we women were required to call the six bosses "Mister."

I shared a small office with a very young mother whom I called Pretty Patty. The space was just large enough for two desks and two typewriters. Because we had no windows, we each bought a large window-size poster of our favorite breathtaking outdoor scene to hang by our desk. Unlike in the Bull Pen, we had piles of daily work, but that didn't prevent us from chattering away more than we should.

During my first days I wasn't aware of any female technicians or engineers. Then I spotted Tony, a diminutive young Englishwoman who always drank tea with cream. There was also a good-looking, young, single gentleman named Tony. To avoid confusion, we referred to them as Girl-Tony and Boy-Tony.

The technicians were required to have time cards allocating minutes worked on their various numbered projects. Every week we secretaries had to add up our team's combined hours for each of the multiple job classifications. In addition to having fun with the technicians, who enjoyed bringing me their glue to sniff, I was glad to take over their job of deciding each day's time allocations.

The engineers and our boss gave us typing jobs, which always featured technical jargon and lengthy numbers. Only our direct bosses employed our shorthand skills, usually for dictation of letters, not reports. I enjoyed correcting the spelling and grammar of the engineers' reports, and sort of liked taking dictation and then translating my shorthand into typed letters, but I hated the plain typing, which was more than 90 percent of what I did every day. *Boring!*

One day, Carter C. Livingston III's boss, Mr. Rules—a fairly new addition to the department—called a meeting in which he chastised the engineers for their grammar and spelling errors.

"The secretaries should not have to put up with your sloppiness," he said, glaring around the room.

I stood up. "Excuse me, Mr. Rules. Honestly, I enjoy getting some work that's challenging. I think the engineers should just concentrate on what they do best, and leave the grammar and spelling to us secretaries."

"No more interruptions, please," he replied with a frown.

I got the feeling Mr. Rules resented my remark and disliked me after that day. I didn't care.

Raises weren't subjective. Every time the cost of living increased, we got an automatic raise. Unless we were able to become technicians (so far I hadn't met a female technician) or land some other classification, our only raises would be due to inflation. None of us secretaries objected because we had yet to find any other workplace that could beat our pay.

On campus, both the SECURITY and the SECRET badges displaying our names and photos were to be worn at all times. To enter our home building only the security badge was needed, but to enter our group offices and laboratories we needed the SECRET badge. To make sure all entrants were qualified, a friendly guard sat on a tall stool at an elevated desk. As I walked up to that desk one day, I found a woman I'd never met before joking with the guard and smoking a cigar. She wore a rather low-cut Daisy Mae[10] look-alike blouse, white with half-dollar-size black polka dots and puffed sleeves. Unlike Daisy Mae, however, she had short, dark, tightly curled hair and olive skin.

"Hi, there," she said, and stuck out a hand. "I'm Roz."

I was immediately drawn to this eccentric young woman, and was surprised to learn that she was an engineer. Out of the thousands of employees at AI, she was only the second female engineer I'd met, which made her one in a thousand.

I discovered Roz was three months older than I, and I was flattered that she chose little-old-secretary-me to be her close friend. She came from a part of the Bronx that had a large Jewish population, and she'd spent the previous four years studying at City College of New York. Unlike us San Fernando Valley girls, who'd all been driving cars since age sixteen, Roz, at twenty, still didn't drive.

"Between the subway and the bus, you don't need a car there," she explained.

Roz's inability to drive wasn't her only problem. "Now that I've graduated college, found a good job and a nice place to live for my mother and me, and gotten braces for my teeth, it's time to find a husband," Roz confided to me. "The problem is, I haven't found a single Jewish man I'm interested in dating, let alone marrying, and I don't dare date someone who's not Jewish, because I might fall in love and want to marry him. That would just kill my mother."

I told her I might be able to solve her dilemma. I was carpooling with three single men—two Jews and one Gentile. "Maybe you'll like one of them," I said.

Roz agreed to hang around with me after work during the brief time my carpool friends and I gathered before we headed home. I introduced her to the eligible suitors, immediately dying to know if anything would come of it.

To my delight, just nine months after they'd met, Roz and carpoolman Joe were married. Fritz and I were the only Gentiles invited to the wedding and reception, both at the elegant Bel Air Country Club.

A year later, however, Roz was an unhappy victim of a cutback at AI. She was terminated even though her seniority was greater and her performance was as good as, or perhaps better than, her male coworkers'. The rationale her boss offered was that the man is the family breadwinner and Roz didn't have that responsibility; therefore it made sense to let her go rather than lay off any of the men.

Indignant, Roz realized that with such a send-off she could sue for gender discrimination. We wondered if her boss was unaware of the recently passed Civil Rights Act of 1964.[11] Nonetheless, Roz feared that a lawsuit might backfire, forever typecasting her as a troublemaker. She was seething, but ultimately chose to go out like a lamb despite wanting to roar like a lion.

When AI implemented a reorganization, I lost touch with my first direct boss, Mr. Akimoto. Crawford Meeks, a former engineer under one of Mr. Akimoto's equals, was my new supervisor. I liked Mr. Akimoto, but had always felt distant from him, so I wasn't upset about the change. Mr. Meeks was more personable than Mr. Akimoto and gave whomever he was speaking to his undivided attention. Uncomfortable with being called by his last name, he insisted I call him Crawford. He always smelled like he'd just gotten out of the shower. In his mid-thirties, he was prematurely graying, his salt-and-pepper hair neatly cut in a flattop. He was fairly tall and nearly skinny, with a sharply chiseled face and penetrating eyes accentuated by black raven-wing eyebrows. His eyes, framed by thick, long, black eyelashes, were as sparkly and blue as a doll's. His face was pockmarked, but his eyes drew me in so completely that I stopped noticing the scars.

Our new group was housed in another of the five buildings, and my new workspace, totally open, was large enough for four desks—mine just a few feet outside Crawford's office door. Various secretaries intermittently occupied the one other desk in my area.

Crawford and I developed a warm friendship. I was pleased to work for him: he treated me respectfully and made me feel like an important member of his team. I felt close to Crawford and wanted to be as helpful as possible to him. I worked more speedily than ever at my boring typing in order to find time to devise a much-needed filing system for the many projects.

When I finally put that system into place, Crawford was grateful for how much easier it made document location—for him and those who worked under him. He rewarded me by treating me to lunch outside our complex, but my greatest reward was his praise: "Alice, you aren't meant to be a secretary. I envision you as an executive someday."

I never forgot those encouraging words. They gave me a mental picture of myself becoming a successful woman in the future.

With Roz no longer around, I became close with my two favorite secretaries, Pretty Patty and Sexy Suzie, who was a gorgeous eighteen-year-old. The first time I watched her walk down our corridor, I saw several engineers and technicians find excuses to leave their offices at exactly that moment, or at least stand near their doorways to gaze at her. Suzie carried herself erect and serenely, like a long-legged fashion model. She was dressed like one, too, in a figure-flattering azure suit. She was willowy, with delicate bones, yet she had voluptuous feminine curves, and her long platinum-blonde hair was set in waves. I met her cornflower-blue eyes—framed by black-mascaraed lashes—and she gave me a smile.

I soon found out that Suzie had become pregnant at fifteen and a mother at sixteen. Upon learning of her pregnancy, she'd married the twenty-year-old father-to-be, but they'd divorced shortly before her second child, a boy, was born, just seventeen months after her daughter. The jealous ex-husband was convinced the second baby wasn't his. Despite this accusation, Suzie told me, he was at her birthing bedside, and when she moaned during labor he chided, "Suzie, you deserve this pain." Later, when he realized that the little boy looked like his Mini-Me, he begged Suzie to remarry him, but she'd already moved on—with no regrets.

Of the three of us, I was the only one without a child. For our group's 1964 Christmas party, Suzie organized some dancing entertainment with five of us secretaries. She brought her adorable three-year-old look-alike daughter, Daisy, to an after-hours practice session. When Daisy tried to imitate our dancing, my heart melted and I was smitten with baby fever.

Per my calculations, Fritz would complete his college degree by June of '65 and be able to begin teaching by September. We already lived in and owned (thanks to Daddy co-signing for us) a small three-bedroom starter home. I figured that if I worked up to a month before giving birth, I'd quit just as Fritz began to teach. I asked him if he'd welcome a baby in early October.

"If I get to keep my den," he answered quickly.

Just as quickly I responded, "Then the baby can have my sewing room."

I stopped using my diaphragm on January 7, 1965—substituted for the pill due to the urgings of my anti-pill gynecologist—and immediately became pregnant. I was overjoyed at first, only to become depressed six weeks after conception. Due to my excessive bleeding, the OB-GYN diagnosed a spontaneous abortion, and told me to immediately resume using the diaphragm for at least three months.

A week later, upon taking out my diaphragm, I found a six- or seven-week-old embryo floating in a pool of blood encased by the diaphragm. I was devastated. I spilled the blood into the toilet and saved my dead dream, which I tearfully and lovingly wrapped in Kleenex and put in a small box. I dug a grave next to the vibrant orange, yellow, and purple birds of paradise behind our house, placed the coffin inside it, and covered it with the loose soil, making a small mound.

I kept my diaphragm clean and continued to use it, but one day when I took it out, lo and behold, it was broken.

My doctor gave me a due date of February 12. I knew I'd have the baby long before that, but I deliberately didn't correct him: AI had a corporate rule that banned women from working during their last thirty days of pregnancy, and I wanted to get paid for the six working days everyone would be paid for over the December holidays.

Because I'd taken a junior college trigonometry class, I'd recently received a small raise and bump in my status, and had been transferred to Rocketdyne, an AI affiliate in the Simi Hills. On January 3, 1966, which I believed would be my last working day for at least fifteen to twenty years, I ran up the hill in my high heels, joyous, to punch the time clock.

Five days later, 7-pound, 8-ounce Jeanette was born.

I sure got that wrong about not working till 1981 or 1986. In 1975, just nine years later, to save myself from more brainless work, I literally bet the house on a new career.

CHAPTER 9
CLEAR WEATHER

I thought ambition was viewed as bad, as wrong.
It turns out it's the key to everything.
—Megyn Kelly, former journalist,
political commentator, corporate defense attorney

E. H. Edwards's brick building seems much older than Wire-Up's sales office. It's not dilapidated; it just has some old-fashioned touches, and there's a certain understated elegance about it, whereas Wire-Up's office is plain Jane. Here at Edwards, I feel gravitas in the air.

Mr. Price is all smiles as he introduces himself. "Why, hello, Mrs. Stiller and Dr. Brown. I'm Peter Price. So glad to meet you. Thank you for coming. I hope we can be helpful in matching your wire samples. I see you brought quite a bunch. It's a good thing you've labeled them. May I take these to the lab now? That way I can give you a tour while the technician does his work."

Instead of concentrating on this fascinating place, where every day thousands of miles' worth of wire are created, I can't stop thinking *can they help me or can't they?* I have more regard for the fact that Peter Price is trying to impress us than I do for how interesting the tour is.

When the tour is done, Peter—he's asked us to call him by his first name—invites us into his dark-wood-paneled office. Bob and I sit in comfortable chairs while Peter sits behind an antique desk. He reaches into his inbox and finds a couple papers, which he scans quickly.

"Well, well," he says. "Just as I thought. We can meet all of these specifications. However, as I already told you, Alice, we can't make those small hundred-pound coils or any of the bale ties either, but I'll give you the names and numbers of the two companies that can. Both have trucks that make weekly pickups here, so they could easily transport our wire to their manufacturing plants and return the final product to our loading dock. I can't tell you how much either of them would charge, but I'll write down their contact information. First, I'll write our prices for the various wire specifications." He scribbles some numbers and pushes the sheet toward us. "Here you go."

I quickly reach for this paper before Bob can get it. Instantly, I note that Karl's kind of wire is priced significantly lower than Wire-Up's. Of course, that won't mean much till I get fabricating information from the two other manufacturers.

Peter continues, "Now the coiler, Schultz Manufacturing, is here in South San Francisco, and the bale-tie manufacturer is in Grass Valley. Hopefully, after you get their prices and calculate each of the products, you'll choose to deal with all three of our businesses. Edwards can give you a one-week lead-time—but I can't tell you what kind of lead-time either of the manufacturers will give you."

Trying to be casual, I say, "So, assuming this can all be put together, on the dates my pickups occur, you'll bill me with a thirty-day due date?"

"Oh, of course."

Hallelujah! Praise the Lord! I hope my face doesn't display too much happiness and my heart's not pounding too loudly. This is still scary, though, because my thirty-day cushion with Edwards will expire before my customers pay me. After all, the coiler and the bale-tie company won't be doing their magic the same day they pick up from Edwards. I can pay Edwards promptly enough only if the Crocker loan comes through thirty-seven days from now—and that is very, very iffy.

Peter's next words jolt me from my thoughts. "As you told me, Alice, time is of the essence regarding the coiled wire. Would you like me to call the owner of Schultz Manufacturing to see if he can meet with you shortly? He's only a five-minute drive from here."

The Schultz factory is depressingly dingy—but so what? Mr. Schultz is a little gray-haired man. He says he needs only a week to complete the job, and gives us what seems a reasonable and workable price that includes the coiling and round-trip transport. I silently rejoice that if I match Wire-Up's price for meeting Karl's specs, there's enough room to allow a healthy profit for Vulcan. Also, Mr. Schultz agrees to thirty-day terms.

I race home and immediately call Karl. When I quote a price higher than what I charged for the earlier substandard wire, he doesn't object, but he does want to know when the new wire will arrive.

"In two weeks," I tell him, my neck tensing.

"It'll be tough to wait that long, kiddo," he says. "Can't you try to rush it?"

"I'll do my best, Karl," I say, thinking that I'm powerless to hasten things.

Karl gives me the order.

Yippee! This venture is going to fly.

CHAPTER 10
THE TICKING CLOCK

All progress takes place outside the comfort zone.
—Michael John Bobak, contemporary artist

I'm still high about today's good news, but it's scary that I'll owe Edwards $1,000 by May 16. Even if I get the Crocker loan, it might not fund that early. I was told at the outset that my loan might take over two months to process. That means I might have no working capital till early June. Owens-Illinois might pay me promptly on May 23, but Karl already told me they usually take more than thirty days. If I can't pay on time, I'll be very embarrassed and more nervous than ever. Also, that would create a very bad beginning with Edwards, and if the Crocker loan blows up in my face, the lack of working capital will sink me. At best, I won't end up in jail.

It's so frustrating to know that my parents could easily come up with the $1,000 I might need. Perhaps I can explain the whole situation and ask them for a short-term loan. After all, they'd have been willing to lend me even more than that if I'd gone to law school. Still, I hate the thought of asking them. Who knows what Mommy might demand? She's always made me so uncomfortable about nearly everything. If I hadn't spent so much time at friends' houses, especially Patty's, my childhood would have been dismal.

Thank God for Patty's place, my home away from home.

After we moved to our new Tarzana home, I was very lonely for a girlfriend. The Silver boys, our next-door neighbors, were nice, but it would have been more fun if they were girls. Mommy made such a big deal when I had anything to do with boys. I wasn't allowed to wrestle or play at anything else she thought was unladylike. Also, she expected me to wear special clothes and have an ugly hairdo if I went anywhere with a boy. I hoped when school started I'd find at least one nice girl who didn't live too far away. It was lonely riding my bike by myself.

Then, one day, there was a girl on a pretty blue Schwinn just like mine. She looked just a little older than I. We stared at each other and got off our bikes at the same time.

"Hi," I said. "My name's Alice. What's your name?"

"My name's Patty."

Within minutes, Patty invited me to her house—just blocks away from mine.

"Mom, this is Alice."

"Hi, Alice. I'm Mrs. Horton. Would you like some cookies and milk?"

"That would be very nice, thank you."

I really liked Patty's mother. She and Patty looked a lot alike—pretty and tall, with long, dark brown hair and big brown eyes. The chocolate chip cookies were still warm from the oven. Just walking into their house, the aroma had made me hungry.

I'd never seen a living room so lovely. The furniture was much fancier than ours. Their kitchen and dining room had beautiful glass-topped tables with curved white legs fluted with gold lines. The chairs had matching legs and colorful floral-print cushions. I felt like I was in a castle—even Patty's bedroom looked like it belonged to a princess.

Patty liked visiting my house, and I was especially glad that Mommy liked her. That hadn't always been the case with my friends. In New York, Mommy hated Becky, and couldn't stand Dee-Dee, the only girlfriend I'd had in Venice. After I told Mommy that Dee-Dee snuck her mother's cigarettes, she said I could play with Dee-Dee only at our house. Whenever she came over, Mommy listened to everything we said to each other. I'd learned my lesson; I would never, ever, tell Mommy another thing about a friend she might disapprove of.

Patty's mother never eavesdropped on Patty and me. Mommy liked to barge into my bedroom when Patty visited; she'd knock quickly and then hurry in before there was time to say anything; then she'd either tell us something or ask us a question or get something out of my high-up cupboard, which Mommy said was for her stuff, not mine. Everything in Patty's room was Patty's stuff.

Patty and I spent a lot more time at her house than at mine. One reason, besides Patty's pool, was that Mrs. Horton so often invited me for meals. Mommy almost always allowed me to have lunch or dinner at Patty's, which I usually wasn't invited to until the last minute. Mommy's rule for having a friend eat at our house was that she must know at least a half day ahead, because she never made more than four portions at a time unless she had previous plans. Anyway, Mrs. Horton's food usually tasted better than Mommy's.

Also, at our house children weren't allowed to touch the TV, but Patty was allowed to turn it to anything she wanted. We liked to watch *I Love Lucy* reruns and some weird shows about grown-up people who did silly things, like pretend another man was a lady's husband and another lady was a man's wife. They said it was great fun.

At home it was against the rules to relax our heads on our living room couch and chairs because Mommy didn't want our hair oils to soil the cloth. Mrs. Horton had pretty doilies on her furniture, and we were allowed to put our heads on them. I begged Mommy to get doilies so we could just relax, but she refused.

Patty's mother spent most of her time sitting outdoors by her pool, where she visited with her friends, painted pictures, or cooked. Mommy almost never went outside or had friends over, and she never painted. She was always walking hurriedly back and forth between the kitchen and the bathroom, where she washed her hands till they were red and raw. Between washings she listened to her records or *Arthur Godfrey* or *Art Linkletter* or radio soap operas, read, played solitaire, cooked, or barged in on Patty and me. When neither Robby nor I had friends over, she liked to sing—sometimes with her favorite records and sometimes with the radio. I was used to hearing her sing *Pistol Packin' Mama, Turkey in the Straw,* and *The Big Rock Candy Mountain.*

The school was finally allowing me to skip a half-year, and I was thrilled to be in Patty's A5 class. Patty and I were both smart, and Carolyn, a new friend I met in A5, was smart too. Now we were beginning junior high, seventh through ninth grades. Even seventh-grade girls wore lipstick, and that made me happy, but I was always scared I'd get *scrubbed*—that was what they called it when an older girl smeared her lipstick all over a new seventh-grader. Poor Carolyn got scrubbed, but so far no one had even tried to scrub me. I wondered if it was because I almost always walked with Patty, and I was sure everyone thought Patty was at least an eighth-grader because she was so tall.

Even though we were only in seventh grade, we went to Birmingham High School because the new junior high wasn't ready for us yet. My favorite thing about Birmingham High was that there was a candy store on campus. At lunchtime we could buy as much candy as we wanted, including a new one I'd never known about before, Fire Sticks. They tasted just like the cinnamon coating on candy apples, but they were flat, thick sticks in candy wrappers. They quickly became my favorite, and I wasn't the only one; in fact, so many other kids liked them that unless you got in line early, they'd sell out and you couldn't get any.

Patty and I discovered that the little store we liked to bike to sold Fire Sticks, so we thought up a great plan: We each used a dollar to buy twenty five-cent Fire Sticks, for a total of forty between us. Then we sold them for a dime apiece. For a while, each of us made one dollar every school day. Then the school candy store started buying enough Fire Sticks for everyone, and we were put out of business and saddled with a bunch of extra Fire Sticks. Not before making ten dollars each, though! And, of course, we'd eventually eat the candy ourselves.

I'd gotten boy-crazy by age thirteen, and all my friends had too. Most of us liked sewing class because we were excited to learn how to make our own clothes. Patty and I loved to go to fabric stores, and Daddy even bought me a fancy sewing machine. My friends and I liked to talk on the phone about boys and what we'd wear to school the next day.

I had no phone privacy in my house. There was only one phone, a yellow one with a curly yellow extension cord, and it was plugged into our yellow kitchen-corner wall above a high stool with a red seat cover. Mommy always pretended to be busy, but she listened to every word I said to my friends, and after I hung up she'd criticize the things I'd said.

Then Mommy decided I used the phone too much, so she made a new rule: only three-minute conversations. She would start our white-sand egg timer as soon as I got on the line, and after all the sand had trickled down I had to hang up—except when she was really interested in what I was saying. Then she turned the timer over and allowed me to continue. Once, I think I got to talk for almost half an hour.

When I reached eighth grade, boys started calling me. If Mommy took a message for me from a boy, I wasn't allowed to call him back. Instead, she told the boy to call again at a time she thought I'd be able to come to the phone. One day, Harvey called back exactly when Mommy told him to, and I explained that I'd been in the shower when he'd called earlier.

"Hang up that phone right now!" Mommy demanded.

I was so embarrassed. "I'm sorry, Harvey. Can you call me back in five minutes?"

As soon as I hung up, Mommy said, "Alice Marie, never ever tell a boy you were in the shower. He might picture you naked!"

I was so jealous of Patty, with her not-nosy mother and her bedroom phone, which she didn't even have to pay for. With my babysitting jobs and summer work, I could have easily afforded a phone in my bedroom, but Mommy and Daddy said that would be ridiculous and wouldn't allow it.

I have to admit, though, that Patty and I did a lot of mischievous things with her private phone. We'd scan the phone book, randomly choose strangers to call, and when they answered, we usually began by politely asking if we were speaking to the person listed. Then, acting like a serious grownup, we asked, "Is your refrigerator running?" To those who didn't hang up on us and answered yes, we followed with "Well, go out and catch it!"

We also enjoyed pretending to sell weird food items, such as pickled pig's feet and chocolate-covered ants. Even though I was shy in front of boys, I loved to flirt when no one knew who I was and couldn't see me. Once, after a long conversation, I agreed to meet a guy at the corner of Lindley and Ventura. Of course, I never showed up. I'll always wonder if he did.

I invented my very favorite crank call after Daddy took Robby and me to the circus. I told whoever answered, "I'm the Laughing Hyena Lady from the Barnum and Bailey Circus." Then I'd shriek with laughter till they hung up. Such fun!

CHAPTER 11
PLANNING AHEAD

I never dreamed about success, I worked for it.
—Estée Lauder, businesswoman,
founder of The Estée Lauder Companies, Inc.

Yesterday I tried to get through to the Grass Valley fabricator three times between 4:30 and 5:00. Today I was again unsuccessful, though I called throughout the morning and afternoon. They don't even have an answering machine for messages. I can't believe any business would be so lax about incoming calls.

In the meantime, I scoured phonebooks for more trash and recycling businesses, as well as miscellaneous paper-product manufacturers and various types of publishers. As I've been doing every day, I keep trying to find out who the key supermarket people are, but all this bale-tie user research is a waste of time if Grass Valley's prices turn out too high.

I've slept fairly well lately, except when worry that the Crocker loan might explode creeps into my head, which still happens. Peter Price has convinced me that Edwards's wire will work for Karl, and he had it ready for the coiler yesterday, just as promised. The bale-tie person turned out to be a woman who'd taken over her husband's business after he died. *Aha—another woman in this wire business besides me!*

She gave me a price low enough that I'll be able to charge the recy-clers a little less than Wire-Up does, which means I'm going to make money from this! I've presented my prices to a number of recyclers and garbage companies over the past couple days, and I think I've persuaded nearly all of them that the wire won't be from Japan. Many seem agreeable to buying from me when they need another batch.

The supermarket bureaucracy, though, is still impenetrable.

I realize, assuming the Crocker loan goes through, that Bob and I will need a very explicit business agreement. The most important part for me is that I'm to get $16,000 a year going back to January 1, after which I'll automatically have annual 10 percent raises. Because Bob doesn't mentor me anymore, he won't get a salary, but at the end of every year, presuming he adds $1,000 to my $9,000 investment, he'll get 50 percent of the profits after all expenses, including my salary.

When Bob comes over he's amazed to see the contract. He's willing to invest $1,000 to my planned $9,000—he says he expects more than $1,000 from his tax refund in a month. I value Bob's moral and financial support. He has me tack on a few items that seem fair and logical, but overall he accepts my terms without argument. After we sign and date the partnership agreement, Bob again gives me effusive praise for how well I'm doing in the business world. "Honey," he says, "I'm impressed with your determination. You'll go far."

CHAPTER 12
DISAPPOINTMENTS

Expect the best. Prepare for the worst.
Capitalize on what comes.
—Hinton "Zig" Ziglar, author, salesman,
motivational speaker

Tomorrow will be exactly twenty-one days since I gave Crocker my loan application. I haven't heard a word from them, but with luck I'll find out the loan has cleared and I'll get my working capital. I try to tell myself it'll all work out and that I'm really not a bad person for the lies I've put on paper. I've never purposely done anything illegal before. I've done some bad things, though. The meanest was when I was thirteen, and Patty and I bullied a girl we thought was strange. After her mother caught us and explained how we wouldn't like similar treatment, I felt ashamed, and I've always tried to be good to odd people since.

I drop in on the Crocker staff for the first time since I presented my application. The branch manager tells me it's very rare for a loan to clear in twenty-one days; he has no memory of it ever happening in the three years he's been with Crocker. He says a good average for a second mortgage is around six weeks, but more than eight isn't unusual. Exactly three working days short of seven weeks, May 16, is when my Edwards debt is due. That's not good—and seven weeks or later is dreadful. If it takes the "not unusual" eight weeks, I'll be in *boiling-hot* water. I hide my distress by acting very casual, but I'm scared witless.

If I'm unable to pay either Edwards or the coiler on time, they'll both think of me as a deadbeat and wish they'd never laid eyes on me. In the worst-case scenario, if Crocker sends me to jail for faking my W-2, I might never be able to pay either of them. Then I'll be worse than a deadbeat; I'll be a cheater—and it won't be the first time.

My head was sprouting slimy, screaming, spitting snakes. I no longer had hair or even a body. I had no arms to yank out the writhing, angry, evil-eyed creatures. Finally, thankfully, I was awake, drenched in sweat but at least not screaming. Fritz was still asleep.

I didn't feel the usual relief of knowing this was just a bad dream, because it was true: I *was* a monster. Worse, I was a sinner. I'd broken my marriage vows.

Until the previous December, I'd always felt committed *till death do us part,* but I'd stopped valuing our marriage shortly after Fritz gave me an ultimatum: The girls and I could spend Christmas with him and his family in L.A., hundreds of miles away from my dream Christmas in our new Dublin home in northern California—or be divorced. At the time, divorce was my worst nightmare, so Fritz had gotten his way. I was not only devastated by the death of my Christmas dream but also dreaded spending Christmas Eve in L.A. Baby Herbie would be there, and I couldn't bear to see him.

I never thought I'd attend a teenage wedding, but there I was watching fifteen-year-old Amy in a hypocritical white gown, walking down Muttie and Papa's stairs to marry sixteen-year-old Herb, Fritz's half brother. Amy, nearly six months pregnant, had no regrets. She supposedly loved Herb, and ever since they began making love in the back of Herb's VW Beetle, she'd been hoping for a baby to love. I thought Herb wasn't too thrilled, though. Both kids were exceptionally attractive, and they could easily pass for brother and sister.

Fast-forward a few months to see them as parents with their adorable three-month-old, Herbie, who looked like an amalgam of both parents. All three had blond hair, light skin, true-blue eyes, and cute little noses. Even though I didn't approve of teen marriages, I had to concede that the trio made a winsome family.

Fritz left our Santa Susana home in Southern California to work in the San Francisco Bay Area as a customer service representative with Crown Zellerbach. The company had advised him not to relocate his family for another six months. Shortly before Fritz's five-month mark, however, he was given the go-ahead to move us, but they said to hold off on buying a house up north till his one-year mark.

We were cramped in our new rental home, but Fritz and I were happy to be together as a family again. The last half-year apart seemed to have worn more on Fritz than on me. The good part was that Fritz was nicer to me than usual, even more so than he was during the half-dozen weekends he came back to our Santa Susana home. I wasn't even lonely for a girlfriend, because Suzie from AI now lived only five miles away from us. She had married one of the AI engineers, and he too had a new job up here.

Herbie's mother, Amy, must have felt dismayed that a real baby required far more attention than a doll or a puppy—because she ran away from Herb and Herbie. The only responsibility Herb took was to call his parents. His mother called Fritz, and Fritz called me. He explained the situation and asked, "Are you willing to take care of an abandoned baby boy? Herb and Herbie are at Muttie's, and nobody there can take care of the baby."

I gasped in anguish. "Oh, Fritz, that's horrible! How could Amy just leave?"

"My parents are sure she wasn't even taking good care of him before she left. Muttie says he was always whimpering, hungry, and dirty."

"I couldn't possibly say no. We can be much better parents than your seventeen-year-old brother and his awful sixteen-year-old wife," I said, my eyes moist.

"My parents will drive him up here in four days." Fritz sounded grim but determined.

"Fritz, we'll give him a good home, and this way we'll have our boy. I'll consider him my Mother's Day gift."

The day after Herbie's arrival, I made a doctor's appointment for him. Dr. Cole at Kaiser Hospital told me, "This infant is malnourished. Even though he's over nine months old, he barely has the development of a baby half that age. He should be sitting upright, but he only slumps. He should also be crawling. I'll show you some exercises to strengthen his body, and with those and a good diet he should eventually develop age-appropriate motor skills."

After a few days, Herbie and I were used to each other and were having great fun with the exercises. I had to work on Herbie's arms and legs eight times a day. As I moved his arms the mantra was, "Stretch them out and *clap;* stretch them high and *clap.*" For his leg-strengthening routine I first pumped them vigorously, saying in a high voice, "Kicky, kicky, kicky, kicky." Then I pulled those little developing drumsticks sideways and back, saying in a low voice, "Doodle, doodle, doodle, doooooo." Herbie joined me with giggles, and we became a musical duo, delighted in our partnership.

Herbie no longer looked sad and weary. Just three days earlier, his light blue eyes had looked vacant, and now they sparkled with merriment. His face was no longer sallow and pale; now his cheeks had a healthy pink tinge. Maybe it was all in my mind, but his straw-colored hair seemed to have gained a sheen as well. I realized, though, that I'd need more time to plump him up. Fortunately, there was no problem with his appetite. He never spat anything out, as my first two had done at his age.

The girls were thrilled to have Herbie in the house. He'd taken over Julie's bedroom, and rather than resent having to share a bedroom, the girls appeared to enjoy being packed into a tighter space. Julie, almost two and a half, was no longer the baby, but she didn't seem a bit jealous of her new little brother. She and Jeanette called him "Boobala," an affectionate name they dreamed up for him.

Everything was copacetic till I arrived home from decoupage group one evening and opened the front door to the odious smell of an overripe dirty diaper. Infuriated, I hissed, "Fritz, the whole house stinks! Why didn't you change Herbie's diaper?"

He answered, "You know I don't like to change diapers. It makes me sick to my stomach."

My jaw tightened. "That's no excuse."

"Alice, I shouldn't have to do something that would make me vomit, and you don't *have* to go to your stupid group."

I was outraged by Fritz's selfish attitude—and torn between disturbing Herbie's sleep to change the diaper right away or risk a diaper rash by the following morning. I opted for cleanliness. Fortunately, Herbie continued his peaceful sleep as I changed him. Watching his slumber calmed me.

Our darling family of five had a memorable Father's Day at Roaring Camp, in the Santa Cruz Mountains. All three little ones enjoyed themselves, with not a single bratty outburst. The weather was perfect; we relished the Big Trees Narrow Gauge Railroad Train ride; and the barbecue and fixings were delicious. Fritz called this the happiest day of his life.

One day, Fritz came home from work and informed me that his boss's boss had just given him the go-ahead to buy a house. He wasted no time; he said he'd found a great, affordable four-bedroom on the other side of town, and wanted me to see it right away. The lady across the street, who was commissioned by the owners, trusted Fritz with the key. We gathered the girls and Herbie into our station wagon and drove straight there.

What an adorable house! It was a yellow two-story fronted by a lush green lawn. It was made to look homey, with white shutters and flower boxes. I stepped inside and was charmed immediately. Fritz said the stairs led to two bedrooms, one for us and one for the girls to share; the lower two bedrooms could be for Herbie and for guests.

My mind conjured a joyous scene of early Christmas morning: the girls running out of their bedroom and down the stairs to see what Santa had brought them. Their eyes glittered, awestruck by the beautifully wrapped presents under a fragrant pine dressed with strands of multi-colored blinking lights, shiny balls, and silver tinsel. Awakened by the happy exclamations, I saw our one-and-a-half-year-old Herbie emerge from his downstairs bedroom and toddle toward Jeanette and Julie to catch their enthusiasm.

We gave our future neighbor a good-faith deposit and told her we'd like to move in on August 1.

Fritz and I applied to adopt Herbie. Of course, the paperwork was a real pain. First we had to become official foster parents till Amy had been gone a full year. Then there'd be more forms to fill out. We'd also have to meet social workers in our home.

Herbie now looked so cute and healthy he could've graced the cover of *Beautiful Baby* magazine. Dr. Cole was very pleased with his progress. Herbie had attained his perfect weight and could stand, crawl, smile, and giggle. He didn't walk or talk yet, but the doctor said he was now normally developed and any day we'd hear words and see him toddling. This meant Herbie had made seven months' worth of progress in only two months. I was almost disappointed when Dr. Cole said Herbie was as strong as he should be; I'd miss our exercise program.

Our little family seemed perfect, and I was content to have my baby son. In a quiet moment, when Herbie and I were alone, I told him softly, "I will always take wonderful care of you, and you'll never, *ever* again be neglected. I love you so much."

On Herbie's first birthday, we all sat around the little kitchen table, with Herbie in his attached baby chair. I'd made my usual chocolate butter-cream-frosted, triple-layer yellow birthday cake with raspberry jam between the layers. I could hardly wait to see Herbie open his presents. I'd had great fun buying and wrapping them, and there were more from Fritz's relatives in Germany and Southern California.

Herbie smiled happily as we sang *Happy Birthday.* We'd finished our cake, and I was about to hand Herbie a big, beribboned box.

Ring. Ring.

I grabbed the phone, expecting a birthday call from one of Fritz's people.

"Hi, Alice. This is Amy. Herb and I are back together. We want to pick Herbie up next week. Herbie will be having a brother or sister, because I'm pregnant again."

"Oh."

"Please tell Herbie 'happy birthday' for me."

I had to get out of there. I dropped the phone. As I sprinted out the door, breathless, I yelled back to Fritz, "Amy's back with Herb and wants to take Herbie away." I raced across the grass onto the sidewalk and wailed, "She wants my baby! She wants my baby!" I don't know how many times I yelled it as I ran around the block, oblivious of who might hear or what they might think.

As I approached home I stopped screaming and wept quietly. Shuddering with every breath, I walked into the house and looked at everyone else still seated in the kitchen. Fritz glanced at me, slumped forward, and dropped his head onto the table.

Phoning various agencies and authorities, I ascertained that my word alone that Amy was an unfit mother wasn't enough to prevent her from taking Herbie. To protect him, Fritz's parents would have to present written testimony, not only against Amy but also against their son. I telephoned to inform them of all this, and they said they didn't want to testify against Herb. I begged them to reconsider. They responded by saying Amy needed another chance. I told them I couldn't imagine Amy being a good mother for Herbie. I reminded them of Dr. Cole's diagnosis. They said they wouldn't testify against their Herb. I hung up and called them ugly names.

I called Fritz at work and asked him to reason with his parents. He agreed with his parents that Amy had probably learned her lesson and needed another chance. He said his mother had had enough stress and he didn't want to add to it. Then he demanded that I not bother her further.

I hung up full of resentment for Fritz, his parents, and above all, Amy and Herb.

After another rough night, I came up with an idea: I told Fritz we should kidnap Herbie and fly our family to Germany. Fritz said that was crazy. I pleaded with him to consider it. He told me to stop talking nonsense and just let all this go.

I at least got sympathy from my mother and my girlfriend, Suzie, but I still felt alone. Hungry for more empathy, I made a final Kaiser appointment with Dr. Cole. When I saw him, he acted like a best friend and wrote me a prescription for Valium. I became aware that taking the pills during the day was horrible—they only made me more depressed, though they helped me sleep at night. I no longer felt joy when I was with Herbie. I felt I was letting him down. Still, I tried to act cheerful around him, even as I wept inside and tried to stop loving him.

I was so sad. If not for Jeanette and Julie, Valium or no, I might have committed suicide.

The black day was here. I awoke the previous night so agitated that I woke Fritz to tell him about my horrible nightmare: Herb and Amy had arrived with no baby paraphernalia and only thirty-five cents between them. I was worried that Herbie would starve to death. Fritz tried to comfort me, but I was inconsolable.

I had packed several sturdy bags full of diapers, clothes, bedding, toys, and nutritious food, and I'd made sure Herbie had eaten the healthiest lunch possible. He was still at the kitchen table, and my eyes continually moved back and forth from him to the clock ticking dreadfully on the wall.

They're here! My heart dropped into my stomach. Through the window I saw Fritz greet them as they emerged from their tiny VW. Amy entered the house first, smiling at Herbie. She picked him up out of his highchair, and thanked me for taking good care of him.

Like a robot, I said, "You're welcome."

Our once-again family of four watched them drive away. When they were out of sight, Fritz formed a handholding, rotating circle with the girls and me. His unspoken message seemed to be that we were now a solid family of four, but in my mind we were broken. Heart pained and throat constricted, I vowed silently to be strong for my daughters.

We had split the cost of a U-Haul with the family moving into our former temporary home. Fritz and the new male tenant helped each other with the heavy lifting. The woman had children, but her friend was babysitting them. Of course, I told her all about Herbie, and she was very compassionate.

I'd never been so glad to be busy. Our new house was 1,800 square feet and felt huge. I'd never dreamed we would have such a big, wonderful house—four bedrooms and two full baths. The kitchen was tiny, with no room for a table, but a high breakfast counter backed the stove and divided the kitchen from the dining room, from which our sunken family room was just a step down.

The fenced-in backyard had an adorable playhouse the size of a small bedroom. The peaked roof, yellow shingles on the sides, and white trim were styled just like the main house. Enthralled with this new abode all their own, Jeanette and Julie furnished it with a tiny dining set and miniature tableware for their dolls and stuffed animals.

We could barely afford all this, so we'd be house-poor till Fritz got a raise. As it was, we'd have to go cheap on any additional furnishings—the only shopping we'd do for a while would be at thrift stores, flea markets, and garage sales.

Fritz's mother phoned to give us what she thought was good news about Herbie. She said he was getting enough food because he was now so strong that when he was hungry he wailed too loudly to be ignored. *It's good news that a one-year-old is compelled to make a ruckus in order to be fed? Hell, he never had to do that with me!* At first he'd been too weak to even whimper for food. By the time he was strong enough to cry, he'd already grown accustomed to getting all the food he needed. The only reason he'd ever acted up in our house was to get out of his crib or to get a particular toy.

Mommy and Daddy came to visit. Fritz and I made our guestroom very inviting. There was a gold-trimmed white bed and dresser set from a garage sale, and the flower-patterned bedspread it came with looked good as new. Wood shutters painted a bright white framed the room's large, long window. It looked out on our well-kept backyard lawn, which led to big light and dark pink oleander bushes against the fence. My folks, especially Mommy, were impressed with our home. "Alice Marie, I'm so happy for you," she said.

With a lump in my throat, I replied, "I'd rather be in the tiny, cramped temporary home with Herbie than in this big beautiful house without him," then changed the subject.

Now that we were settled, I had a welcome distraction from grief: my girlhood friend, Linda, was getting married to Mr. Right. The wedding would be the Saturday after Thanksgiving. Linda had chosen me as her matron of honor, and Jeanette was to be her flower girl. Linda had trusted me to pick out patterns and fabrics and sew both our dresses. I was also going to decoupage her wedding invitation as my wedding gift.

I didn't know whom this wedding was better for, Linda or me. It felt good to be back in the church where Fritz and I were married. It was the nicest day I'd had since just before Amy phoned me on Herbie's birthday. Linda was a lovely bride, and her new husband was a handsome, friendly man.

Jeanette walked down the aisle with perfect poise, and I was so happy she'd been honored with this glamorous little-girl role. I only hoped tiny Julie would have the same privilege at some future time. Julie didn't seem to envy Jeanette, and later was delighted when Linda gave her a festively wrapped box containing a little yellow ducky jigsaw puzzle. Jeanette's gift was an embossed pink faux-silk purse. Neither girl wished she had received the other's gift, thank God.

The wedding behind us, we visited Fritz's parents. While the girls and three of their cousins played in another room, Fritz's family and I sat around the coffee table. I was in a big soft chair facing the sofa, where Muttie sat between Fritz and his sister Elke. Papa and Elke's husband sat on comfy chairs on either side of me. We were all relaxed after another of Muttie's tasty German meals.

Out of the blue, Muttie said, "Fritzie, you will be back here for Christmas, won't you?"

"No," I said quickly. "We'll be in our Dublin house."

"Hold on, Alice," Fritz said. "We've always spent Christmas with my family except for the time we were stationed in Fort Hood, and that was only because I couldn't get enough leave."

My stomach clenched. "But, Fritz, we have the perfect place for Christmas. Ever since I first saw it, I've looked forward to spending Christmas there. Also, I can't bear to see Herbie yet. I need more time."

Muttie nearly jumped out of her chair. "What! You should be glad to see Herbie. I thought you missed him so much."

"That's the problem," I said, my eyes burning. "I miss him too much, and it makes me too sad to think of him with a mother like Amy."

"Oh, Herbie is getting enough food now," Muttie said. "You should see him, Alice. He's nice and plump."

"Plump isn't that great. Is he fed nutritiously? Is he fed without having to demand food?"

"What does it matter?" She waved a dismissive hand in the air. "He's strong and he's growing."

"Well, those things matter to me," I said, heart pounding. "And I can't believe he's loved enough by a mother who once ran away from him for months. I simply can't handle seeing him, knowing I'm helpless to attend to his needs."

Now Papa joined in: "Family is more important than anything. The family must be together for Christmas."

"Yes, Alice, think of family," Elke chimed in.

"Alice, we need to be here for Christmas," Fritz said, his voice firm. "Remember, we're a family."

Close to tears, I pleaded, "Fritz, don't you understand?"

"I understand that our family being together for Christmas is more important than you think it is. We just have to be here." His jaw was set.

"I really don't want to be here on Christmas, Fritz."

Everyone glared angrily at me. I doubted I'd get any sympathy if I added, "Please don't force me to watch Herbie with those two loathsome people." Instead I said, "I'm still trying to heal. Please don't reopen my wound."

Obviously stone deaf to this, they continued to glare at me.

They don't give a shit! They're heartless! In my mind I heard a broken record of *The Farmer in the Dell* with endless repeats of "the cheese stands alone, the cheese stands alone." I had never felt so lonely. Even my husband was against me.

Previously, I'd always enjoyed Christmas Eve with Fritz's family. Now I was there only because I didn't want a divorce. My heart felt no joy, only angst.

Herb came in first, followed by Amy, ready to pop out another unfortunate babe. Herbie was in her arms. He was fat enough, true, but his coloring was sickly, and he looked sad and didn't talk. He gave me a blank look.

Amy was nice to me and gave me a recent photo of Herbie. I thanked her, to which she graciously replied, "You deserve it." I hoped silently that I didn't deserve the fact that Herbie looked no happier or healthier in the photo.

Fortunately, Herbie and his inadequate child-parents had to leave early. Herb and Amy said their good-byes, Herbie in tow. I had managed to put on fake smiles the whole time, but as the door closed behind them, I broke down.

Fritz put his hands on my shoulders. "Stop that, Alice. Don't ruin Christmas for everybody—I mean it!"

I had nowhere else to turn, so I clung to him, still sobbing. He continued to speak sternly to me. Even though I kept holding on to him, I began to *hate* this husband.

Christmas Eve had been an even worse nightmare than I'd feared it would be. Five months earlier, Herbie had been my bouncing, bubbly baby. Since then, every drop of healthy red blood and happiness I'd infused him with had been drained away. Even his brain cells seemed to have deteriorated. Dr. Cole had said he should be talking any day, yet I hadn't heard a word out of him. *Biology be damned! Why do the courts hold the law above common sense?*

Our legal system is cold and cruel. Who made the law but slimy lawyer-politicians? If I couldn't fight them, I'd have to join them. As the saying goes, "Fight fire with fire." I needed to work to change the ridiculous rules that gave more rights to natural parents than it did to their innocent, neglected offspring—if not for Herbie, then at least for future Herbies. As the law currently stood, DNA-related mothers had the option to treat their babes as mere stuffed toys to be jostled around and eventually tossed aside.

I had to do something constructive. I had to fight with all my might. First, I needed to understand the law. Then I'd be able to wage war to defend the little ones out there. That meant I needed to go back to college and complete my bachelor's degree. After that: law school. My New Year's resolution would be to become a lawyer ASAP, whatever it took.

I fumed about the power Fritz held over me that December: he manipulated me by threatening divorce if I didn't go to L.A. for Christmas. I felt trapped when I wasn't strong enough to hold my ground. I resented the overly high value I'd placed on our marriage. I wanted to believe I could have my choice of wonderful men—men who'd appreciate me too much to make such a threat.

I needed to be sure other men found me attractive. I started by purchasing some inexpensive but cute outfits. My favorite was a white polyester dress with a fitted top and flared miniskirt, which I wore with white faux-patent-leather Nancy Sinatra boots and white tights. When I saw male heads turn in approval, my confidence shot up.

As we filed out of our Law and the Poor class one day, a handsome but macho policeman named Rex made small talk with me. As Fritz had twelve years earlier, Rex went out of his way to walk me to my next class. Unlike Fritz, Rex wasn't shy, and neither was he single—he was married with two kids, as I was. I felt guilty to be so attracted to him.

After our final exam was over, Rex and I agreed to meet a few days later. I spent the intervening time excited and apprehensive in equal parts. Would I really meet him? This was just harmless flirtation. Of course I wouldn't meet him. Oh, but I would—and I did.

We met in the school parking lot, where Rex invited me into his station wagon. He drove us to a wooded area with no other cars or people in sight. My heart fluttered as he kissed me for the first time. We moved to the back of his car. Without completely removing our clothes, we enjoyed each other. Rex worked hard at stimulating me, and our con-summation was quick but satisfying.

As I put myself back together, I felt shocked by what I'd done. After being so diligent at protecting my virginity with Fritz, I had allowed this? Was I in love with Rex? Was I still the same person I'd been an hour ago?

No, I wasn't.

A week later Rex phoned me during lunchtime to arrange another meeting. The only phone in our home was in the kitchen, and the girls were there. In front of them I said, "Bonnie, I'm really busy and I can't talk now—maybe later."

A few days later he called me again. This time I said, "Bonnie, I don't think that would work. I'm really busy these days."

I never heard from Rex again.

After that tryst my head was split with contradictions. Did I love Fritz or Rex? Both of them—or neither? My husband was such a Jekyll-Hyde. Before my fall from grace, every time Fritz had been loving and adoring I'd felt like the luckiest wife in the world, but after betraying him, I felt little pleasure and a lot of guilt when he was sweet. And when he was mean, I usually escaped into romantic thoughts of being with Rex. Above all, I no longer lacked assurance that I was still physically attractive to other men. I trusted I wouldn't buckle the next time Fritz bullied me with a divorce threat.

When the time came to plan for Christmas again, I didn't feel ready for a divorce. Instead of picking a fight, I actually said something like "I guess we'll be spending Christmas in L.A. again." On hearing me say that, Fritz acted grateful and showed me a little extra affection. Fortunately, I was spared seeing Herbie and his baby sister that holiday.

Around the second anniversary of our taking Herbie in, Fritz be-gan to complain about his job and simultaneously griped that I wasn't working. He said he wanted to quit. I suggested that he take sick or vacation days to job-hunt. Fritz replied that taking time off wouldn't work because word would leak to Crown Zellerbach, and then they'd either fire him or make his job more difficult. I told him that was a risk he should take, but Fritz was adamantly against it. Then, in the summer of '73, he pulled the trigger: he left his job, with no new prospects on the horizon. I was furious and frightened.

Later that week, while we shopped for some basic items, Jeanette pointed out a ninety-nine-cent colander; ours had recently fallen apart. In view of future cash problems, I eschewed this needless purchase. When I came home, Fritz greeted me with the news that he was going salmon fishing with his buddy. They periodically enjoyed these $25 fishing expeditions and always brought home salmon—but only the equivalent of what might cost $3–$5 at the store.

Hysterical, I told Fritz he was crazy to indulge in this luxury when we didn't know when he'd next earn money. Each of us tried to drown out the other till Fritz calmly said, "Alice, I want a divorce."

"You've got it," I yelled. I yanked off my wedding ring and ran upstairs to put it in my jewelry box.

I must put a halt to dismal thoughts. I have to think positively. After all, six weeks is the norm. I must calm down and try to sleep. The loan will come… The loan will come… The loan will come.

CHAPTER 13
FORECAST VERSUS REALITY

The real test is not whether you avoid failure, because you won't.
It's whether you let it harden or shame you into inaction, or
whether you learn from it; whether you choose to persevere.
—Barack Obama, 44th President of the United States

After a lot of research into professional truck pickup and delivery, I find I can get Karl's wire transported for only $45. Were Bob and I to rent a truck again, we'd use a five-step program: 1) drive to the rental place; 2) drive to Edwards to get the wire; 3) drive the load to Owens-Illinois; 4) return the truck; and 5) return home. All that would cost us $36 for the truck and about $4 more for the gas. All that hassle would save us only $5. Because we get credit from the coiler and the trucker and give credit to Owens-Illinois, we could operate very efficiently without having to pay anyone immediately or worry about not collecting immediate payment from Owens-Illinois. Now I realize the beauty of doing business on a credit basis.

I've scheduled the trucker to make Karl's delivery tomorrow afternoon. Just to make sure all goes smoothly, I decide to call the little-old coiler guy to confirm that the coils will be ready tomorrow.

"Hi, Mr. Schultz. It's Alice from Vulcan Metal Joining Consultants. I just want to verify that the coils will be delivered to Edwards tomorrow morning."

"Oh, sorry," he says. "They won't quite be ready tomorrow. I've been pretty busy lately. But call back in a couple days."

"What!?" My voice goes into high-pitched mode. "You promised me any orders I gave you would be ready in a week. What happened?"

"Like I told you, I've been busy lately," he says calmly. "Don't worry. It'll be good and ready Friday."

As if scolding a child, I say, "That's two days too late. My customer even asked if I could deliver it in less than two weeks on the day I scheduled with Edwards and you. Edwards met their promise. Why can't you meet yours?"

"Take it easy, Alice," he says, still unruffled. "Everything will work out just fine. I'm sure your customer can wait a couple more days."

"Well, now that you'll be two days late, I'm going to try to get the trucker there in the morning right after you complete your job. Exactly what time will you have it there?"

"Probably around nine, but I can't promise before noon. Schedule your guy for afternoon, okay?"

"Okay, but I wish you could do better than that." I almost bang the phone down.

I had everything planned perfectly, and now that damned coiler man is letting me down. He doesn't even have a valid excuse.

Karl will be *furious*. For all I know he might finally be getting a late delivery from his original vendor. He's probably been pushing them without telling me. Now that I'm not meeting my obligation, if Karl gets his regular wire, he has a right to cancel his order with me. I won't blame him if he does. I won't even blame him if he yells at me.

It's a good thing I have no appointments today, because I'm so upset I have a stomachache. I can't think straight. Before I call Karl, I'm going to allow myself a one-hour bike ride to calm down.

"Hi, Karl. It's Alice from Vulcan."

"Hi, kiddo. Is my wire coming today?"

I take a breath. "Karl, I'm so sorry. There's been a delay. It won't be till Friday."

"Oh, shit! Can you at least *promise* it'll be here then?"

"Yes, Karl. I promise."

"Well, it better be, and it had better work, or I'm done with Vulcan."

"I understand, Karl. Please forgive me. Have a nice day. Goodbye," I say as though I'm a contrite naughty child.

I hang up feeling relieved; at least he didn't cancel his order, but now I'm too nervous to get back to work, and my stomach still hurts. I'll just do housewife activities the rest of the day. I'll invite Bob to a home-cooked meal for a change—spaghetti. He and the girls had better love it. I need a win right now.

It was a nice distraction to cook my spaghetti and hear Bob's grateful praise. Now I'm back to being scared that the coiler man won't have my wire ready on Friday. I think Karl meant it when he said that if it didn't arrive by then he'd be done with Vulcan. That means he'll cancel his order, which in turn means I could owe money for wire I might have no use for, especially if it's partially coiled and therefore too awkward to remake into bale ties. A disaster. At least the Fire Sticks Patty and I were stuck with in junior high were inexpensive—and edible. The wire is neither.

Worse, if Karl gets disgusted with me, he could blackball me in the boxboard industry. He knows many of the plant managers who use this kind of wire. Today and tomorrow I'll try to find as many recycling places as possible that use the 12-gage annealed wire for bale ties. I'll also revisit or phone the companies I already know that use those ties, and I'll ask when they think they'll need more. I don't want to dwell on the worst-case scenario, but I know it's smart to have a backup plan.

Good news: The coiler guy has assured me the wire will be ready by noon tomorrow. The trucker has also assured me he'll pick up and deliver tomorrow afternoon. I think I'll sleep well tonight.

I call the trucker just before 5:00 on Friday to verify that all went well. He tells me the wire was picked up but not delivered due to the horrendous weekend traffic. Then he promises me a Monday morning delivery. Seething, I say, "Traffic or not, you should have kept your word!"

I try to call Karl, but he doesn't pick up. I can only leave a message and hope he's not furious with me and really not through with Vulcan. At least he'll know his wire is on the road once he hears my message.

I hope future transactions won't be this cumbersome. I don't know how to discipline an adult, other than to dump him or her. I know I can always find a different trucker, but I doubt I can find another coiler close enough to Edwards to easily commute between their plants. Even if the Crocker loan comes through and Karl absolutely loves his new wire and forgives me for the delay, I deplore this dismal business of babysitting adults who don't do what they say.

Maybe I should have continued with my law school plans after all.

Karl took my call and complained only mildly that his wire arrived early this morning rather than last Friday. He said it looked fine and that he's already put two of my spools on the baler. "So far so good," he said, but he's not yet ready to give me any further orders or recommendations.

I've slept well the past couple of nights because devising price and customer charts all weekend exhausted my brain. I worked myself round-the-clock and relaxed only at mealtimes. I have a helpful chart from Edwards that shows how many running feet there are per hundred pounds for each of the gages, and used it to figure out the numbers.

To calculate coiled wire costs is simple; technically, a sixth grader could do it, but it's an arduous procedure to calculate bale-tie costs. First I have to figure out the respective cost of 10–20-foot-long bale ties with gages between 11 and 14, including every gage and a half. Second, add half a foot to each designated length for making the loop and the twist. Third, determine whether said bundle will have 125, 150, 250, or 500 bale ties in it. Fourth, calculate the weight of each bundle in order to know my cost from Edwards, since they charge by the pound. Fifth, add my Grass Valley per-bundle cost, which is determined by the bundle, the length, and the quantity of wires in the bundle. Sixth, for those potential customers who expect to pay by the "delivered" bundle, calculate the trucking fees (based on weight) and divide by the number of bundles.

I found some tablets of multi-columned spreadsheet forms at the stationery store. I use a two-foot-wide page for each of the eight gage sizes. Then I list the potential customers on the left and put my costs where the gage and length and delivery figures are applicable.

I'm as busy now as when I juggled school, childcare, and my other domestic responsibilities. During regular work hours I do all my phoning and visits. During non-business hours and weekends, I do calculating and other paperwork.

Karl didn't respond to my call today. I was so hoping for great news from him now that he's had a couple days to try out my wire, but I'm still excited about a recycler giving me my very first bale-tie order. It's only for ten bundles, but at least it's the same 12-gage wire Karl uses. I should have enough left over from my spooled wire to make a couple of bundles, but I'll need to place a second order with Edwards. Even with a sizeable profit margin, I'll make only $100 from this job, but if I can eventually get a good number of small orders like this, they should add up nicely.

This morning, Karl takes my call. He says he still isn't 100 percent convinced my wire is good. To be absolutely sure that it works well, he tells me, he needs to have it loaded on at least four of his ten running spools.

"I'll have used up two more of my old spools by tomorrow afternoon," he says. "I'll replace those with Vulcan wire and see what happens."

He invites me to drop by at three o'clock, and if my wire's doing well, he'll give me another order and some referrals. Now I'm so anxious that I might not be able to sleep.

I'm flying high! Karl gave me an order—not for just thirty-six coils but 108! He also gave me six referrals, each of which is a Fortune 500 company. He said there are probably many more places that use this kind of wire too, but I'll have to ferret them out myself. The frosting on the cake is that he totally scrapped my "lousy wire" from my first sale, saying he just wanted to get rid of the "crap," and he didn't demand a refund. I'm off the hook.

Next week I have appointments with five of Karl's six referrals. The sixth plant manager, in Sacramento, is on vacation. I'll also visit some bale-tie users, a few for the second time. I'm learning firsthand how advantageous it is to cite Owens-Illinois as a satisfied customer. Both of the Fortune 500 company men I saw today responded positively about maybe giving me their next orders. One even told me to call back in a week, at which time he might place an order. I wonder if, in the meantime, he plans to call Karl to verify that I'm truly doing business with Owens-Illinois.

During my 9:00 AM visit I got an order for 108 coils—just like that! I also revisited three bale-tie places to brag about doing business with my two household-name customers. During another visit I got my second bale-tie order, this time for twenty-five bundles. The money I'll make from the four orders I received in these last eight days is more than I'd have made in eight days at Mervyn's had they promoted me—possibly even more than they pay their buyers.

Oh, stupid me! Despite my good reception in San Jose, I've been disillusioned today. Until old Mr. Schultz informed me that there's always a waste factor for the spooled wire, I'd anticipated every bit of my Edwards wire being produced in salable form. I'm angry with myself for not having considered the fact that when I get large coils weighing 800–1,200 pounds, unless those coils are perfectly divisible by one hundred, there'll be leftover unusable wire—those coils of spooled wire must weigh exactly 100 pounds each. Of Edwards's four large coils, which weighed a total of 3,799 pounds, the waste factor was 229 pounds; that boils down to a net prefabricated-wire cost increase of 6.03 percent.

I need to factor in waste for the bale ties too. When the large coil has become diminished to a length too short for a bale tie, the remainder is unusable. Also, the coiler's remnants are unusable—resetting the bale-tie machine for less than hundred-pound increments is too labor-intensive for it to be worthwhile. I'm so dismayed I want to slap my head. I'll still make a healthy profit on my existing orders—but not nearly as much as I'd imagined.

CHAPTER 14
THE CLOCK KEEPS TICKING

*Have the end in mind and every day make
sure you're working toward it.*
—Ryan Allis, CEO and chairman, Hive Global

I just discovered that all sorts of businesses, including manufacturers and major users of wood-based products use balers—even IBM. They certainly don't use as much wire as Owens-Illinois and its competitors, but they're definitely worthwhile. I simply need to get on the phone and make enough inquiries to find out who's responsible for ordering baler wire.

I still haven't been able to make an appointment with a chain supermarket's decision-maker, but after being transferred from one person to another, I was able to set up a meeting at IBM in less than half an hour. There are so many accessible bale-tie users that I can schedule appointments with less than a twenty-minute drive between them. There's so much gold out there… but will I get my tools soon enough to stake a claim?

This has been the busiest and most fruitful week of my new career. So exhausted with Vulcan activities, I've dropped off to sleep easily despite my worry about the Crocker loan, but Edwards's due date is too close to ignore. A week from today—three days before the seven-week mark—I'll owe them a little over $1,000. I think I'll pop in on Crocker this Monday, exactly six weeks after my loan request. I told them I wanted the money to improve my home, so it shouldn't seem out of the ordinary that I'm antsy. With my recent successes, I almost believe those false income statements are true. Also, I feel confident that Crocker hasn't smelled a rat, since someone contacted Bob regarding my employment and income weeks ago.

I got a 108-coil order from one of Karl's recommended Fortune 500 leads. All I did was phone the man to follow up, which he requested I do last week when I visited. As long as Crocker comes through in time, I'll have a very successful business.

The bank's loan officer told me to assume that everything is working out fine, and that second mortgages take six to eight weeks lately. He doesn't want to investigate the status till the eight-week mark. I hope my apprehension didn't show. I still hope to get the loan no later than this Friday, early enough to drive a check over to Edwards and meet my thirty-day deadline. I don't want to lose the respect I've received from Peter Price. Holding my head high is very important to me.

If it weren't for working a menial job and using food stamps, I might be in law school right now. As an over-thirty woman working as a waitress, I felt inferior to my friends with their college degrees and professional careers. I hated the humiliation of wearing that short little uniform and bending over subserviently to take lunch orders. I preferred to work as a legal secretary, but with the good tips my restaurant work was more lucrative. My customers were generous, perhaps because I enjoyed them and found it easy to smile.

The truth is, the straw that broke my back about law school wasn't vocational embarrassment or discomfort with borrowing more money from my parents and brother. It was a mortifying incident at Albertsons.

Thanks to my two buddies, Gary the produce manager and Norm the store manager, Albertsons had become a sort of home away from home for me while I finished my undergrad degree. To get a little fresh air and exercise, I preferred to leave the car at home and ride my bike to the store; I'd affixed a big basket on either side of the rear wheel to stick the groceries in for the ride home.

Often stressed from the intensity of homework during this period, I found that talking with either Albertsons friend helped me unwind. Immediately upon entering the store, I relaxed and enjoyed the music as I shopped.

I usually paid with food stamps. Even when his wasn't the shortest line, I chose Norm to ring me up. I hadn't seen him that monumental day, and I assumed he was off duty. All the lines but one were very long, so I got in the shortest. A woman who looked vaguely familiar was operating the cash register. By the time it was my turn, at least half a dozen people were behind me. As a box boy from our neighborhood bagged my groceries, and the person I was behind still fumbled with her purse, I handed the checker my food stamps.

"You need to get a job," she said loudly, and looked at me disdainfully.

"I have a job," I replied, feeling like she'd just slapped me. I glanced around—everyone within earshot was staring.

"Then you need to get a better job."

My face felt hot. I tried to stay calm. "I plan to," I said politely. "But now I'm attending college."

"Well, if I were you, rather than use food stamps for my groceries, I'd look for a better job, or at least a second job."

I didn't say another word; I just got the hell out of Albertsons as quickly as possible.

What a bitch! Maybe I shouldn't go to law school. That would mean over three more years of food stamps—and of being a waitress getting deeper and deeper in debt.

My $1,000 bill from Edwards is due three days from now. I'm tempted to ask my folks for a short-term loan. Before I completed my bachelor's degree, it was actually their idea to lend me money on a monthly basis till I completed law school. They knew that to fund my education and living expenses, I would otherwise have to sell my lovely house and our Lake Tahoe lot, split the proceeds with Fritz, and then move the girls and myself into an inexpensive apartment. They wanted us to remain in our good neighborhood, so they offered financial help—as long as they made as much interest as they would if they'd left the money in their savings account.

Prior to the Albertsons incident, which took place just nine weeks before graduation, I'd planned on law school. I had majored in political science, an impractical and nearly useless major for anyone but a future lawyer. Until I began full-time job-hunting, I hadn't realized what little earning clout my degree gave me.

Now that Robby is married, he's trying to accumulate down-payment money for a house as quickly as possible. My parents have nearly disowned me because they don't approve of my lifestyle—namely, the fact that I'm dating and sleeping with Bob Brown. Otherwise, if I wanted to resume my law school plans, I'm sure they'd offer more loans. Currently our communication is very limited, and they know next to nothing about how I spend my time.

When Mommy first learned that Fritz and I were divorcing, she said, "I don't know what we should do with you now. I thought our job was over when we gave you your wedding." And boy, did she ever want to take charge of that wedding—my dress and everything else!

I wanted an evening wedding, but Mommy insisted on afternoon. I acquiesced without argument because of her explanation that it would be far less expensive to serve only hors d'oeuvres than a full dinner. I always respected my parents' financial limitations.

For years I'd been brainwashed into thinking that braces and a wedding were mandatory for a girl, and a superior education was mandatory for a boy. I'd already benefited from my expensive orthodontic care; otherwise, the orthodontist said, I'd have looked like Eleanor Roosevelt—too many big teeth in a small mouth. Robby's teeth were less than perfect and would remain so.

Another contested wedding issue was the church. St. James, our fairly new, oversized Tarzana Presbyterian church, didn't appeal to me. Only two of its twelve tall, narrow windows were stained glass; indoors, it looked like a work in progress, which it was.

I spotted an adorable, smaller, less airy church in Encino, the adjacent town. The dozen shorter but much wider kaleidoscope-colored windows bathed the interior in a romantic, fairy tale-like aura. An extreme contrast to the cold, impersonal interior of St. James, this inviting, cozy place also had a charming exterior of softly rounded gray stonework, which gave it an old European flair.

Mommy wouldn't hear of the Encino church. She was upset that I'd even suggested not using Tarzana's. She had two good reasons to forget about getting married in Encino: 1) that church would cost more because we weren't members; and 2) it would be a slight to our pastor, Reverend Duncan. I accepted her financial reasoning, and I didn't want to hurt Reverend Duncan's feelings. Sadly, I backed off.

Regarding my wedding dress, however, I thought I should have what I wanted, even if I needed to chip in to make that happen. At the start, Mommy and I had fun shopping together. Perhaps the subtle lavender scent in the bridal specialty store helped soothe our mother-daughter tensions. For about an hour we were relaxed as we leafed through the snow-white, fit-for-a-princess gowns, each of us quietly putting aside the ones we found most appealing.

I collected half a dozen dresses, and Mommy chose only one before we entered the dressing room, which immediately felt small and snug with the gossamer billows of the gowns hung all around us.

I tried on my six selections. None felt right. "Well, Mommy, I think we need to go to another store," I said with a sigh. "None of these dresses makes me look good enough."

"Oh, Alice Marie, look at this sweet gown." She held up the one she'd picked out. "Try it on."

"I don't know, Mommy, I think it has way too many of those little ruffles."

"Just try it on, Alice Marie," she said in her bossy manner.

"Oookay, Mommy." I put it on and let her zip me up.

One look in the mirror was enough. I made a face. "I don't like it."

"Oh, Alice Marie, you look like a perfect bride!"

"But Mommy, I look more like a little girl playing dress-up than someone who's going to be married."

"Don't be silly, Alice Marie. It's the most beautiful bridal gown imaginable. Look at the price tag." She held it up in front of me. "It's only $99,[12] and most of the other dresses here cost over $100."

"Well, please don't buy it for me," I said, frowning. "I'm sure I can find a better dress somewhere else. If it costs more than $99, I'll pay the difference. I want to feel good in the most important dress of my whole life."

"It's time to go home now, Alice Marie. We'll both think about it."

I could tell that as far as Mommy was concerned, there would be no more shopping trips. I was sure she planned to persuade or blackmail me. She knew affordability was my soft spot, and at only $99, her choice met the financial test.

A week later I went shopping again, this time with Patty, my future maid of honor. *Eureka, I've found it!* No silly ruffles, but lots of sophisticated scalloped lace over a full tulle skirt with hundreds of seed pearls sewn into the lace. The price was $125.

I could hardly wait to get home with my joyous news.

"Mommy, Mommy, I found my dress!" I sang out as I burst through the door. "It's gorgeous! When can you come see it with me?"

Mommy shook her head. "Alice Marie, there's no need for me to look at any more dresses. We've already found your perfect gown."

"I told you, I don't like that dress." I prepared for battle.

"Ridiculous. You couldn't look lovelier in any other dress. Besides, it costs only $99."

"That's not true," I said. "It makes me look like I'm in a cheap movie pretending to be a bride. Don't worry about the cost. I'll be glad to pay the extra $26."

Mommy wouldn't budge. "Alice Marie, you're being unreasonable. We'll talk more about it when your father gets home."

The moment my father walked in the door, I pounced.

"Hi, Daddy, guess what? I found my wedding dress."

He didn't smile. "What does it cost?"

"It costs $125, but—"

"*Criii...minnn...inly!*" Daddy said in his high-pitched, whiny voice. How foolish could you be to want a $125 dress?"

"Daddy, you would only have to pay $99. I'd pay the rest."

He looked at me like I was crazy. "Do you think I'm foolish enough to pay $99 for a dress?"

"Well, Mommy thinks it would be okay," I said, sounding like a petulant child. "She wants me to get a stupid dress that costs $99."

"George," Mommy stated, "$99 is a reasonable price to pay for a wedding gown."

"The hell it is!" Daddy bellowed.

"Most wedding dresses now cost over $100; $99 is an excellent price," she calmly replied.

"Well, I think you both need to shop some more and find a dress for less," he retorted.

"Daddy," I chimed in. "Whatever you think is reasonable and are willing to pay, I'll pay the extra."

"It's the parents' duty to pay their daughter's wedding expenses," Daddy said, in his normal voice. "A daughter should never have to pay for any part of her wedding."

"Well, I guess that settles it," Mommy said smoothly. "Alice Marie will get that lovely $99 gown."

"I'll settle the whole thing and save you both money," I spat out angrily. "I'll pay for my $125 dress, tax and all."

"No, Alice, we can't have you pay for your wedding dress," Daddy said. "That wouldn't be proper. Chalky"—his nickname for my mother, due to her white skin—"just go ahead and get her the $99 dress. I don't want to talk about this anymore." He walked into the bathroom and closed the door.

"I'm not getting married in that ridiculous dress!" I yelled. "I don't see what's wrong with you both! Can't you just let me buy my own dress?"

"Calm down, Alice Marie," Mommy said. "You are going to have a beautiful wedding, dress and all."

"You're both just plain mean," I shouted, tears streaming. "I'd think you'd want me to be happy on my wedding day." I hurried down the hallway to my bedroom, slammed the door behind me, and fell onto the bed. As I bawled I imagined myself in the tasteless, gaudy dress, a sharp contrast to the joy of imagining myself in the beautiful $125 gown.

After a while both my parents walked in, and Mommy said soothingly, "Okay, Alice Marie, you can have your dress, and your daddy's going to pay for it."

I guess they love me after all.

CHAPTER 15
TOSSING AND TURNING

Courage is being scared to death but saddling up anyway.
—John Wayne, Academy Award-winning actor, filmmaker

S till no word from Crocker. As of today I owe Edwards almost $3,000, and by the day after tomorrow over $1,000 of it is due. Now I'm wondering if Bob's hefty tax refund might come in before Crocker's loan. I'm so anxious I almost can't function.

I'm still thinking about asking my parents for help. I might be able to handle Daddy's practical questions and advice… but Mommy's a different story. She thinks business owners are a vulgar sort, and she might even hope my wire venture gets nipped in the bud.

Mommy knows nothing about business and has no respect for entrepreneurs. She disdainfully exclaimed, "*Nouveau riche!*" as she jealously discussed the various affluent merchants in our Tarzana neighborhood and social groups—as if she belonged to the upper class. She's no socialist; it's just that she doesn't appreciate the value of prosperity based on hard work and a grasp of supply and demand.

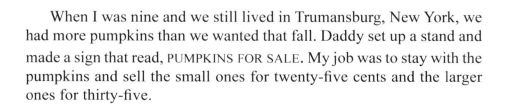

When I was nine and we still lived in Trumansburg, New York, we had more pumpkins than we wanted that fall. Daddy set up a stand and made a sign that read, PUMPKINS FOR SALE. My job was to stay with the pumpkins and sell the small ones for twenty-five cents and the larger ones for thirty-five.

One of our pumpkins was head-turning huge. A very nice lady stopped by and asked how much that enormous one cost. When I told her thirty-five cents, she was incredulous. She asked me to bring my mother out so she and Mommy could discuss it.

Mommy begrudgingly left her indoor sanctuary and verified that the pumpkin's price was only thirty-five cents. The lady said we could make far more than that if we entered it in a fair, and that it would probably win a prize. The lady said she thought the pumpkin was worth a dollar, but she would be happy to pay us fifty cents. Mommy seemed irritated that the lady wanted to pay her that much, and adamantly restated our asking price. With a sigh, the nice lady paid us. The pumpkin was so big that she needed her teenage son's help to get it into her trunk.

A few years later, when I was in the ninth grade, I worked hard to get straight A's. When my report card came, Grandma wanted to reward me with money, but Mommy refused to allow it. Daddy refused to interfere with anything between Mommy and her mother, so I was out of luck. Mommy said I should work hard just because I should, not for money. "You like money too much," she told me with a look of distaste.

A year after that, one of my girlfriends asked me if I'd be interested in babysitting two horrible eight-year-old twin boys. She said she couldn't stand them, but she knew I was more interested in making money than she was and that the twins' parents paid extremely well. Because I was five months away from sixteen and not yet eligible to land a $1-per-hour minimum-wage job, I decided to give the boys a try.

6:30 PM

Those identical twins were cutie-pies. I wondered why Michelle said they were devils. I'd brought my usual arsenal of books to help entertain them. Their mother had set her kitchen table with three plates, each holding a steak, a small, steaming baked potato, and green beans. Beside the place settings were glasses of milk. In the center of the table were three bowls of chocolate pudding and, oddly, a roll of paper towels. All I had to do was butter, salt, and mash the potatoes slightly and cut each child's steak into bite-size pieces. I was directed to sit at the head of the table, with the boys across from one another on either side of me.

The parents begged me not to telephone them unless something critical happened, like a fire or a broken bone. As they left, they kissed their boys and asked them to be good and go to bed nicely at eight o'clock.

When the door shut behind them, I looked at the boys. "Well, Jack and Joe, it looks like your mother's made us all a wonderful meal."

"I hate green beans," said Jack.

"I hate them too," said Joe. He got an evil look on his face, put a couple in his mouth, chewed for a few seconds, and then aimed a squirt at me. Jack followed suit.

I scooped some green goo off my shirt with a finger. This explained the paper towels on the table. "Stop it, boys! That isn't nice."

They continued, laughing between squirts. Apparently they planned to drown me in green spit till all the green beans were off their plates.

"If you don't stop that right now, I won't read you any stories before bedtime," I said in what I hoped was a stern voice.

"I don't like stupid stories anyway," said Jack. *Squirt!*

"I don't either," said Joe. *Squirt!*

In a minute both their plates contained only potatoes and steak.

I grabbed some paper towels and wiped the slime off my face and my plate and the table. Then I looked from one boy to the other with a forced smile and said, "Once I get the butter on these potatoes, they'll be yummy. Don't you think?"

"I guess so, but I'd rather play pirate," said Jack. He picked up my steak knife and lunged at me, much too close for comfort.

Simultaneously, Joe and I made a grab for the knife. I'm usually not strong, but my adrenaline kicked in and I wrested it from Jack's grip. I stood, holding the knife high in victory. In a second both boys were now my height as they stood on their chairs to reach for the knife. I backed away and put it on top of the green-slime-speckled refrigerator.

"Boys!" I yelled. "Stop being spoiled brats. Now go to your room. If you don't, I'll take that knife and cut you into a million tiny pieces." I snarled this part so menacingly I actually believed my words.

The little monsters ran to their room, and the door slammed shut. I guessed they believed me too. I retrieved the knife and decided to cut up our steaks while I was safe. I ignored the thumping sounds that emanated from their bedroom, and chose to eat alone in peace. I looked at my green beans and envisioned the gunk I'd recently cleaned up. I stood, scraped the beans into the garbage disposal, then sat down and plunged into my steak and potato.

One bite and peace was over. The twins emerged.

"I'll be good," said Jack.

"I'll be good too," said Joe.

"Do you promise?" I asked.

"Yes," they said in unison.

"Okay, then, let's be friends and finish our dinner together. Can you do that?"

"Yes," they said together.

We all cleaned our plates, and then I started to pass out the bowls of chocolate pudding. Overeager Jack quickly reached for his bowl—and accidentally propelled his milk over to his brother's side, where it spilled onto his lap.

Joe yelped, "Jack, you got me all wet!"

"Don't be a big baby about it!" said Jack.

"Don't you be a big baby either," Joe said, and catapulted his own milk toward Jack.

"I'm not a big baby, and I'll teach you a lesson," said Jack. He flung a spoonful of pudding at Joe's face.

"I'll teach you a lesson too," said Joe, mimicking his brother with his own pudding toss.

"Boys, the pudding is yummy," I yelled above the din. "If you don't stop, it will all be gone."

At last they stopped, but the pudding had diminished by half and I foresaw a twenty-minute cleanup job in addition to the ten-minute green-bean scrub I'd already planned on. I tried to enjoy the momentary silence and postponed cleaning the mess till I got them bedded down.

I hoped that by listening to my good books the boys would be able to unwind, but they couldn't sit still and began another fight. At least I could be thankful they weren't ganging up on me.

I looked at my watch and saw that it was only 7:35. I wished it were later. *Can I last another twenty-five minutes with these imps?*

"Boys, it's time to get into your pajamas and brush your teeth," I said, managing a calm tone.

"No, it isn't," Jack said. "We don't have to get ready for bed till 7:45."

"Yeah, that's right," Joe said.

"Okay, you have ten minutes more to play," I said, reluctantly giving in. "Do you want to play hide-and-seek and make me find you?"

"Okay," they both answered gleefully.

"You have to close your eyes and count to twelve, and no fair peeking," Jack said.

I promised to oblige, and savored my twelve seconds' tranquility, all the while hoping they'd split up and keep quiet.

"Here I come, ready or not," I announced when I'd reached twelve. I took my time looking in various places, each time saying loudly, "I'll bet you're here in this closet. I just know you're under this bed. You've *got to be* behind this curtain…." I prayed I wouldn't find either brat until 7:45. When I got close to one boy, I heard a muffled giggle. I pivoted away. *Easy,* I thought. *I'll just avoid each giggler till 7:45. Finally, something that works!*

8:10 PM

Those last twenty-five minutes took forever. They peed, brushed their teeth, and had their last sips of water. I closed their door with them in bed, but they weren't asleep. I heard arguing, pillow fighting, and banging.

8:33 PM

Peace! Thank God. I'd never been so content to clean up without distraction. I actually looked forward to my dull required school reading. I wanted no sounds from a radio or TV, just some quiet time.

11:50 PM

Mr. and Mrs. Smith came home and asked me how the evening had gone. I told them the sordid truth. They apologized for their sons being such a handful and told me how much they appreciated all my work. Before Mr. Smith drove me home, Mrs. Smith handed me a $10 bill. I told her she owed me only $2.75 and I had no change. Mrs. Smith said she knew how difficult her children were and hoped the extra money would make it all worthwhile for me.

"I'd like to give you more babysitting jobs in the future," she said. "Would you be willing to come back another time? I always want to pay you well," she added quickly.

"I'd be happy to!" I said just as quickly, thinking of how much money I'd just made.

Mrs. Smith seemed very happy, and so was I.

I was so proud of myself the next day that I made the mistake of bragging to Mommy and Daddy how much I'd made the previous night. Mommy was horrified. She said it wasn't ethical for me to accept that much. On my fourteenth birthday she had allowed me to raise my former thirty-five-cent-an-hour wage to fifty cents. She knew that Michelle and some of my other friends charged seventy-five cents an hour, but she thought that was way too high—even when I told her the other girls didn't bring good children's books like I did.

"The most you should have accepted was $3," she said.

"But Mommy, she really and truly wanted me to have the $10 because she knows the twins are so much work," I protested. I told her all about the night's irksome events, then said, "If I can keep only $3, I won't ever baby-sit there again!"

Mommy must not have understood my logic, because to this she merely said, "Well, that's your choice to make, Alice Marie."

I tried to get Daddy to change her mind, but he said it was between Mommy and me, and he wanted to keep out of it.

In the end, Mommy took the $10 bill from me and gave me ten $1 bills. Then she drove me over to the Smiths' and waited in the car while I knocked on the door. I declined the invitation to come in and sadly delivered my news.

"My mother says I'm allowed to keep only $3," I said, and tried to hand her $7.

"Oh, please, Alice, keep all the money," she said. "I know how much work the boys can be."

I looked down. "I'll get in trouble if I don't give you the money, Mrs. Smith."

She sighed and took the bills. "Are you still willing to return another time?" she asked hopefully?

"I–" I glanced away. "No, I don't think so. I'm really sorry."

As we said goodbye, Mrs. Smith's face crumpled.

If neither the Crocker loan nor Bob's tax refund comes through tomorrow, I'm *cooked.* I feel paralyzed: I don't want to leave the house for fear of missing Crocker's call, and I don't want to tie up my phone line, but that's just as well, because I have zero interest in research or selling. It's good there's no additional paperwork to keep me busy, because I couldn't concentrate if I tried. I can't even enjoy a good book.

All I can do is mindless housework. At least I'll have a sparkling-clean home, just the way it was before I resumed my schooling—back when all I could think of was my baby Herbie. I'll always remember my neighbor, Sally, admonishing me a few months after I had to give up my sweet little guy. "Alice, your house is too perfect. You're a disgrace to womankind. You should either get an interesting job or go back to college. Use your intellect and stop wasting that brain of yours on grieving and cleaning, grieving and cleaning."

Now I'm pacing and cleaning, pacing and cleaning.

It's so frustrating to know that Mommy and Daddy could easily come up with $1,000 if they wanted to. The big question is: would they want to? Definitely, neither would like the idea of this wire venture, but for very different reasons.

Mommy abhors anything that even hints of masculinity for women. Her ideal life for me would be as a stay-at-home housewife and mother, but even before Fritz and I separated, she was agreeable to my child-advocate attorney plans, probably because she considers anything to do with children very feminine. Then, after I gave up on law school, she was probably pleased to think I was on a clothes-buyer career path—another fairly feminine pursuit. I'm sure she'd consider my Vulcan dealings inappropriate, though. A "proper lady" wouldn't be caught dead negotiating costs and prices, selling greasy black wire, and traipsing into machine-filled factories—or worse, sinking her heels into smelly junkyard soil.

And Daddy wouldn't be thrilled about my being self-employed. He tried his hand at that a couple of times and failed. I'm afraid he'd think that if he couldn't earn a living without a big organization behind him, I certainly couldn't.

A bad Friday for me: I'm now an official deadbeat. I wonder if Edwards will call me first thing Monday morning. I think I'll be unavailable and just hope to get funded before the day ends. If I still have no working capital by Monday, perhaps, much as I hate the thought, I should just give in and try to get my folks to help out, but everything in me is resistant to the idea. I'm sure Mommy's controlling demands would do me in. She's always jumped at every chance to run my life, and she'd relish the opportunity to make stipulations. Even though I truly married Fritz for love, I remember that joyful free feeling of no longer being under Mommy's thumb. Until I said, "I do," she'd been overbearing. I'll always remember that episode when I was a lonely country girl in New York.

A new girl moved to our neighborhood when I was nine, and I was so happy! Her name was Nelly Peoples. She was one year older than I. Mommy told her mother not to allow her to play with Becky. When Mommy thought I wasn't listening, she told Mrs. Peoples that Becky's mother was bad because she wasn't really married to Becky's daddy. *Mommy sure is mean,* I thought.

Mrs. Peoples allowed Nelly to play with Becky anyway. Her rule was that Becky was only allowed to play with Nelly inside Nelly's house and in the front yard. I decided Mrs. Peoples wasn't mean like Mommy.

Nelly and Becky liked each other more than they liked me. They ganged up on me one day and said I was too babyish. Then they sang, "Baby, baby, baby."

I ran home.

"What's wrong, Alice Marie?" Mommy asked me. "Why do you look so sad?"

When I told her, she said I should go right back and tell them they weren't being nice and to never be mean to me again. I didn't want to, but she made me go. I walked back to Nelly's house, but didn't knock on her door. Then I walked back home and lied to Mommy; I told her I'd said what she wanted me to say. Even though I'd told a lie, I didn't feel bad, because I didn't think it was any of Mommy's business what I said to my friends.

My loneliness ended shortly after we relocated to California's San Fernando Valley, but Mommy still wanted to control me. She didn't want anyone else to cook in her kitchen, and that bugged me; a lot of my friends were allowed to cook. Mommy made me do lots of stuff, like set the table, and put Crisco on cookie sheets and muffin tins, and wash fruits and vegetables, but she never let me make anything on my own.

At last, after I'd begged for weeks, I got permission to make chocolate chip oatmeal cookies and have some girlfriends over to eat them and drink lemonade. I used the recipe on the Quaker Oatmeal box. Mommy drove me crazy because she kept on telling me what to do.

"I can read the directions just fine!" I said indignantly—and with all my strength, I pushed her out of the kitchen and closed the door.

"Okay, Alice Marie," she said, anger in her voice. "You're on your own!"

I was so glad she was out of there.

My cookies were delicious, and everybody loved them. Later, Mommy said she was very proud of me.

One day, Patty and I discovered a really good deal. A makeup place called Merle Norman gave us a facial treatment and applied makeup for free. We liked it so much that we bought their cold cream and facial-mask kit, and some lipsticks too. When Mommy observed that I was using cold cream, she insisted a teenager shouldn't put cold cream on her face and made me give mine to her. *I could have killed her!* I'd bought that expensive cold cream with my very own hard-earned money. I fumed. *She had no right to take it away from me!*

Shortly thereafter, Mommy also downsized my friendships, albeit inadvertently. Patty and Carolyn were going to summer school, and Mommy wouldn't let me go. She insisted summer school was only for dummies. She knew Patty and Carolyn were smart—smarter than I was, in my opinion—but when I argued this fact with Mommy, she told me she didn't care what my friends did and summer school would be a waste of my time.

I felt like she was wrecking my friendship with Patty and Carolyn, first by not letting me join them in summer school, and then by never letting me to go to good movies with them. She always consulted that stupid *Parents Magazine,* and if it said kids under seventeen shouldn't see a movie, then I was forbidden to see it. Sometimes Patty and Carolyn and the other kids talked about how good those films were, and I always felt like a dummy not knowing what they were talking about.

In the past, Patty and I had done almost everything together. Even if one of us wanted to visit another friend, the other usually came along. Now she and Carolyn were closer, and I felt like an outsider. And Mommy didn't even seem to care that she was ruining things for me.

Now, as an adult, I still ponder which is worse: being an extreme deadbeat—I already am—or risking hell by asking for help from my folks. Mommy would no doubt expect more blood from me than Daddy, who almost always goes along with anything Mommy wants, though he did wholeheartedly side with me once.

I knew my mother wouldn't be thrilled with the news, so I delivered it as quickly as possible: "Mommy, guess what! I've got a twenty-hour-a-week file clerk job that pays me $1.25 an hour. To accommodate my college class schedule, the boss will give me two hours every Monday, Wednesday, and Friday, and seven hours on Tuesdays and Thursdays. Isn't that wonderful?"

"Alice Marie, that won't work out for me," she replied, frowning. "I've finally been able to keep up with things now that you have time to help me with my housework on Tuesdays and Thursdays. You'll have to turn that job down."

"What? I can't believe you! It's bad enough I can't live on campus like all my friends. I might as well make a good substitute for the fun time I won't be having in a sorority or visiting in the dormitory."

"You don't need to make any more money than you already do with your babysitting and summer jobs," Mommy said, her voice even. "It's bad enough I can't have much help from you in the summers when you work full time."

"Well, Mommy, if I can't go to this job and keep on living with you, then I'll move out and work full time. I can support myself on a dollar twenty-five an hour if I work forty hours a week. Randy, a girl who works there, is supporting herself, and she has her own apartment."

Mommy took a deep breath. "You will do nothing of the sort, foolish girl!"

As if scolding a naughty child, I said, "Mommy, you are mean and selfish. You're not going to school. You're not working anywhere. And you don't have any little kids to take care of. You shouldn't need much help from me."

She narrowed her eyes and pointed down the hall. "Go to your room, Alice Marie. No talking on the telephone for the rest of the week, and don't let me hear any more of that rude talk. When your father comes home, he'll set you straight."

"I'm eighteen, and I can work if I want to, and you and Daddy can't stop me," I yelled as I ran to my room.

An hour later, upon hearing my father's clomp, clomp into the house, I ran out to intercept him before my mother could. "Hi, Daddy!" I chirped. "I found a twenty-hour-a-week file clerk job that pays me $1.25 an hour. Management is willing to accommodate my college schedule. Don't you think that's wonderful?"

Mommy didn't give him a chance to answer. "George, I already told Alice Marie this job is out of the question. It simply won't work out!"

He gave her a confused look. "Why not, Chalky?"

She let out an exasperated sigh. "I need Alice Marie to help me with my housework. During these last two weeks since she's been back in school with two available weekdays and not working at her damnable summer job, I've finally caught up on things. Remember, we showed Alice Marie how she could get her sixteen units packed into a three-day schedule, not only to save gasoline but so she could help me on Tuesdays and Thursdays. Besides, she was fresh with me."

"Oh, Chalky, Alice will be busier than ever with this job, and we've always agreed idleness is the devil's playmate. If she can keep up her grades, I think this will be a good experience for her, especially since she's never worked in an office before."

Mommy's jaw was clenched. "I already told Alice Marie she can't take this job. I need you to agree with me."

"I don't think I ever told you this before," Daddy said, "but whenever I interview recent college graduates, I always expect them to have had some kind of a job alongside their college attendance; if they merely went to classes without a part-time job, then I don't want to hire them. Besides, a part-time job will force Alice to budget her time wisely."

Mommy looked shocked. "Golly, George. I can't believe you let me down." She stomped away without another word.

Perhaps I should steer clear of Mommy and interrupt Daddy at work tomorrow to explain that I need a short-term loan of $1,200 due to a financial emergency. But he's sure to ask for details, like why I need so much and why so quickly and how I'll be able to pay it back. I don't dare mention Bob's tax refund, because referring to Bob will probably lead to Daddy's getting me off the phone as soon as possible. Also, he's too savvy to think that I could possibly qualify for a second mortgage with my current income, which means I'll have to admit to the falsities on my loan form and how Bob assured them I make far more money than I've ever made. Then he'll tell me how ashamed he is of me and later tell Mommy, who'll also shame me.

I could try another tactic: Say nothing of Bob or Crocker and just explain my business opportunity; indicate that I can get 1,200 dollars' worth of wire tomorrow, and an hour later sell it for a $500 profit. To keep it simple, I can just explain that my customer, Owens-Illinois (that name should impress Daddy), won't pay me for at least thirty days, and I can add that once Owens-Illinois pays me, I'll be able to repay Daddy.

This plan involves lying by omission, however, and I haven't told a lie or broken a promise to Mommy or Daddy since I was nine—just before we left New York for California.

One day Daddy came home and had to tell Mommy some bad news: he'd been fired from American Airlines. That meant we might have to move.

I wasn't supposed to tell anyone, but the very next day I told Daddy's secret for class news. When I got home from school, Mommy asked if I'd been able to keep our secret, and I said of course I had.

At that, Mommy told me I'd done two bad things: First, I hadn't kept the secret, and second, I'd told a lie. Just a few minutes earlier,

Miss Sterling had called her to ask if we were really going to move away.

Mommy had a big talk with me. She wouldn't stop staring into my eyes. She looked so sad that I'd have liked it better if she'd been mean and given me the worst spanking in the world or a punishment worse than I'd ever had, but all she did was talk with that sorrowful look on her face.

I felt so ashamed. I decided I would always keep a secret and never tell a lie for the rest of my life!

Good and bad news—the bad is that my loan won't be granted today; the good is that it'll be granted tomorrow at ten o'clock. Tomorrow I'll find out if the news is mostly good or mostly bad when I hand the late payment to Peter Price, plus another, slightly early, payment that I hope will make him decide to forgive me.

To expedite tomorrow's Edwards payment, I deposit a $20 personal check into my brand-new Central Bank business account.

CHAPTER 16
ALMOST READY TO SAIL

A goal is a dream with a deadline.
—Napoleon Hill, author of *Think and Grow Rich*

Hip, hip, hooray—today's my day—the loan came through! I first deposit the Crocker check into my personal account, and then make out an $8,980 check to deposit into the Vulcan business account. It feels so good to write the $1,200 check for Edwards. In addition, I write a $700 check for Edwards that isn't due till June 5. I plan to tell a white lie—that I was so busy I overlooked Friday's due date, and to make up for the oversight I'm paying the $700 bill sixteen days early.

Bob and I drive to Edwards together. We hope to find Peter Price before he leaves for lunch. Peter greets us and acts as friendly as can be. And that's before he knows we're going to pay our bills. After I hand him the two checks, he points out that if I had mailed them Friday, they might not have arrived until today anyway, and adds that Edwards generally doesn't phone regarding overdue bills until five to ten working days after the due date.

A business doesn't expect to receive payment by the due date? This is news to me.

Peter asks Bob and me if we're free for lunch, and of course we are. Peter brings along an associate to create a foursome.

After a congenial lunch, Bob and I, ecstatic, decide to make merry in bed at his apartment. After our love fest, Bob looks at his mail—and finds that his $1,500 IRS refund has just arrived. I remind him that $1,000 of that money is promised for our partnership seed money. I also make it clear that I don't plan to spend one penny of my Crocker money for anything other than paying off my family loans, spartan living expenses, and working capital.

"Let me take you and the girls out to celebrate with a fancy dinner tonight," he suggests. "My treat!"

Bob takes us to one of the nicest restaurants I've ever been in. The girls and I are clearly impressed. They have their first-ever Shirley Temples, and all four of us are in our own heavens as we finish off our chocolate decadence desserts. I'll sleep well tonight—I'm not a deadbeat!

It felt good to know I'd no longer be in debt to my family or Fritz. I assume that Crocker submitted Fritz's payment shortly after I signed the final papers. I bet Fritz will be pleasantly shocked when he opens his mail and sees that big fat check paying off his mandated share of the home equity. Receiving it is probably the last thought on his mind, since he knows nothing of my second mortgage. The amount wasn't legally due till Julie's eighteenth birthday in January '86, over ten years from now.

In addition to the principal I owed Robby, I decided to give him 50 percent of the interest he'd have made had he invested the money he lent me in a savings account, even though he said he didn't want interest. I called it my token of appreciation. The deal with my parents, of course, was to pay exactly the interest they'd lost by withdrawing funds from their savings account. It felt so good to be free of any financial obligation to those two, especially to Mommy.

After funding Vulcan and reimbursing my family, my personal account is left with $350—barely enough to cover personal expenses till I begin receiving payments from Vulcan's sales invoices. It's time to start selling again. I like this job I've created, and I'm raring to work hard tomorrow. There are more potential baler-wire customers out there than I can contact in the next few months—perhaps in the next few years.

CHAPTER 17
SAILING

You have to find an opening or unmet need within a market and then fill it rather than try and force your product or service in.
—Small Business Administration (SBA),
US government agency that provides support to
entrepreneurs and small businesses

The answering service says Chris Hale of International Paper is on the line. I've never heard of a Chris Hale. Of the two IP facilities I've visited, I don't recall meeting anyone with a name even similar. My contact at the San Jose location expects me to call him next week, and the other location won't need wire for at least another month.

I take the call anyway, of course.

Chris Hale, in a not-at-all-friendly yet not-rude monotone, speaks quickly, as though in a great hurry. He places a sizeable bale-tie order for the exact price I quoted Jeff Johnson at San Jose a while ago. He doesn't mention Jeff, and I wonder if Jeff instructed him to call me or if he's just taken Jeff's place. Bob has taught me that when I get an order it's best not to ask unnecessary questions or volunteer unnecessary new information—just thank the person for the order and skidoo. It seems weird to get an order without struggling for it. My stomach is tight with excitement, but I think I successfully fake my astonishment and master a casual business-as-usual tone. I see my hand shake, however, as I write down the purchase-order number. As I say thank you and goodbye, my previously calm stomach is rumbling.

I suddenly feel sharp contractions similar to those I experienced during childbirth. My hands are still shaking. I clutch my stomach, then stand up quickly and run the few steps from my desk to the toilet. Sitting, I bend over with more pain till my bowels are emptied and the cramps are gone.

I emerge from the bathroom and head upstairs, hoping to reach the bed before I faint. *This isn't how I imagined success would feel.*

CHAPTER 18
NOT SO EASY

Be realistic at the beginning, and start with enough
money that will last you to the point where your
business is up and running, and cash is actually flowing in.
—Small Business Administration

Peggy Penny of Valley Bank is on the phone.

"Hello, is this Alice Stiller?"

"Yes, it is," I say, in a carefree tone. "What can I do for you, Peggy?"

"There's a problem. We have two checks you wrote totaling nearly $2,000 dollars, and we can't process either one until May 27, next Tuesday, when the five-working-day hold ends on the nearly $9,000 you deposited three days ago. We'll have to charge you for two bounced-check fees."

My heart sinks. "I can't believe you're doing this to me. That $9,000 is secure money. It came from Crocker Bank. I never dreamed Valley Bank would do such a despicable thing."

"Mrs. Stiller, five-day holds are the way we always do business. We can't make any exceptions."

"Are you aware I can't run an effective business with such stupid rules?"

"We can't make that our problem. We must send those two checks back."

"This is unacceptable," I say, my volume increasing. "I need to speak with your boss."

"Our branch manager, Mr. Sweeny, is busy right now—and I'm sure he won't be making an exception for you." Her tone is sharp now.

"Well then, I'll be right over to convince him he *needs* to make an exception for me."

I slam the phone down and quickly choose my nicest pantsuit, an expensive-looking beige knit Fritz chose for my twenty-ninth birthday. While I dress, I stew over my conversation with Peggy. This isn't the first run-in I've had with her.

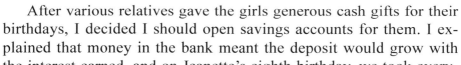

After various relatives gave the girls generous cash gifts for their birthdays, I decided I should open savings accounts for them. I explained that money in the bank meant the deposit would grow with the interest earned, and on Jeanette's eighth birthday, we took everything she had—a little over $100—and went to Valley Bank, where we opened a savings account in her name.

"In a year," I told her, "we'll come back to see how much money you've earned."

Fifteen days later, on Julie's sixth birthday, I did the same thing for her. Two years younger, she had two fewer years of accumulated birthday money—a little under $100.

On Jeanette's birthday a year later, our bank visit was a lot of fun. Jeanette enjoyed seeing her name on the bank booklet, and she especially liked seeing how much interest she'd earned. She was very happy to deposit that year's birthday money.

Fifteen days later, however, when Julie and I arrived at the bank anticipating an experience similar to Jeanette's, we were dismayed. Julie presented the booklet to the teller, Peggy Penny—only to receive a harsh explanation that not only was she ineligible for interest, but it was requisite to deduct a fee for savings accounts with balances under $100.

Julie looked as if she's been slapped for doing a good deed; then she burst into tears. Flummoxed, I couldn't figure out what to do other than cuddle and comfort my little girl.

Mr. Sweeny suddenly appeared at our side, looking concerned. "And why is this little one so unhappy?" he asked kindly. When I told him, he pursed his lips. "Well, I don't want a nice little girl to be sad on her birthday," he said. "I'll overrule that minimum deposit standard immediately."

His instructions to Peggy Penny to implement the changes required to make Julie's account an interest-bearing one were music to our ears. Julie immediately broke out into big smiles. Mr. Sweeny had saved the day.

Now, four months after the fiasco with Julie's account, I hope Mr. Sweeny will again overrule that heartless, bull-headed Peggy Penny. If not, it'll take all my strength to avoid a sad scene—and I'm sure I won't look nearly as cute doing it as little Julie had! I'll end up either being Mr. Sweeny's biggest-ever fan or causing him a lot of embarrassment. (If he denies my request, I'll unleash a loud tirade that will either leave the other customers openmouthed and paralyzed or send them scattering to escape the madwoman.)

When I enter the bank, Mr. Sweeny is seated at his desk behind the tellers, and he's not on the phone or with another customer. Still seething, I wait in line— fortunately not Peggy Penny's. When I reach the window, I ask to speak with Mr. Sweeny, and the teller excuses himself to walk over to him. My hopefully hero-to-be looks up and smiles as he invites me to sit in front of his other desk in the reception area, where I face away from the tellers while he sits facing them.

After pleasantries I explain the situation. Mr. Sweeny asks me several questions about Vulcan and then excuses himself, presumably to look at Vulcan's and my recent personal banking records. I forgo the temptation to turn around and face the action behind the counter. After five minutes, I wonder if Mr. Sweeny is phoning his boss, or perhaps even Crocker Bank. *Does he know I once received my food stamps here?* I'm certainly not going to volunteer that information, but I'm concerned that Peggy Penny might. I continue to steel myself to not turn around; I want to appear relaxed and sophisticated, but my stomach churns frantically, and I'm terrified I'm about to have another diarrhea episode.

Mr. Sweeny comes back with a smile on his face, and says, "I'll forgo the five-day hold for this recent deposit and future ones up to $5,000, as long as you never make an overdraft."

I try not to show just how happy I am as I thank him, but I'm not sure I succeed. On top of my relief, it feels great to get Peggy Penny overruled for a second time.

Trouble again! I've had my head in the clouds! Maybe I'm a dizzy blonde having too much fun selling and not thinking. Until today, I didn't realize I hadn't done a proper cash-flow forecast. By June 18, I won't be able to pay the $3,600 I owe Edwards. I should have taken more heed of what I learned in business classes: most new businesses fail because of inadequate working capital. I thought I had enough. *Wrong!* I must work this out, because I can't afford to fail. Thank God I've been miserly with every penny in my possession.

A couple of days after Bob got his tax refund, I got mine, and that $300 refund is still safely untouched in my personal bank account. How ironic that I'll have to use all of it and still not be able to pay Edwards till thirteen days after their June 18 due date. And then I'll have enough only if that recycler pays me on time. If he doesn't pay me within two days of his due date, I'll be over two weeks late with Edwards. *This Vulcan game isn't fun anymore.*

I ask Bob at the end of the day if he can offer any bright ideas. "Bob, I've been too upset to get much work done today, and I didn't call you because I didn't want to mess up your schedule with my worries," I tell him.

"What's wrong, honey?" he asks, full of concern.

"I've done a cash-flow forecast, and it's so scary. Now that I've learned I won't receive payment for most of my sales invoices till thirty-five or more days after the sales, I'm right back to big-time money problems. Even worse, because of the additional time needed for fabrication and trucking, my Edwards bills will always be due two to three weeks before I get paid for the wire I've bought from them. It seems that the more I sell the deeper in debt I'll be before I can pay off my debts, not just to Edwards but also the fabricators and truckers. I know it sounds crazy, but on paper my projected gross profit is nearly $6,600, and I've not used a cent of it for personal expenses, yet in twenty days I won't be able to pay Edwards what'll then be due."

"Calm down, A.M.," Bob says gently. "First, you shouldn't insist on limiting yourself by never making a late payment. You heard Peter Price say they don't bug people till the bills are five or ten working days overdue. You need to take advantage of that. Also, if and when Edwards gives you a reminder call, just ask them to *work with you.*"

I draw a deep breath. "I guess that makes sense."

"Second, I know of a way you won't even need to use the *paper* profits for living expenses. You can just let Vulcan grow for a while."

"Bob, are you crazy? What in the world are you talking about? My only scheduled income is Fritz's child support payments, and they don't even fully cover Jeanette and Julie's costs. Also, Fritz's pay habits are erratic."

"Just let me talk. Sit down and relax." He waits a moment and then goes on. "You know I spend more daylight hours at your house than at mine, don't you?"

"I guess so."

"You know I want to marry you, and the only reason we're not married now is you're not yet legally divorced. Also, you're afraid the marriage tax would take away some of the Vulcan profits, right?"

"Right." *Actually, I'm not really sure I want to pledge the rest of my life to you, but I'm not telling you that!*

"Well, wouldn't it make a lot of sense if I moved in with you and the girls and let you have my apartment money instead of wasting it on a place I don't spend much time in?"

I frown and shake my head. "It just seems wrong, Bob. Even Robby ended up having a mainstream wedding before he moved in with Cindy, and he's the rebel in the family."

"Don't be so old-fashioned. All your friends and neighbors won't think any differently of you. You know that, don't you?"

Won't they? "I'm not so sure."

"It's okay for people who love each other to live in the same house. More and more people are doing that these days."

"Bob, it was only last year that Robby got married. Before that, when he said he'd never marry anyone unless he lived with them first, it seemed to me like he was talking blasphemy. I was glad he ended up getting married like a decent man without first just living with Cindy. I thought her refusing the *just-live-together* idea was sensible."

"Your brother obviously married a prude," Bob says with a chuckle. "But that's neither here nor there. This is about us and about your financial difficulties. We love each other, right?"

"Right." *Not as much as I once loved Fritz—though that was when I stupidly assumed his love was as giving as mine—but it was such bliss before the blinders came off.*

"A.M., don't daydream on me—listen! We're already sort of living together when I spend the night and sometimes two or three nights in a row, right?"

"Right," I admit reluctantly.

"So what's the big deal? You'll be doing nothing new—just more of our time will be together. And the frosting on the cake will be you'll get my rent money instead of the greedy apartment owner getting it. In fact, we can eliminate the section in our Vulcan contract where I get a small reimbursement for my office space. That'll make Vulcan even more profitable. Also, I'll help pay my share and *then some* for the utilities and groceries."

"You've made some good points," I concede. "Let me think about it."

"In the meantime, let's take advantage of the girls being with their father. Tonight I'll take you to any restaurant you want and then we'll go see *2001: A Space Odyssey.*"

"Sure. Sounds like fun."

It's a fascinating movie, but I can't concentrate on it. Bob's financial help might be the only way my wire venture can succeed. It's not like I chose Bob for his money—*but it is only for his money that I'd let him move in with me.* I'm worried the neighbors might talk more than ever. Every one of the homes on my street houses a married couple. I'll be the *white trash* of the neighborhood if they all know my boyfriend's living with me.

On the other hand, I'm a grown woman, legally separated from her husband and almost divorced. I doubt anyone expects me to live like a virgin, but maybe some people do. If so, I've already offended them by allowing Bob to spend nights with me. So far, though, none of the girls' friends or their parents has stigmatized any of us, and I would think that if Bob did move in, those who never cared that he slept at my house wouldn't care that he lived there, and those who were already offended wouldn't be any more offended.

If I refuse Bob's offer to live with me, then I'm just as silly and hypocritical as Cindy. I'll always remember that day, shortly before she and Robby were engaged, when they visited Fritz and me. Trying to be hospitable, Fritz offered them our guest bedroom, and Cindy indignantly spat, "I'm no bunny!" I thought she was being ridiculous and mean, because I was aware that she and Robby frequently went on trips together, and both were in their late twenties, for God's sake. Even my parents believed they were having sex. Daddy felt sorry for Cindy because her deceased father wasn't around to insist that Robby marry her sooner. Both Mommy and Daddy, convinced that my *nefarious* brother had taken sweet Cindy's virginity years ago, were ashamed of him for "using" Cindy rather than marrying her.

Before dating Cindy, Robby once brought a Japanese divorcee home for dinner. Mommy was openly hostile to her. Robby mistakenly thought the hostility was race-based, but it turned out to derive from Mommy's determination that Robby marry only someone who had never "gone all the way" with anyone else.

I've often wondered if my parents placed equal value on my wedding-night virginity and Robby's top-notch education. After my marriage to Fritz, I found out that when I was twelve or thirteen, Daddy told Mommy to make me stop trying to do splits because he feared I would break my hymen. I also discovered that if Fritz and I hadn't married when we did, my parents would have sent me away to Grandma's, in Oklahoma, to put a damper on my sexual yearnings.

Mommy was also horrified at Reverend Duncan's judgment when I told her about our mandatory premarital consultation. He asked us if we wanted a baby right away, and when we replied no, he asked what kind of birth control we planned to use, to which we both answered, "the pill." Mommy thought it was highly inappropriate that Fritz and I had even discussed such a delicate issue before marriage. She also said it hadn't been very professional for Reverend Duncan to bring up such a private matter. I later learned that Daddy agreed with her. How shocked they'd be if I told them that a couple of months before our wedding day, Fritz had driven me to the doctor for my examination and prescription.

When I asked her what she and Daddy did, she said, "Your Daddy quietly excused himself to go to the drugstore before we went to bed together." Mommy too had been under pressure to postpone pregnancy when she married Daddy; she was still finishing her bachelor's degree, and just before her wedding night, her mother warned her: "Don't you embarrass me and have a baby in nine months."

After Fritz and I separated, Mommy told me I shouldn't date for at least a year. She was dismayed to learn that I was dating and probably sleeping with Bob half a year later. I'm sure both she and Daddy will be aghast and depressed if Bob and I choose to live together "in sin."

I hate to disappoint my parents—but I'm a thirty-three-year-old woman, for God's sake! After the movie ends, I'll give Bob the go-ahead.

CHAPTER 19
MAN ON BOARD

*In the '50s, too many women, even though they
were very smart, lived to make the man feel
that he was brainier. It was a sad thing.*
—Ruth Bader Ginsburg

We're still adjusting to Bob's living here. Some things are good and some are bad. One good thing is that he's helped improve Jeanette and Julie's disrespectful behavior toward me. They now treat me as nine- and seven-year-olds should treat their mother—at least, they do when Bob is around. I think Fritz belittled me so much in front of them that they assumed I deserved their disdain as well. Bob does what a good husband and father should do: he puts his foot down whenever they speak contemptuously to me. He never goes so far as to send them to their rooms, but he rebukes them sharply. I wonder if he would treat them more harshly if he were their biological parent.

Another positive force from Bob is that he's improved the girls' table manners. I confess that I've been too lax with them; though they've never embarrassed me with company or in restaurants, their eating habits at home left much to be desired. Fortunately, they've quickly buckled down to Bob's expectation that "Sunday manners" apply Monday through Saturday.

One bad thing is Bob's attitude toward anything to do with Fritz. He doesn't want to let Fritz enter our house, not even to use the toilet. He also thinks it's improper that I keep in touch with Fritz's relatives. I stand my ground on these issues because I want a friendly relationship with Fritz and his family. There's no way I want to dump them out of the girls' lives—or even my own. As a little child, I wished I could see more of my father's sisters and their families, and I resented how my only-child, bratty mother would sometimes keep us from visiting Daddy's people. Bob doesn't care about my reasoning, and I don't care much that he boils with frustration over this issue. *Too damn bad!*

Another bad thing is that Bob insists I wear pantsuits for customer and vendor meetings. He considers dresses and skirts unprofessional. When he moved in he bought me a very elegant pantsuit, but one is his financial limit. Before that I had only four pantsuits because I refused to spend more on clothes due to Vulcan's ongoing cash-flow problems. Now, for out-of-home business dealings, I stick to wearing my five pantsuits when Bob's in town. I save my skirts and dresses for when he travels. Bob is content, and I'm thrilled with my new outfit, so it's not all bad.

Another mixture of good and bad is that I now have a home office, but my lovely guest room is no more. Bob needed a home office, and luckily the hundred-plus-square-foot room easily accommodates two desks. Bob scouted out an inexpensive used one for me, and he already had his own. I operate much more efficiently now that I have all my Vulcan paraphernalia constantly at my fingertips instead of having to move the documents I need back and forth between the guest room and dining room. I also like being able to open and close the door to my workplace when not working, even if for just while I make and eat dinner. For Vulcan, I'm in a better mindset businesswise, but for hospitality and aesthetics, I lament no longer seeing the inviting bed with its gay floral spread.

I certainly can't complain about food: Bob treats us to eating out more than ever, so it doesn't bother me that other than barbecue, he never offers to make a thing—Fritz at least made omelets.

Bob eschews domestic chores in general. He's already hired a gardener to give my yard a needed spruce-up. Bob won't lift a finger for housecleaning, but he's extremely neat and does indeed pay more than his fair share of utilities, so I can't complain on that account either.

CHAPTER 20
DESPERATE FOR HELP

*Are we limiting our success by not mastering
the art of delegation?*
—Oprah Winfrey, media executive, actress,
TV producer, philanthropist

I'm so glad tomorrow is Sunday, the only day I take time off from Vulcan. On Mondays through Saturdays my only free time typically consists of one or two bike rides. The first, sometimes only, ride is to the post office. The hoped-for second break is to the bank to deposit a check or two. Most days I squeeze in a grocery trip to Albertsons on one of these two fresh-air escapes.

I feel like an overworked slave to my new company. Bob takes us out for half of our meals, but when I cook I feel pressured to prepare the food and eat it as quickly as possible—that way my Vulcan taskmaster will allow me more sleep than if I took longer. Sometimes I stay up till three in the morning. Sometimes I get up at three in the morning. But usually I work from just before sunrise to shortly after sunset, plus an hour or two after dinner. I frequently have insomnia due to fear that something might upset a customer to the point of dumping Vulcan. Sometimes I wake up in the middle of the night and worry that I won't get any more orders. Other times I worry I'll get too many, and my business will implode.

I've discovered that running a business requires a lot of nickel-and-dime expenditures that unfortunately add up to dollars. I've invested in customized letterhead, envelopes, three-ring binders, business cards, invoice forms, a Vulcan address stamp, a date stamp, a stapler, spread-sheets, pencils, pens, carbon paper, onionskin, Wite-Out, erasers, and more.

When I found myself raking through all sorts of papers, I realized I needed file folders. Then, when the folders grew so numerous that they'd become unwieldy piles, I bought cardboard file boxes for them. After accumulating four tightly packed file boxes, I invested in a four-drawer metal file cabinet. Any day my empty file boxes will be needed again to take on the overflow.

Soon I won't have any time left to continue expanding Vulcan—but if and when the growth curve stops its steep angle upward and plateaus, I'll be able to cash out a chunk of the profits I've earned. There are times when my bankbook looks substantial and the impressive numbers nearly burn a hole in my pocket, but when I do a cash-flow forecast, I realize that in two or three weeks I'll need that money to pay my vendors. I now enjoy some proceeds, however, even if only a fraction of Vulcan's true earnings. My one splurge was for clothes—six back-to-school outfits for each daughter and one more pantsuit for me. That shopping spree, though, was helped by a check I recently received from Fritz; the biggest ever, it covered both his overdue child support and final alimony.

Bob complains that I spend too much time working. He misses our former Saturday night movie dates, for which I'm now either too tired or too busy, and says I should get some paid help. I agree, but to find someone competent to do what I've been doing will take some thought and organization on my part.

I tell my dear friend, Suzie, to whom I always tell everything, that I'm getting frazzled and close to a nervous breakdown because I feel I'm falling farther and farther behind and not sleeping enough.

"I need help," I tell her. "But I'm nervous! I've never hired or man-aged anyone before—unless babysitters count."

"What if I help you out in my spare time?" she asks.

"It's so sweet of you to offer," I say. "Thank you! But first I need to figure out how you could be useful. Can I let you know soon?"

"Of course," she says.

What a dear she is!

After the traumatic Herbie period when my marriage went downhill, Suzie's close proximity and friendship was a godsend. Without her I might have truly gone insane. She later told me she was appalled and disgusted with how Fritz treated me during that terrible time. She also told me she thought I should have left him earlier; she couldn't stand how Fritz tried every which way to prevent me from resuming my college education.

Suzie may have withheld her thoughts from me, but I suspect that Jeanette overheard her talking to her husband, Ed, about Fritz's ill treatment of me when she was babysitting once. Jeanette came home that night and stated in front of Fritz and me that Fritz should act nicer so I wouldn't leave him and find another husband. Both Fritz and I were shocked, and Fritz thought she'd been privy to a conversation of mine. At that point I had neither desire nor energy for divorce and actually felt sorry about Fritz's mental anguish. I lovingly insisted that such thoughts had never entered my head, which was true at the time. To this day I don't know if he believed me.

After I turned thirty, such thoughts *did* enter my head. At breakfast on that birthday, Fritz, six months older than I, said, "When I turned thirty I didn't feel old, but now that I have a thirty-year-old wife, I feel really, really old."

I was devastated. That afternoon I went on a driving errand with the girls. Without thinking, I ignored a stop sign, and a policeman pulled me over. I told him I had no excuse, that I was just depressed because I felt over the hill due to my thirtieth birthday. Of course, he asked to see my driver's license.

"You really are thirty today!" he exclaimed, clearly surprised. "For a birthday present I won't write a ticket; but be more careful so you can keep those precious little girls of yours safe and sound."

That was the nicest thing that happened to me on March 19, 1972.

Less than two months later, when I had my affair with Rex, Suzie was my understanding confessor. In fact, she was especially sympathetic because she then told me about *her* extramarital affair. We became soul mates in our neediness for sexual love outside the home, caused by our husbands' not meeting our needs. With Suzie it was sex, and with me, respect and appreciation. Ed insisted Suzie's sex hunger was nymphomania, whereas Fritz didn't respect my educational goals, desire for better sexual foreplay, or general feelings. Before my infidelity, I begged him to meet with a marriage counselor, but he refused. Worsening his birthday insult, shortly thereafter he danced around me as he talked about the delightful nymphets at his office. I smiled sadly, and wished that I could be someone's nubile young maiden.

Suzie and I enjoyed being sex goddesses outside of marriage, but the duplicity caused me more distress than it did her. It drove me crazy, and I began to want a divorce. The day Fritz and I separated I felt an immediate, euphoric freedom. The disappointment and despondency was there too, but relief counterbalanced it. Suzie and Ed, meanwhile, have stayed married and are compatible outside of their bedroom. Suzie calmly accepts that it's vital to get her sexual needs met by someone other than her husband.

Suzie also needs even more masculine attention than I do. She not only relishes compliments from the opposite sex but expects them. I think the reason she passed her part-time legal secretary job on to me in the summer of '73 was because Bill, the attorney, never told her how nice she looked, no matter how attractively she dressed. Even though I too tried to dress attractively, it didn't bother me in the least when Bill treated me with an all-business attitude.

In terms of Vulcan, Suzie would love the attention she'd get from selling; but new sales have already added to my paperwork nightmare. It's the bookkeeping that's crushing me. I must step back and analyze all my clerical jobs. I suspect I'm not doing everything as efficiently as it could be done. Even though I did well in college business classes (Principles of Accounting I and II, Income Tax Accounting, Principles of Economics I, Theories of Management), I don't apply everything I've learned. At first it would have been overkill, but now I should think of my Vulcan dealings as a regular business. Before I try to introduce any improvements, I decide to contact the Small Business Administration, which helps startups for free.

When I get in touch with the SBA, I'm informed that I'll be meeting with a group of retired gentlemen who'll expect me to bring a summary of my business and be prepared to ask and answer any pertinent questions. In the days that follow, I make a balance sheet of Vulcan's net worth, which, along with cash flow, has grown from the original seed money thanks to my frugality, Bob's financial contributions, and, above all, fantastic sales. In that balance sheet I have an entry for Taxes Due, which includes sales taxes and a rough calculation of year-to-date unpaid state and federal income taxes. My diligent work in the Income Tax Accounting class comes in handy here.

The day of the meeting soon arrives, and I find myself in a room with four old men—far older than Daddy, perhaps all in their seventies—each balding or gray. They pounce on the Taxes Due entry, stating that I should keep up on my taxes. They can't understand my reasoning—that the deadlines haven't yet passed, and I plan to pay my debts within the time limit. I quickly realize that these businessmen lack the sophistication to understand accrual and tax accounting; probably, they all dealt with cash-only transactions and blindly passed on the paperwork to their accountants. I know that my daily entries aren't done very professionally, though, so I'm humiliated when one geezer says, "Your bookwork is… is… it's *Mickey Mouse!*"

I know he's right, but I had trouble applying my book knowledge efficiently, due in part to a lack of ledgers but also to my hurried sloppiness. The men tell me I can find ledgers in any stationery store. I just hadn't looked for them, but before the end of the day I've secured the account books, and for several tedious days I pencil in entries, beginning with my original wire purchase. This exercise is a tremendous sleep-robber and puts a halt to attempting new sales, but I know it'll pay off in the long run. I also design and pay for copies of new order and requisition forms, whereas before I'd simply put the information on blank sheets of paper.

Finally I have an efficient system—no longer *Mickey Mouse.* The time I've invested in organizing all this will make my life easier, but I'd still be overworked without office help, so I'm thrilled to have a teachable plan to relieve me of at least a third of the boring office drudgery!

Other than brief tasks not worth delegating, I can have Suzie do the more time-consuming but simple work. Bank and mail runs qualify, but my great escape is to ride my bike on these trips. The fresh air and light exercise is so invigorating, even in the rain, that I always feel energized afterward. *I'm not giving that up for anything!*

I learned in Theories of Management class that no matter how good a typist the boss is, he or she should delegate all the typing jobs. The example proffered posited an attorney who typed 60 wpm but assigned all typing to his secretary, who typed only 50 wpm. The attorney still produced fifty dollars an hour for legal services—more than seven times the cost of his seven-dollar-an-hour secretary. Accordingly, Suzie can do 100 percent of the typing. She can also do most of the filing, as well as the nasty job of hounding the late payers. Lastly, she should be able to make all the data entries related to checks received, sales, sales taxes, and especially a lot of the columns in the customer and product spreadsheets.

Non-daily tasks will continue to be my weekend jobs, but with Suzie's assistance the daily jobs should be whittled down. When I originally got into this business, all I saw were the dollar signs; I never imagined the accompanying drudgery. I hate the process, but I love the results. Apart from bike rides and visits and phone calls with my favorite customers, my only relaxation these days is the nirvana I feel as I gaze at black-and-white evidence of super sales and profits.

CHAPTER 21
FIRST FEMALE SHIPMATE

Leadership is the art of getting someone else to do something you want done because he wants to do it.
—Dwight D. Eisenhower, 34th President of
the United States

Suzie absorbs the knowledge I throw her way like a sponge. She saves me only ten of her twelve weekly clerical hours, since we chat for half an hour each of the four days she arrives. Still, I'm so happy to have her help—and at minimum wage—that the socializing feels like a bonus. Her wages are affordable, and ten net hours a week gives me time for extra sleep, selling for Vulcan, and even a movie date with Bob now and then.

It's Suzie's third week, and she has the records in order. Now she convinces me she's acquired enough familiarity with the wire products to sell them, and she'd like to be a salesperson a few additional hours every Tuesday, late morning to early afternoon. I've decided to take her into the field on an outing.

We go to a substantial recycling center in Richmond managed by Jim, a personable, lean and handsome black man. I tell Suzie that Jim buys enough wire to justify a Vulcan-paid lunch, and if he seems receptive, I'll invite him to join us. I reveal to Suzie that I haven't yet taken any customers to lunch, and will feel more comfortable about it if she's with me. Jim seems to be a sociable guy. *And is he ever!* He asks enthusiastically if we can go to his favorite nearby haunt, where everybody knows him.

As we walk in, I note that all the restaurant's customers are Caucasian; their coloring ranges from pasty white to California sun-tan. Jim seems oblivious of being a minority, and apparently revels in being ensconced between two leggy blondes. Two hours later I gulp inwardly when I note the total on the bill, due in part to Jim and Suzie downing two glasses of wine apiece. I, meanwhile, struggled to finish half a glass, as wine always tastes like rotten grape juice to me. As we leave, Jim loudly thanks the waiter for treating him and his *girlfriends* right. Suzie and I giggle.

These last four months with Suzie's help have been a godsend, but now I'd like more work hours from her than she's willing to give. At least her help will keep me out of the funny farm while I deal with Thanksgiving preparations on top of my Vulcan work. Even then, I may have to put in some Vulcan time after dinner tomorrow before I start on my special turkey stuffing and pies.

Then Suzie blindsides me: "I won't be able to come in tomorrow," she says as we're wrapping things up today. "I have so much to do for Thanksgiving. I'm sure you understand."

"What? The hell I do!" I reply, feeling punched in the gut. More calmly, I continue: "Since you've been helping me, with the extra time I've gained, I've accumulated more customers than ever, and now I need more help than ever. Suzie, I'm counting on you. The supermarkets are overwhelmed with Thanksgiving needs; the boxboard plants are making more box material for Christmas; the manufacturers and retailers are gearing up for Christmas; and the recyclers are getting more holiday-related recyclables from everywhere, so if you don't come in tomorrow, I could have a nervous breakdown."

"But Alice, I'm going to be so busy getting ready for Thanksgiving," she says in a pleading tone. "I really can't come in to work till after Thanksgiving."

In an equally pleading tone, I say, "Suzie, don't you think *I'm* busy getting ready for Thanksgiving too? Please don't let me down."

"Please try to understand," she says firmly. "I just can't help it. I'm sorry."

"I'm sorry, too," I say—matter-of-factly, but with some venom added. "I'm going to end up a nervous wreck on Thanksgiving. Doing your work and making my pies tomorrow will keep me up till at least 2:00 AM. Then I have to get up by six to stuff my huge turkey so I can get it into the oven on time."

"I'm sure you understand," she says.

I'm so overwhelmed I feel like I might explode. *A fine time to desert me, you fair-weather friend,* I almost shout at her out loud. Instead, almost spitting poison, I snap, "Well, Suzie, I understand you're letting me down *big-time.*"

"I'm sorry, Alice. But try to be happy. It looks like I'll be getting another customer for you before Christmas. Gotta go."

I slump in my chair when she leaves, thinking *oh, go to hell!*

Bing… Bing… BING.

God damn that alarm! It seems as if I've just lain down, but at least all of Vulcan's customers are taken care of. I guess Suzie doesn't think of her assistance as a real job—after all, she's only paid minimum wage, a far cry from what we both got paid at AI and later up here for our legal secretary work. I should be thankful that she's been willing to work for such minor remuneration—especially because she doesn't need to make money, given her husband's great job and all the financial goodies they get from his parents.

Suzie's also made money for Vulcan by picking up a couple of customers—not big ones, but every little bit helps. Based on her few selling hours every Tuesday, her commissions probably amount to a pinch above minimum wage. Even if she doesn't calculate her hourly pay, I'm sure she's happier selling than doing clerical work. With her poise, confidence, and head-turning good looks, she probably gets a fantastic reception from every man she meets.

I shouldn't forget that she's doing me a favor, and if she really needed a job she could do far better than Vulcan—unless she was willing to be more devoted to selling rather than only dabble in it. My bottom line, though, might be that it's not a good idea to have a friend work for me, especially when the money means next to nothing to her. She'll probably skip out on me at Christmastime too.

So far I've been able to financially absorb Suzie's twelve weekly hours easily enough. If I can get a high school student to cover the office two and a half hours every Monday through Friday afternoon, I think things will go much more smoothly for me. Unlike Suzie, a youngster who values office-work experience would likely appreciate making a nickel or a dime over minimum wage, but training a student will probably be a lot more difficult and time-consuming than training Suzie was. Also, I don't have the time to scout, interview, and break someone in right now. After the girls' January birthdays, I should be able to concentrate on it. In the meantime, I must remember to be thankful for Suzie's valuable assistance—even if I can't rely on it. Sure hope I can survive Christmas!

At least I won't have to do the twelve-hour roundtrip down south this Christmas: Mommy and Daddy refuse to allow Bob and me to sleep together at their house, so Bob refuses to visit them. I'm sort of glad, because it means the girls and I will finally spend Christmas in our Dublin home. Of course, it's sad that there'll be no Herbie or a loving Fritz, plus, the girls are now privy to the reality behind the Santa fantasy, which takes some of the magic out of the holiday. Still, I'll enjoy our first Christmas in our house.

Finding cash for Santa presents this year isn't a problem because the main gifts are free—a seven-week-old puppy for each girl. Bob is the one who searched out these doggies and purchased a doghouse—they'll have to live outdoors because of Jeanette's asthma. Bob also found the perfect cardboard box and red blanket for the pups to nestle on. Tomorrow morning, they'll be hidden in the box.

When the girls gallop downstairs, giggling, Bob directs them to the unwrapped but red-bow-topped box. Jeanette picks up the lid and gasps. "Oh Julie, look. Real puppies! I want the black one." She gazes lovingly at the long, sausage-shaped canine.

"I want the white one," says Julie, awestruck, as she pets the dog with the big tan spots, which has a more ordinary mutt's body.

"This is my Shatzi," Jeanette says—that's "honey" in German—and I will love her more than I'll ever love my very own children."

I laugh out loud. *Boy, will I ever have fun kidding her about that in fifteen to twenty years.*

"I'll name my dog Brownie," Julie declares, gathering the puppy into her arms.

These shaking little littermates don't look a bit alike, but they're both small dogs, roughly the same size. Our new little mutts made this Christmas sparkle.

Whew! I got through the holidays without having to go to the funny farm. Before Suzie (predictably) skipped out on me a couple of working days before Christmas, she insisted that I buy an adding machine with tape. It also subtracts, multiplies, and divides—and the printed tape certainly prevents errors. Those things are expensive, and I hated spending the money, but it did help make Suzie's absence easier on me.

Suzie will be back to her regular grind tomorrow, and fortunately won't be likely to skip out on me while I prepare for the girls' birthday celebrations. If and when I find her replacement, I doubt she'll mind getting canned. After all, she'll always have the option of using her newly freed time to sell on commission.

CHAPTER 22
FEMALE SHIPMATE NUMBER TWO

The really expert riders of horses let the horse know immediately who is in control, but then guide the horse with loose reins and seldom use the spurs.
—Sandra Day O'Connor, former Associate Justice of the US Supreme Court

Yum, bakery bliss! How sweet of Bob to insist his New Year's resolution is on Saturday afternoons to buy Sunday morning pastries for us when we don't plan to brunch at the Refectory, my former waitress haunt. I haven't indulged in a cherry strudel since just before Fritz quit his job.

"Hi, you two. Can I help you select something?" asks a buxom, baby-faced teen. I admire her perky voice and clear pink complexion, complemented by her pink rosebud-patterned apron. Her curly, honey-blond hair makes me think of a spun-sugar halo. A miniature of this little blue-eyed cutie would make an adorable cake decoration.

We come in one week later, and the same darling girl is behind the counter. The people she's waiting on seem very fond of her and call her Betty. I'll remember her as Buxom Betty. It might be a good idea to steal her for Vulcan. I promised myself to seriously look for an assistant after the girls' birthdays, and Julie's eighth birthday party was just yesterday. I'll ask Bob what he thinks of my idea, and we'll surreptitiously interview this bubbly Buxom Betty next time.

"Hi, Betty," I say when we approach the counter.

"Oh, how nice of you to remember my name," she says, beaming. "May I ask what your names are?"

"I'm Alice," I say, smiling back.

"And I'm Dr. Brown," Bob says.

"I'll remember your names, too, Alice and Dr. Brown."

"Hi, Alice and Dr. Brown," Betty chirps when we enter the bakery this morning. "It looks like you're regular customers now. So glad to see you again."

She certainly has great manners. I'll bet she'd be terrific with customers on the phone. I decide to get some intel: "Hi, Betty. It looks like you work here every Saturday. Do you work here any other days?"

"Oh, yes. I work every Sunday morning too. I come straight from church."

"Is it because of your school schedule that you don't work Monday through Friday?" I mentally cross my fingers that this isn't the case.

"I wouldn't mind working right after school," she says with a shrug. "But they're not busy then, except for Fridays, when the baker helps his wife behind the counter. They're very nice people. They pay me five cents over minimum wage."

"Have you ever thought of doing office work?"

"Oh, I'd love to work in an office… hopefully someday. I'm a good typist."

I decide to spring the trap. "Well, Dr. Brown and I have a business called Vulcan Metal Joining Consultants that we operate out of our home, about a mile from here. I have an opening for part-time office help, two and a half hours every Monday through Friday. The pay would be ten cents over minimum wage. Would you be interested in working for us?"

"Oh, yes. I could get there every day about five minutes past three. Would that be okay?"

"Perfect," I say, with a grin.

We agree on her start date, and off we go!

Bob and I are very pleased with Betty. And she's pleased with us— I'm sure of that, because we were the only non-relatives invited to her high school graduation. Now she's out of school till she begins junior college in September. I'm spoiling myself by increasing Betty's twelve and a half weekly hours to twenty, 2:00 to 5:00 for office assistance and 5:00 to 6:00 for cooking our family meal, whether or not Bob is out of town. Though only eighteen, Betty cooks as well or better than I do, and while she's in the kitchen, I'm in the office; sometimes I even finish tasks I formerly had to do after dinner. Betty's happy with the extra income, and I'm happy producing enough to afford her additional services.

Bob plans to spend his tax refunds this year for the four of us to vacation in Maui. He says it's about time I took a week's vacation. The girls and I have never been to Hawaii, and we're all excited. We'll leave in late July.

While we're gone, Betty can do some of my daily tasks in lieu of her current one-hour cooking job. In bits and pieces, I teach her the extra jobs and substitute her work for mine to make sure she can operate competently. I plan to set up some hypothetical situations to prepare Betty to think on her feet before we go. I'm thrilled to go on my first vacation in ages—but I'm also nervous about being gone from Vulcan for a full workweek. I hope Betty can handle everything in my absence.

We've only been back a week, and Hawaii is now just a soothing memory of warm ocean water; sweet-scented flowers; alluring scenery; Polynesian singing; hula dancers; and the aroma of Kalua luau pork served alongside pineapple, mango, watermelon, and papaya. I even enjoyed the purple poi more than the bland white rice—though the others didn't. Our tropical days passed way too quickly. It seems Vulcan ticked on without me well enough, thanks to Betty being such a smart, personable young lady.

Yesterday I noted that July's phone bill was extraordinarily high, due to lots of calls to one particular phone number during the week we were away. Betty didn't tell me about any problems or situations that would demand so many calls to one place. The calls added up to nearly $35. *Hell!*

I called the number, hoping to get to the bottom of things.

"Hello, Smith's Printing."

Smith's Printing? Oh, yes. That's where Betty picked up our new letterhead while I was in Hawaii. "Hello," I say. "This is Alice Stiller from Vulcan Metal Joining Consultants. Was there a problem with our recent order?"

"I'm sorry, I have no idea. May I pass you on to our customer service man, Romeo?"

"Sure." I wait. "This is Romeo."

"Hi, Romeo. This is Alice Stiller from Vulcan Metal Joining Consultants. We recently purchased 200 sheets of letterhead from you. Was there a problem of any sort with the transaction?"

"Oh, no, ma'am. We finished the order exactly when we promised, and your representative said all was perfect."

I frown. This doesn't make any sense. "Well, I'm looking at a phone bill with seventeen calls made to your business in one week. Do you have any idea why that is?"

"No, I don't, ma'am. As I said, we gave you excellent service and excellent quality."

"Thank you, Romeo. Goodbye."

Hmm. I think I see the picture. Now I remember that young Romeo fellow from when I visited the shop. He had looks that could kill; I'm guessing he's just Betty's type. She's not shy, and probably pestered him while I was away, and he was too chivalrous to tell me. Either that or he enjoyed the attention; some of those calls lasted over fifteen minutes, after all.

This romance amounts to a $35 expense for Vulcan. Betty knows my rule is no personal calls at work. I'm afraid that when the cat was away, the mouse chose to play.

As she walks in, Betty cheerily greets me, "Hi, Alice. Got any new sales?"

"Yes, Betty, but I have something important to ask you. Why did you make all those personal calls while I was away?"

"Personal calls?" she repeats, looking wide-eyed and innocent. "I've never made any personal calls at Vulcan; I know you don't allow them."

"I'm afraid you did make at least sixteen personal calls." I hold up the phone bill.

Her face remains blank. "I have no idea what you mean."

"I mean you called Romeo of Smith's Printing seventeen times, and there was no business reason to call him for at least sixteen of those expensive calls. I figured that out after I studied the phone bill and personally called Romeo to ask if there were any problems with the letterhead we ordered from Smith's Printing. Romeo assured me there were none."

Betty's usually rosy face turns white. "How much do I owe you?" she blurts out.

This girl is too good a liar to remain with Vulcan. *Damn! I'll have to let her go.*

CHAPTER 23
SHIP FULL OF WOMEN

If you really want to grow as an entrepreneur,
you've got to learn to delegate.
—Sir Richard Branson, British business magnate,
investor, author, philanthropist

Knowing how pleased one of my customers was with a young employee he found through his local high school, I decide to give that a try too, and *voila*—Mature Mary!

Mary is a very serious sixteen-year-old high school sophomore. Though she's two years younger than Betty, she's far more mature—or at least she seems to be so far. Mary is rather plain, with no outstanding physical features. She wears conservative, mostly earth-tone clothes over her average teenage body. She's a dishwater blonde, and I have to look carefully to note that her eyes are a forgettable gray and her skin has a few freckles. Unlike Betty, Mary doesn't generate charisma, but her telephone style is cordial enough—just not as engaging as Betty's warm chitchat. Most important, Mary seems every bit as smart as Betty.

I miss Betty's buoyancy, however, and I miss her cooking, too. Mary has no interest in cooking or in the five extra weekly hours, so I've hired another high school girl, Skinny Sandy, who not only cooks but also eats with us and cleans up afterward. Sandy isn't a bad cook, just not as good as Betty. She's a pixie-faced, anorexic-looking brunette who'd be prettier—and sexier—with a few additional pounds.

During the week with no clerical help, Bob persuaded me to obtain cleaning services. First, I put up with an incompetent ninny from Merry Maids. I was greeted with a high-pitched, "I don't do windows." I thought if this meant she also didn't clean toilets I'd send her on her way, but when I asked, she smiled sarcastically and replied, "Yes, I clean toilets." I thought if I were cleaning houses I'd rather clean windows than toilets—but I didn't plan on asking her to clean my windows anyway. After she left I realized she hadn't cleaned the house properly. Then I regretted I hadn't immediately dismissed her for having such an impertinent attitude. I asked Merry Maids for my money back, but they refused to either refund or send me another person at no charge. I resignedly touched up the places neglected by the Merry Maids misfit. *So much for Merry Maids!*

A couple weeks later I tried another agency, which sent a great lady, Elaine, a real keeper. Also, Elaine willingly cleans windows. Perhaps she's so hardworking because she's a single mom with a boy in first grade. Elaine looks as neat and clean as she makes our house. She wears a crisp pink uniform that sets off her slightly freckled face and perfectly coiffed strawberry-blonde hair. She doesn't tie me up with incessant talk, but says just enough to let me get to know her a little better with each cleaning session. Best of all, she gives me several more hours a week to work, sleep, or enjoy my loved ones.

Skinny Sandy has been with us for a month when she gives her notice because she's having trouble keeping up with her schoolwork. *Probably needs extra sleep to make up for not eating enough, poor thing.*

Now I have Over-Salting Oprah, another tall, but not skinny, fifteen-year-old. Despite being a redhead, she's not temperamental. In fact, because she's so sweet and interesting, I don't have the heart to fire her for not immediately heeding my low-salt instructions. The meal following this stipulation, I salivated at Oprah's lightly cooked green peas, but nearly spit them out when I tasted only salt.

I know I'm a weird one, hating salt so much. Unlike most people, I never sprinkle the stuff on eggs or corn-on-the-cob, and rarely appreciate the briny soups others rave about. I guess my taste buds allow the salt to overpower other natural flavors. I think I'm entitled to expect under-salted food because I'm the employer.

It's taken me a while to accept the fact that I am indeed a boss. I've always taken umbrage with bossiness. I don't necessarily have problems with authority; I've just never wanted to be thought of as bossy. I remember thinking how obnoxious the power-grabbing student hall monitors were when they commanded the other kids who ran in the grammar-school hallways to stop and walk. I don't recall being chastised by any of them, but still thought they were foolish to act so self-important. When my sixth-grade teacher asked me to be a hall monitor, I turned him down, determined never to stoop so low as to be one of them.

Initially, I suffered hurt feelings when I heard Betty refer to me as her boss. Then I realized there was no better term. On the other hand, I don't want my vendors or customers to think of me as an owner or partner at Vulcan but rather as a representative of an established, substantial business. In fact, I've taken great pains to hide the reality of my shoestring operation. Before I hired Suzie, when I did business letters I always typed my name below the area for my handwritten signature—and then, two spaces below my typed name, I lettered *AS: mw.* This stood for Alice Stiller for having dictated the letter, and Mystery Woman having been the typist, but the recipient was supposed to think *mw* indicated Mary Williams, Mona White, or some such—certainly not Mystery Woman. Thankfully, that bit of subterfuge has been unnecessary ever since I had my typing taken over, first by Suzie, then Betty, and now Mary. *Yes, I'm thrilled to have outgrown that type-type-typing job at AI.*

CHAPTER 24
MY GODFATHER

I have learned more in the streets than in any classroom.
—Don Vito Corleone, fictional Mafia chief in
Mario Puzo's novel *The Godfather*

This San Francisco garbage company is huge. I'll bet they buy lots of wire for their recycling division. It took me months to get a visit with this Angelo guy who's in charge of recycling, though he now seems very welcoming.

Somewhere around fifty, a cigarette dangling out of his mouth, Angelo has a winning, lopsided smile in a weather-beaten face framed by wavy gray hair. He's very tall—at least six foot two, big-boned, and almost skinny. His blue-gray-green eyes appear kind and calm. He's craggy looking, with a large nose, and his breath and clothes stink like an ashtray, but there's something strangely attractive about him. Could it be his coarse and calloused hands, his soft-spoken, laid-back manner? Or do I find his poor grammar charming? Whatever it is, I feel very relaxed around this lumbering type-B personality.

He tells me he used to haul garbage, but now he's a stockholder and on the board of directors of Bayshore Salvage's parent company, Sunset Scavenger.[13] He says every stockholder and board member used to be a can carrier. Most of them have a son or sons who are currently hauling garbage and will, upon their fathers' retirement, be entitled to their fathers' stock and board memberships.[14]

Angelo shows me his baler, which uses those big 1,000-pound silver spools. He says they also buy bale ties for some of their customers, and gives me the specs. I tell him I'll get back to him with quotes. I note all sorts of garbage trucks coming and going and ask where the garbage is. Angelo walks me over to the pit.[15]

It gets stinkier and stinkier as we walk. Angelo points about a hundred feet beyond us and says he's seen and smelled enough garbage for a lifetime, so he'll remain in place, but if I'm still curious I may continue on.

"Be very careful," he warns me. "One man accidentally fell in that trench a few years back and drowned in all the crap."

What a way to go! I walk closer, feeling strange in my high heels and full-skirted dress. About ten feet away, I can see the increasingly nauseating, multicolored contents of the poor fallen man's enormous burial site. I walk another yard and gag. I pivot away and, despite my constant dry heaving, feel like I'm running faster than a professional athlete could. I see Angelo smile and suppress his laughter.

Angelo is now one of my satisfied bale tie customers, and I've stopped by to see how much he has on hand so I can calculate when he'll place another order.

"Now that youse knows more about garbage, would youse like to learn more about recycling?" he asks me.

"Sure, Angelo."

"We already have lots of recycling customers, but we want lots more. I think youse could do a good job of getting them. There's big bucks in recycling. For every customer youse gets, I'll give youse half—fifty-fifty. Are youse interested?"

"I'd like to give it a try—that is, if you don't mind if I work only one day a week. You see, I'm pretty committed to Vulcan."

He shrugs. "I'd rather youse leave Vulcan, but I'll take a day a week. I'll tell youse more about recycling after I tell our deal to the board. They'll probably want to meet youse before youse starts."

"You got a deal, Angelo. I think it'll be fun."

"Okay. Come back in a week by four o'clock, and I'll show youse to the board."

The following week I show up fifteen minutes early and greet Angelo with a smile. "I'm ready to meet your board."

"Youse looks nice. I hope the board'll like youse. Most will, but some don't want a woman in there." He grimaces. "Youse'll be the first woman invited."

"Wow, Angelo! What an honor."

"Just act nice and it'll all be okay."

"I'll be a good girl."

"I know youse will. Hope youse won't mind when they speak Italian."

I shake my head. "I won't mind. I used to put up with my former in-laws always speaking German. Later my ex told me they were saying things like "Too bad she's not German, because American women don't make good wives." Maybe the board will say too bad I'm not a man because women don't make good salesmen."

"They already know I think a cutie like youse'll get our deals better than a guy." Angelo chuckles. "They'll all be in the boardroom in twenty minutes. Let's get there early. Just up the stairs here. Good! A couple guys're here already." He leads me over to them. "Hey, Dino. Hey, Tony. Here's Alice."

"Hi, Dino." I stick my hand out.

He grasps it and shakes. "Hi, hon. Glad to meet you. You've got a nice handshake for a dame."

"Thanks." I turn to the man next to him and offer my hand again. "Hi, Tony."

"Hi, hon. Nice to meet you."

This place is splendid. It has beautifully textured wood panels for walls, a long wooden table, and a sparkling ashtray in front of each of the padded chairs; there's even a fancy bar with lots of bottles.

"Want a drink, hon?" Dino asks me.

"Do you have a Coke?"

"Sure, but don't you want some rum in it?"

"No, thank you. I probably have a much longer drive home than you all do."

"Yeah, we all live pretty close. We used to have to get up in the dark to be here on time for our garbage routes."

I look at the wall behind Dino and see a framed black-and-white photo of a naked lady. I quickly avert my eyes, but the image of her shameless, gorgeous face and provocative smile sticks in my mind. With her chest puffed out, her breasts look freakishly huge. She's in the middle of strutting, the length of her legs accentuated by her high-heeled pumps. Her dark, fluffed-up pubic hair contrasts sharply with her platinum tresses.

Approaching us is the best-dressed man of the lot; he wears a starched, long-sleeved white shirt and tie, while the others all wear short-sleeved patterned shirts, and most are tieless.

Angelo sidles closer to me. "Here comes our president," he whispers. Then, in his normal voice, "Hi, Lenny.[16] Meet Alice."

"Hi, Alice, a pleasure to meet you. How do you like it here?"

"I'm delighted to meet you, Lenny," I say with a big smile. "And I'm impressed with this elegant meeting room."

"At the end of the day we all need to kick back and relax, so we set this place up real nice. It reminds us that garbage is beautiful."

"Hey, Eddie, Marco, come meet Alice," Lenny says to the fellows walking in.

A haze of cigarette smoke fills the room, the burning odor competing with store-bought male fragrances. The quiet is replaced with loud English and Italian words punctuated with clinking glass. After a few minutes of this, Lenny says, "Time to get seated, guys."

Angelo gestures for me to sit next to him. Another man comes in, glances at me, and heads toward the bar.

Now that we're all seated, the conversation begins, all in Italian. One of the men switches to English and, with a smile on his face, ribs Angelo for being Sicilian. "Even though you're not a true Italian, you're one of us and a good guy."

A man with a beer belly bellows, "Hey, Alice, do you know why most of us have raised right shoulders? It's because of how we hauled our cans. Those were tough days."

"Now that you aren't doing that anymore, what do you do for exercise?" I ask.

"Ho, ho, ho, ho. Now I have more energy for something fun. I get lots of exercise, if you know what I mean."

I shoot back, "But I read that doesn't burn any more calories than climbing two flights of stairs."

Oops! What did I say? Me and my big mouth.

It seems like they're sneaking peeks at me, and now they all speak Italian again—I sure wonder what they're saying.

Lenny gets up and walks toward the bar behind me. He removes the naked lady picture from the wall and, glancing my way, runs around the table carrying the pinup at eye level. He circles three or four times as everybody laughs, including me. The whole scene is so comical that I'm having too much fun to blush—and my high school friends used to call me Pinky because of that. Was this a test? If so, I'm pretty sure I've passed.

I love going to the Emporium,[17] my favorite location for business and to shop and eat. I usually just window shop, but often break down and buy something irresistible. The store custodian, Armando, is always welcoming and a very loyal bale-tie customer. I just wish that when I occasionally take him to lunch, he wasn't averse to dining in the Emporium's gorgeous, glass-domed dining area. I guess he needs to get away, since his job is to keep the whole store in perfect condition.

Now Armando is giving me his recycling business, which Angelo should be very happy about. This account should be almost as, or perhaps even more, lucrative than the Federal Reserve Bank business, which I got four weeks ago, greatly impressing Angelo.

I'm thrilled to see my recyclables monthly commission check of $1,178—not bad for just one day a week of work with minimal phone and transportation expenses. Also, no related vendor debts to counterbalance immediate spendability. So far I've brought in nearly $2,000 in commissions. My biggest customers are the Federal Reserve Bank[18] and the Emporium. Together, they amount to roughly 90 percent of this month's pay.

Every first Thursday I visit Angelo, and he always treats me to lunch, along with his paper broker or some other business contact of his. Every time the bill is presented, he and his male guest have an arm-wrestling fight over the bill; the winner gets the honor of paying.

Having left my car in the parking lot, I'm halfway to Angelo, who's standing by his gigantic baler, when a crazy driver in a sleek blue Mustang speeds past me. After screeching to an abrupt stop less than three feet from Angelo, a big blond man jumps out of his car and starts to shout at him.

"Hey, Angelo, you asshole. You took my goddamned fuckin' Federal Reserve away from me. I could've taken it to Golden Gate, but I always came to you, and now you've double-crossed me, you fuckin' prick. How could you do this to me, you cocksucker? See if I bring my shit to you anymore. I'm out of here, and for good! If I don't get to you first, choke on shit in an asshole, motherfucker."

I watch with my mouth practically hanging open. This is about *me*. I procured Federal Reserve's recyclables for Bayshore Salvage, and it's a juicy account, my biggest yet.

Angelo says something back to the angry guy, but says it quietly, and I can't make out the words. The antagonist jumps back into his car. By now I'm hugging the side of the office building between the parking lot and the recycle center. The car seems to jump just before it squeals away.

I wonder if he knows I'm the one who landed Federal Reserve? I hope not. At least he didn't seem to give me even a passing glance. Stunned, I remain frozen by the office building.

Angelo walks over to me. "How are youse, Alice?"

"Well, I was fine till just now. I'm scared, Angelo. That guy is so mad I think he'd bash my head in if he knew I was the one who stole the Federal Reserve from him."

"He wouldn't dare touch a hair on youse's pretty little head."

"Why the hell not? He threatened you."

Angelo looks entirely unconcerned. "That's all just a load of hot air. He'd never harm either one of us. He knows that would be the end of him."

"Why would he think that?" I shake my head. "I'm scared for my life!"

He gives me a reassuring smile. "Don't youse worry. He knows he'd be in big trouble if he even touched youse. He'd end up smashed inside one of our one-ton bales going to Japan—just like Jimmy Hoffa."

I glue my eyes onto Angelo's. He looks down at me, smiling.

"Youse thinks I'm in the Mafia, don't youse?"

I swallow. "Well, are you?"

"Youse just wonder."

Angelo just handed me my second $1,000–plus check from Bayshore Salvage! After I deposit it, I'll love looking at the Vulcan checking account more than ever. The downside is that I haven't acquired as many new monthly wire customers as I used to. Even though a lot of new-customer wire business always looks great on paper, it's a hardship to pay for the goods before receiving payment for them. Before getting these glorious commissions, my exponentially growing wire sales translated to diminished temporary cash flows.

"Thanks, Angelo," I say as I slip the check into my purse. "I just got another customer for you, but it's just an itty-bitty one—a mom-and-pop grocery store."

"That's good news," he says, "but I've gotta tell youse to lay off The Emporium."

"What do you mean?" I ask in a high-pitched voice. "The Emporium is my second-biggest customer, and the client there is one of my favorites. He's real happy with me and Bayshore Salvage."

"Sorry, Alice. The Golden Gate Disposal guys had the account for a long time and got real mad at me for taking it away from them."

"But they're your competitor, not your partner. Isn't that right?"

"Well, youse're sorta right—but youse just can't keep the Emporium no more."

My stomach clenches. "Golly, Angelo, that's nearly half my paycheck. It would take at least six regular customers to make up for it." I know I'm whining, but I can't help it. This money is huge for me.

He shakes his head. "Well, youse just can't have the Emporium no more. Sorry, Alice."

Boy, am I mad and sad about giving up the Emporium. It made me almost as much money as the Federal Reserve, and I was able to kill two birds with one stone by getting both Vulcan bale-tie orders and Bayshore Salvage recycling orders there. It looks like there's too much baggage regarding the big-money recycling customers—the work is either dangerous or short-term. Now that Vulcan's cash flow is healthy, I think for most of my Thursdays I'll concentrate on wire sales and just keep up the rapport with my existing recyclers.

I come to see Angelo as usual, and he hands me a check for barely over $500.[19] *I guess I should feel lucky to make this much money for such little effort.* "Thanks, Angelo," I say, a bit subdued.

Angelo takes a deep breath and blurts out, "Alice, I don't want youse to work for us no more."

I'm disappointed, but a little relieved. "Oh, Angelo. I'm sorry about that. But you'll still buy my wire, won't you?"

"Sure, kid. I still want to be friends."

"I do too, Angelo."

And with that, my career in the recyclables business comes to an end.

CHAPTER 25
MAN OVERBOARD

Because I am a woman, I must make unusual efforts to succeed. If I fail, no one will say, "She doesn't have what it takes;" they will say, "Women don't have what it takes."
—Clare Boothe Luce, US ambassador,
author, politician

Nine-year-old Julie has again neglected her daily chore of empty-ing the wastebaskets into the big trashcan in the garage. Bob, who always expects perfection, is furious. He orders the three of us into the family room. He commends Jeanette for faithfully getting the dishes rinsed, placed into the dishwasher, and put away. Then he rebukes Julie and asks her why she didn't perform her simple task. The usual little-kid answer of "I don't know" follows.

Bob changes his harsh tone to that of an understanding, sympathetic uncle, and says, "I know it's hard to remember some things every day, isn't it, Julie?"

Julie relaxes a little and nods her head.

Bob smiles. "There are lots of things you like to do every day, aren't there?"

"Oh, yes," Julie answers, smiling back at him.

"What do you like to do more than anything else?" Bob kindly inquires.

"Doing things with Mama," she replies, reflecting Bob's friendly smile.

"Good!" he snarls, squinting into Julie's big trusting eyes. "No doing things with Mama for the next month. That should help you to remember to empty the wastebaskets."

Julie bursts into sobs, and I bend down and hug her, saying, "Don't you worry, honey, I'll keep on doing things with you. We'll think of a different punishment than that."

Jeanette joins the hug, and our tightly knit threesome glares at Bob as *the other*. He looks mortified—appropriately so, I think.

This unacceptably harsh punishment, which doesn't fit the crime, is the last of the nails Bob's hammered into his coffin. I decide he has to leave—and soon!

When Julie regains her composure, I stop pitying her and start to pity Bob, whom I see as a defeated, shrunken monster. I even identify with him, recalling how it felt to be *the other* at Fritz's parents' house, when I didn't want to spend Christmas there and everyone glared at me.

Bob never displayed mean-spiritedness till he was well settled in with us, but since then he's often acted like a misanthrope. I wonder if he gets a sick thrill from being spiteful. Once, he even brought a waitress to tears: the sweet young thing was covering a crowded restaurant when Bob chewed her out for not keeping his coffee hot. I wanted to get up from the booth, hold her, and say, "Just ignore him. He's probably had a bad day." Instead I sat mutely and wished I could disappear.

Bob's frequent critical comments about various people's looks and facial mannerisms don't exactly endear him to me either. At least his victims are always unaware of his disdainful remarks—he comes across as charming till out of their earshot, when he thinks he can tickle my funny bone with inane imitations of their well-intentioned smiles and other expressions.

I still can't figure out why he's been so hostile to Julie in particular. Awhile back, I blamed her for something only to later discover she was innocent. When I realized my error, I apologized. She looked up at me with an adorable smile and said, "We all make mistakes." I melted with love as I hugged her.

Later, alone with Bob, I bragged about her sweet forgiveness. Instead of being touched, Bob said something about her being phony. I thought, *Look in the mirror, Bob.*

After he pulled his trick on Julie tonight, I now see Bob as cruel and devious. The way he tried to trap her was more brutish than Fritz's verbal putdowns of me ever were. It's only fair to my girls that I rid them of Bob's evil presence, just as it was fair to myself to get away from Fritz's attempted domination and insults a few years back.

I'm ashamed I didn't dump Bob three years ago, when I first realized his duplicity. Now I'm lifting the rug and reexamining his dirty lies—the "free" consulting fee, the fifty-fifty split, and the "successful three-man partnership." I've had enough of his complaints about Fritz and his objections regarding the gifts I send to Fritz's little niece and nephews. Just a few months ago, to avoid Fritz, Bob even tried to separate me from my girls by sending them away.

"Now that you're making good money along with me, we can afford to put the girls in boarding school," he said one day. "I could pay half the cost. You wouldn't be so busy and tired all the time, and Jeanette and Julie would get a better education."

"What?" I was shocked. "No way! I was so relieved when Fritz agreed they should mostly live with me. I couldn't imagine dumping them in a quasi-orphanage."

"Oh, A.M., you'd be able to be with them every other weekend, and the weekends that Fritz has them we wouldn't have to be disrupted by his visits. I hate him snooping around here and using the bathroom."

I stared him in the eyes. "Bob, I'm not putting my daughters in boarding school. I don't want to hear another word about it. Case closed!"

Bob is also a shameless thief. One afternoon I discovered an insurance representative in our living room with him. *Bob missed his calling as an actor,* I thought. He was so believable: lamenting how appalled he was that his expensive suits, ties, and shirts had been stolen out of his car while he was in a restaurant during a business trip.

Bob had put on a lot of pounds since he moved in with us, and had outgrown his clothes. He had decided that this would be a handy way to replace his wardrobe. After the man left, Bob acted like I should be proud of him for the hoodwinking. He was chagrined when I said his actions were "just plain wrong"—but that's all I did, and then tried my best to forget about it.

After the girls are in bed, I give Bob his pink slip.

"Bob, honey," I say gently, "I'm afraid we have to break up and you have to move out."

Looking me in the eyes, sadly but sympathetically, he replies, "I saw that coming. The student has outgrown the teacher. You don't need me anymore."

Until this moment I hadn't realized I was no longer his protégé. Solemnly, I return his look and nod. "Yes... but that's not why. The reason is that we don't have a happy home. You need to find another place by the first of next month. I'm really sorry, Bob."

"I'm sorry too, A.M. I'll miss you a lot."

We get in bed, and Bob starts to cry. I put aside my disgust and wrap my arms around him. I feel like I'm putting down a rabid dog. I realize I've been feeling like a frog brought slowly to a boil. The writing was on the wall even before he moved in two years ago, but I pushed aside my disdain for his crooked ways. If this evening's incident hadn't happened, I might have let our relationship drag on for several more months.

The big bad wolf is gone. At least Bob and I parted amicably, and Julie can breathe easier now. She was never bratty to him, but he sure was to her. *What a bully!* Jeanette probably doesn't care one way or another. I, meantime, don't miss his bed warming at all, and I certainly don't miss watching him scratch his pubic hair like a monkey every time he took his clothes off at night. Ugh! Thank God I never married the weasel. I should've dumped him long ago. I guess I was too in need of compliments—and too poor.

I'm now Vulcan's sole proprietor. In lieu of making payments to Bob for his share of the profits, I've signed an obligation to take over his monthly car payments; these total a little more than I otherwise owe him, but won't deplete Vulcan's now-healthy cash flow. Knowing that I have control over these payments, I can also rest easier, since I cosigned for Bob's auto loan, as his recent bankruptcy had made him ineligible.

What I'm nervous about is breaking the news to my E. H. Edwards contacts. I've led everyone there to think of me as Bob's assistant, so they might feel dubious about my assuming Vulcan's helm, but if they can accept my running the show, my fabricators will fall in line—and my banker and truckers won't even know the difference.

I owe it to myself to never again be sneaky, so it's paramount that I own up to my new status as soon as possible. *God, I hope Edwards will be okay with this.*

"Hello, Peter. Alice Stiller from Vulcan here," I say in as natural and friendly way as I can muster.

"Why, hello, Alice," Peter says warmly. "How are you? Do you have another order for me?"

"Sorry, I don't. I need to have an important meeting with you and any of your coworkers who are interested in Vulcan. Could we meet tomorrow?"

"Certainly, Alice. You know we appreciate your business," he says, a tinge of concern in his tone. "I hope nothing's wrong."

"We"—*oops, without Bob, perhaps I shouldn't say* we *unless Mary counts*—"appreciate your business too. Nothing's wrong, but I prefer to give you some news in person."

"You've certainly got my curiosity going. Would you like to meet at your office? We could take you out to lunch."

"Since you're willing to drive out to Dublin, how about meeting tomorrow morning at the Howard Johnson's for coffee? I'll already have eaten breakfast." *My stomach will be too knotted up to enjoy a meal with them.*

"Great. Let's meet at nine thirty."

"See you then."

My God! There are three of them, all seated in the booth already; this can be my excuse not to shake hands—I feel sweaty all over, and my hands are as cold and clammy as they've ever been.

The men begin to rise.

"Gentlemen, hello," I say hastily. "Please don't get up."

I'm flattered that all these big, well-dressed men drove all the way here from South San Francisco to meet little-old me. *Oh, I forgot—they were expecting Bob too.*

I try to act unflappable as I sit down next to the lone man seated on the left side of the table. *Shoot!* The two men across from me reach their hands out to shake. How embarrassing to offer my unpleasantly cool, moist hand. Then the man next to me, whom I've never seen before, introduces himself and offers his hand. These damned hands of mine have just ruined my hope for a good, powerful impression, but at least I'm tastefully dressed: cultured pearls around my neck, and a conservatively high, open-collared pink dress with a full skirt topped with a three-inch-wide belt. I've been on a hypoglycemic diet lately, and have lost a lot of weight as a result. My pantsuit bottoms fall so low now that I trip on them—so this dress is as good as it gets.

Now that I've accomplished gathering these men, I wonder what they think I've called them here for. Maybe they think I'm going to ask a favor, like sixty-day terms, or try to negotiate lower prices. Will they believe that I can manage Vulcan alone? I decide to ease into the conversation. "How nice of you all to meet me here in Dublin. The one good thing about Howard Johnson's is the big insulated coffee pot always on the table."

"Oh, we've always liked the HJ restaurants," Peter says graciously. "May we treat you to breakfast, too?"

"Thank you," I say, nodding. "I could go for a small pancake order," I pretend hunger only so they'll be comfortable eating in front of me. "Big men like you probably need more than a couple of pancakes, though." I square my shoulders. "Gentlemen, before the waitress gets here, I'd like to tell you the purpose of this meeting. Bob Brown and I were partners in Vulcan Metal Joining Consultants, but we've dissolved the partnership. I hope you won't mind dealing only with me, because I'm now the sole owner."

"Oh, we won't mind at all," Peter says immediately. "We always thought you were the sharper one. We'll be happy to deal with you as the head."

"I'm delighted to hear that," I say, trying to hide my giddiness. "I promise I won't let you down."

"We won't worry about that at all," says the man next to me. "We appreciate your business and want to continue to work with you."

"And I appreciate your good wire and service and your friendly attitude," I say as I nod confidently and make eye contact with each of the three.

"Let's lift our coffee cups to that," says the man across the table.

Now that this has gone so smoothly, I should be able to swallow my pancakes without getting a stomachache.

CHAPTER 26
SO MANY FISH IN THE SEA

You have to kiss a lot of frogs to find your prince.
—Unknown

Only days after Bob moved out, my neighbors introduce me to their bartender friend whom I now think of as Boozy Bernie. The fact that I'm a borderline teetotaler, repelled by the smell of alcohol on anyone's breath, makes for a short-term relationship.

Julie's friend Barbie's father, whom I call British Brady, is a friendly English chap who prides himself on always wearing slacks, never jeans as most American men do. He tells me that he's been having an international love affair with his wife's former best friend who lives in England. She supposedly wants to ditch her husband—but only if Brady will leave his family to unite with her in England where the romance began just before Brady left for the USA. Brady says his family is too important, and I suspect that centers on Barbie, the youngest of his three children. Brady and Barbie have an exceptionally close relationship. In fact, they seem to idolize each other.

While the girls are in Julie's room, Brady remains with me, seated on the couch in my living room. I chat with him about my nonsensical affair with Boozy Bernie and how I want to get out of it without hurting Bernie too much. Brady says it's good timing, because a friend of a friend of his just arrived from Southern California. He says this man, Ned, just broke up with his girlfriend and moved north to make a clean break, and he thinks the two of us would get along well. Ned was an engineer, like Brady is, but left engineering to make a killing in real estate. Supposedly he's a very successful salesperson. Brady convinces me I'll find Ned good-looking and wants to know if I'd care to be introduced to him next weekend.

Ned and I have a whirlwind romance. His religion is a hedonism that revolves around marijuana, magic mushrooms, and nudism. When he realizes he can never persuade me to savor psychoactive stuff or to toss my fig leaves, he concludes we don't have enough in common. I'm dumped—and anguished over the breakup.

After I tell all to British Brady, he's angry with Ned for being a scoundrel to me. But in the whole scheme of things, it's obvious Ned and I weren't meant to be a couple. I'll get over this.

Brady has become my platonic boyfriend and fast-dancing partner. A few months into our friendship, I discovered via Jeanette that we're suspected of being lovers. He's not even a physically compatible match for me, and the thought had never even crossed my mind. An affair with Brady would be a messy situation. Above all, I value his friendship, and being sexual would ruin our very comfortable relationship. He seems hopelessly in love with his British girlfriend, and she's begun to think of leaving her family in England to live with Brady here in Dublin.

Right after Christmas, I decided that I needed to stop missing Ned, even though I know it's silly to miss someone who's so wrong for me. I saw a newspaper ad for a dating service and the price was right, so I signed up. The deal is that every subscriber has a face-to-face interview with an older lady who then decides which woman would be compatible with which man. She then gives the man the woman's phone number. I'm about to have my first date, and I sure wonder what this Oscar will look like. He sounded interesting on the phone. He called me last Wednesday, and we agreed he could visit me at my house this evening after the girls are in bed. That way I won't need a babysitter. I'll just serve him tea—no goodies that late.

Oscar looks a bit old for me—probably Ned's age, but not as vigorous or as handsome. I like the fact he's tall and thin, even if he lacks

Ned's muscular physique. He comes on almost as strongly as Boozy Bernie, but won't tell me his vocation; he says, "It's personal."

I can't believe this guy expects me to accept his romantic advances when he won't even tell me what he does for a living. He spins nonsense about how physically compatible we are for each other, but I could never be attracted to someone so secretive. His groping is just short of a wrestling match. He doesn't repulse me, but I'm not tempted either.

Oscar finally seems to realize I need to know more about him, and tries to impress me with his Olympic Club[20] and Bohemian Club memberships; he tells me former governor Ronald Reagan is a member of one, and adds other details that have less impact on me than he'd like.

Shortly before he leaves, Oscar asks for another date. "Come meet me in San Francisco," he suggests, "at the Olympic Club. I'll show you around and then take you to lunch."

My curiosity is aroused just enough to agree.

This place is full of stodgy old men; they're all dressed to the nines, and they either converse quietly or read newspapers silently. I'm early, so I'll just mosey around. I hear faint splashes, so I walk in that direction. A door opens, and I see an indoor pool. I go in to look at the swimmers. Moments later, an older man approaches me.

"Young lady, who do you think you are?" he demands in a paternalistic tone. "Don't you know this is a men's club?"

"I'm Alice Stiller," I say, "and I'm here to meet my friend Oscar."

"You must leave, young lady," he says, pointing toward the door. "Women aren't allowed in this pool area."

"Can't I remain here for just another minute or two?"

He presses his lips together with displeasure. "No. The men must feel free to disrobe should they choose. A woman here is unacceptable."

"Well, all the seats in the entranceway are occupied, so I have no place to wait."

"That is not my concern, young lady. Please vacate these premises."

"Okay. If you see Oscar, tell him I'm unimpressed with the unfriendly attitude here."

I walk out of this creepy place. *And come to think of it, Oscar is creepy too.*

I date a police detective. He has interesting stories about his job, especially about the prostitutes he's crossed paths with. He says a lot of men prefer paid sex with women below average in looks. I wonder if he's telling the truth. Though I'm not particularly attracted to him, I date him a few times to hear about his adventures. Eventually, he stops calling.

During the five years since Fritz and I separated in '73, I've had only go-nowhere relationships, but today I feel positive vibes for the man I'm meeting right after I collect my $5,000 from that obscure Walt Osgood jerk with the shiny wood staircase.

I was probably a big letdown for this poor blind date. All I could do was jabber incessantly about my bizarre bumping-down-the-stairs experience at Osgood's company. I'm sure I appeared to be Ms. Wrong to him. No more looking for Mr. Right while I can only think of Osgood, my $5,000, and my ruined business reputation.

CHAPTER 27
CHRISTENED BY THE GARBAGE MEN

*Historically, our number one growth driver has been
from repeat customers and word of mouth.*
—Tony Hsieh, CEO of Zappos

I f Osgood's check doesn't arrive soon, I won't have enough money
for many new customers to make up for losing his business. It's been
two days since his secretary phoned to assure me that the check was in
the mail; I hope that was the truth. Perhaps Osgood thinks I won't carry
out my *see-you-in-court* threat if I don't get the money; or, he might
reason that if I sue him, his best defense would be that of course he
paid me, in fact right after I rudely interrupted his meeting. If indeed
the payment was mailed the day before yesterday, I might receive it
today. That would be manna from heaven, but only short-term. If I get
it, then I just might be able to build Vulcan back up by working harder
than ever, day and night.

Today I mean to be productive, but no selling yet, just paperwork. I
can't even think of planning visits, but tomorrow I'll research and plan
marketing to untapped industries. If I bang on enough new doors out
there, I just might make it.

I might start off with an overnight trip to Fresno via Modesto and
Merced. Those faraway customers are exceptionally friendly and always lift my spirits. My favorite, that darling Modesto man, Rudy
Bonzi, is almost due for a visit and an order. Even though his garbage
business has a big recycling division, I'll bet he's too far away from

Osgood Recycling to have heard about my brouhaha. Anyway, I think he likes me too much to dump Vulcan.

God love Rudy. He and his wife, Mary, are adorable. Rudy is a dwarf, and Mary, about his height, is, unlike Rudy, normally proportioned. They're wealthy now, but when they were first married they were nearly dirt poor. They had an old truck that Mary drove while Rudy hopped off at various houses and businesses to pick up the weekly trash and empty it into his pickup. When their first child was born, the little one rode with them. Eleven years ago, they bought a 128-acre site for their Modesto business.

It's always fun to visit them and take Rudy out to lunch. Sometimes he also has me drive him to various locales to pay his bills so he can save on postage—or so he says. He's an eccentric, fatherly character with an unbelievably loud voice for such a little guy. When he fondly calls me Little Alice, I fondly call him Big Rudy.

I've never been so anxious to see what's in my post office box. I open it to find an envelope with Osgood Recycling on the upper left. I rip it open—and here's a $5,000 check. *Thank God!* Breathing room. No cash-flow problems—at least for a while.

Just as I walk into my home office the phone rings, and Mary, my secretary, answers. *Rudy Bonzi of Bonzi Sanitation,* she writes on a notepad so I can nod my head yes or shake it no to his call. It's too soon for Rudy to place an order. He couldn't be in Osgood's good-old-boy network because he's too far away from him. *Maybe he wants to place an order after all.* He always wants to talk to me personally when he calls, so I pick up.

Before I can even say hi, Rudy asks in a concerned tone. "Alice, are you all right?"

"Hi, Rudy. Yes, I'm fine. How are you?"

"Let's not worry about me. Are you injured at all from your fall down the stairs at Osgood's?"

Oh, crap! He knows—and he's at least seventy-five miles away from Osgood. How did news travel so fast? I proceed with caution: "No, Rudy. I'm not injured."

"That's good." His voice is warm. "I've been worried about you. Everybody's talking about your stair tumble. They know Osgood doesn't like anybody who stands up to him, and nobody does because they're all scared of him. He's a mean son of a bitch. One guy died of a heart attack because of Osgood yelling at him. People don't like him. I have a lot of friends who want to meet you. We're all calling you The Little Lady with Balls."

I let out a relieved laugh. I want to yell, *I'm popular with people who haven't even met me!* Such a reaction was beyond my wildest dreams.

"The guys say you should become an associate member of our garbage club, the Royal Order of California Can Carriers—R.O.C.C. for short. If you do, I'll introduce you to a lot of guys who'll buy your wire. I called Osgood to find out if the rumor about you was true. He said he didn't mean to drop you and was going to pay you anyway; said your check was mailed only half an hour after you left. That means you'll have the money to join our club. Membership costs $300. What do you think, Little Alice?"

"I'd love to join your club," I say, deliriously happy.

"I'll send you a form and some info. There's no big rush because our convention isn't till September, two weekends after Labor Day. We're meeting in Reno. It's lots of fun. You should join and meet my friends. Oh—and my friends all pay on time. Anyway, they know not to mess with you. Ha, ha, ha."

"Sounds great, Rudy, thank you."

"I'm so glad you're all right, Little Alice. By the way, get me another hundred bundles—same price as last time, isn't it?"

"Yes it is, Rudy. I'll have it ready for you in just a little over two weeks. Thanks a lot."

I feel like just as I was about to be run over by a train, a band of angels lifted me.

I wander the Peppermill Hotel in Reno, Nevada, searching for the Capri Ballroom. As I step into the enormous room, the smoky air reminds me of my time as a waitress at the Refectory Restaurant, though the raucous laughter and clink of glassware is many decibels louder. There are hundreds of people here, mostly men in black suits with white shirts, open to expose black curly chest hair tamped down with glittering gold chains. Their lapels sport one-inch golden garbage cans with multicolored jewels, some piled a quarter-inch high; others spill out of the elegant receptacles.

I concentrate on finding Rudy or anyone else I know. The sexes are separated, with fewer women than men. I congratulate myself on being appropriately dressed in my amber-brown cocktail dress and golden, sandal-strap, three-inch heels.

At the far end I notice a semicircle of men and wonder if Rudy, with his short stature, could be hidden amongst them. I enter the group, which, I discover, is centered on a man slurring his words. He staggers toward me and pulls me into his personal miasma, which smells like rotten eggs tinged with vomit. I'm not quick enough to push him away, and my lips suffer a sloppy, drooling kiss.

"Stop that!" I command, with my eyes narrowed.

"You should be proud," a man chides me. "He's our R.O.C.C. president."

"Yeah, and he owns ABC Garbage Company, the biggest in L.A.," another says.

"That doesn't give him the right to kiss me," I reply angrily.

"Anyway, he's drunk. Give him a break," someone else admonishes.

I feel a gentle tug at my elbow and am arrested by the most beautiful, pure green eyes I've ever seen. They belong to a strikingly handsome man who appears to be under thirty. I notice his shirt is buttoned and he's wearing a necktie.

"Let's get you out of here, okay?" he says.

I acquiesce and leave the group with my rescuer.

"That was certainly a bad beginning for me," I say to him. "Thanks for pulling me away before I did something stupid."

"I could see nothing but trouble could happen if you stayed there. Tomorrow all the guys will be sober, and the old guy might not even remember the incident." He gives me a questioning look. "What are you doing in a place like this, anyway?"

"I sell wire for their balers, so I was invited to become an associate member as a vendor."

"Well, that makes two of us. My father owns a factory that manufactures parts for their garbage trucks. I'm here to represent his business. My name's Mike. What's yours?"

"I'm Alice," I say, and shake his hand as we walk by a room filled with people. Some are nibbling, while others drink or dance. "That looks like a wedding party with plenty of food to spare," I point inside. "By now we've missed out on our prepaid R.O.C.C. dinner. What do you say we be party crashers? I'll bet everybody will think we're just a couple of people they haven't yet met. Are you hungry and daring enough to give it a try?"

He grins. "Sure. Let's go for it."

Sated with shrimp, deviled eggs, a hodgepodge of other delicacies, and spiked punch, my whole body perks up to Chuck Berry's *Johnny B. Goode*. Mike notices my head bobbing and asks if I want to dance. We caper to other high-energy golden oldies and sit out the slow ones. Not a soul converses with us, and neither do we feel particularly noticed. We finish our intrusion with tiny, delectable pastries and more spiked punch, then return to the ballroom to find everyone seated and listening to speeches as waiters clear the dishes. We seat ourselves quietly and separately. When the speeches end, I get up and continue to look for Rudy. I finally find him at a table, and he beams when he sees me.

"Hi, Little Alice. So glad to see you."

"You too, Rudy." I return his smile.

"I heard Drunken Dino planted a wet one on you." He laughs. "They said you were real mad and left. Don't be upset. He was so tanked that tomorrow he might not even remember kissing you. Keep in mind he's our R.O.C.C. president."

"I know all that, Rudy, but if a man acts like that when he's drunk, then he shouldn't drink—plain and simple!" I shake my head.

"There's no chance any of us macho Italian guys will stop drinking. Please try to get over it, kid, okay?"

I relent. "Okay, Rudy. For you, I will. Remember, you promised to introduce me to a bunch of your friends."

"Sure thing, Little Alice. But I'll do that tomorrow. All the guys want to either gamble or go to bed now."

"That makes sense. Well, I'm going to head to bed too. I look forward to seeing you tomorrow—and remember to introduce me to your friends."

"Don't worry, Alice. You're a famous lady, so they want to meet you too."

CHAPTER 28
FINALLY LAUNCHED

A dream doesn't become reality through magic; it takes sweat, determination and hard work.
—Colin Powell, statesman,
four-star General of the US Army (RET.)

I love those garbage men! Thanks to my stairs episode and Rudy, I've more than made up the loss of business from Osgood Recycling. In the months since the S.O.B. dropped me, my notoriety gained me half a dozen new recycling customers, and a couple more thanks to the R.O.C.C. convention. Since I've discovered a few tricks for breaking through bureaucracies, I've landed a couple of juicy supermarket accounts, too, and more paper-related and general industry accounts. Now I feel less apprehensive about a slowdown in orders.

My love life, meanwhile, is going nowhere, though I keep hoping. It's nice to go dancing on a Friday or Saturday night with British Brady when I don't have a weekend date.

Because he knows how well Vulcan is doing, Brady talks me into buying myself a present—something extravagant. He says I must treat myself now that I earn more than enough to make ends meet. I follow his advice and choose a lovely Black Hills gold ring with wee golden grapes amidst a swirl of three leaves—one peach-colored of pinkie-nail-size, and two apple-green smaller ones. This is the only frivolous purchase I've made since before Fritz quit his job five years ago. In a way, I feel this splurge is a gift from Brady.

In late September the dating service sets me up with Les, a sweet gentleman who's forty-five, nine years my senior. An established attorney with two partners and a shared legal secretary, he's an only child and a second-generation Persian. I like his café-au-lait skin and his big brown eyes. Otherwise his looks are ho-hum—average features, height, and weight. I appreciate that he doesn't mind my lack of enthusiasm for alcohol and marijuana, and I'm glad he's not a jealous sort. He accepts my friendship with Brady right away, and we three enjoy occasional lunches together and even go on a three-person date to a football game.

After countless fun dates of dining and dancing, Les makes me a candlelit dinner at his apartment. His place is small and nondescript but tidy.

It's early January now, and I've just reciprocated with a dinner for Les. The girls are with their father, so we have the house to ourselves. In the evening Les proposes marriage, and I accept. It's nice to have a stalwart companion and a stable future to look forward to.

It's early February, and tomorrow I'm having a hysterectomy due to complications from a tubal ligation. For months I've been preparing for my time off, but very concerned with what not being in top form for six to eight weeks will do to Vulcan. I'm more nervous about that than about the surgery itself. I appreciate that Les has been understanding of my not wanting to go out these last two evenings. I've been looking forward to our only date this weekend: a relaxing lunch at the nearby Yellow House. After this we can fool around a bit before Fritz returns the girls around dinnertime. I'll feed Jeanette and Julie, and then take them to stay with some friends who live down the street, where they'll remain till I return from the hospital in a week. Les will transport me to the hospital and back, so he'll stay with me through Monday morning.

Now we're at the Yellow House, and Les is acting edgy. I wonder what's bothering him, poor guy.

"Are you not feeling well?" I ask.

"I'm fine," he says stiffly.

"Is something wrong?" I press.

"I said I'm fine," he snaps.

Our talk is stilted, as if we've had an argument. We leave the restaurant earlier than usual. As Les pulls out of the parking lot, he nearly hits a parked car and swears under his breath. He's taciturn when I again try to draw him into conversation.

When we're a block away from my house, he pulls over and stops. "I want to break off our engagement," he blurts out. "I can't take it anymore. My wife had a hysterectomy and moped around the house like an invalid for half a year. After she stopped moping, she didn't seem like a woman anymore. I can't handle you doing this to me—I don't want this all over again!"

I'm stunned. "So this is what's been bugging you? I had no idea." I'm hurt and want to get away from him. "It's been nice knowing you, but please get me home now," I say quietly, a lump in my throat.

Wordlessly, Les drives the additional block, parks in my driveway, gets out, and opens the door for me. I get out and quickly say, "Goodbye, Les." Then I run into the house and feel crushed. Funny, though, my heart isn't exactly broken. I'm only hurt.

Before eight o'clock my neighbor, Jan, who offered to take me on her way to work, drops me off at Kaiser's Hayward Hospital. The admitting clerk tells me I need to reschedule because my doctor isn't coming in today.

Loud enough to create a scene, I respond, "What? I've had this operation scheduled for six months, and have been preparing for it all that time. I'm not leaving this hospital with my uterus! Understand?"

She tries to shush me. "Please, you must understand your doctor isn't in today."

"Then get another doctor to remove my uterus," I say, "because I'm staying here till it's out of me."

By eleven o'clock I'm in the hospital bed and Dr. Oza, a petite, pretty Indian lady, introduces herself. I like her much better than Dr. Burns, who admonished me for fearing a scar above my bikini line, saying, "You're almost forty, so in a few years you won't care how you look in a bikini." What a misogynistic insult! In contrast, sweet Dr.

Oza, says, "I'll do everything possible to do the operation vaginally, and I don't anticipate a problem with that."

With time on my hands, I call some customers to explain that I'm in the hospital for surgery and will be out of commission for two months. I get orders from one of them and relay the information to Mary at the home office.

Just after I get off the phone with Mary, a handsome, blue-eyed anesthesiologist visits to discuss his part of the process. I tell him about the nightmarish anesthesia experience with my tubal ligation, when the instruments on the top part of the wall became monsters trying to attack me.

"What kind of imagery would you enjoy thinking about?" he asks me kindly.

I think for a moment. "The ocean?"

"Well," he says, "let's try for that."

I call more customers and get more orders just before I'm wheeled into the OR. Soon I gaze up into the anesthesiologist's dreamy blue eyes. They become the ocean, warm and easy to float upon. Euphoria!

I wake up to two friends staring at me, Janice and Brady.

"Alice, you look so pale," Janice says.

"You look just fine," Brady says.

I feel my tummy and am relieved there's no bandage. I remember my transcendent *going under* and yearn to experience it again—or at least have another look at those magical blue eyes. Between morphine shots to relieve the pain, I try to hypnotize myself into revisiting my azure sea. I hope I'll get another chance to see the dreamy anesthesiologist.

A couple of days after the operation I have two unexpected visitors: one of my suppliers, Craig, and later a psychologist friend of Les's, whom I vaguely remember. He says he asked Les if it was okay to ask me out, and Les gave his permission. He gives me a book about how positive thinking aids healing. I plan to read the book, but not to date him—just not my type.

Five days after my surgery a doctor I've not met before introduces himself and declares me fit to go home tomorrow.

"But I don't want to," I say. "They said I'd be here for a week, and I'm counting on all seven days."

He's clearly taken aback. "I've never met anyone who wanted to stay here longer than they had to," he says.

I explain. "A couple of years ago I bought an insurance policy that retroactively pays $100 a day if I'm in the hospital seven or more days. If I leave early, I won't get paid!"

He laughs and says, "As you wish."

He laughs even harder when I tell him I always wanted to be paid $100 a day just for lying on my back.

Craig of Weld-Lock visits again before I leave the hospital and asks if he may visit me at my house after I'm released. I'm beginning to think he's romantically interested in me. I remember Bob Brown asking me if Craig was "the other man," and I laughed it off, but now I see him in a new light—as a potential love interest. The first time we met was a year ago, when he convinced me to become a Weld-Lock plastic strapping distributor. Now I notice his tall, muscular body and appreciate his wry sense of humor.

Les's psychologist friend visits again too, and we talk about the book he gave me. I thank him and say it seems to be working because I feel great and will go home tomorrow. I feel so rested that I look forward to doing a lot of the medically suggested walking.

A day after I'm back home, Les calls to say his psychologist friend said I was healing quickly. He also tells me that even though we've broken up, he'll keep his promise to help get Vulcan incorporated pro bono. I need to incorporate to keep my income taxes down.

Les comes over tonight, and I've made myself as attractive as possible—I want him to feel sorry for having dumped me. I'm no longer hurt, however, because I'm enjoying Craig's attentions. Les gives me papers to sign and some legal advice. I'll be incorporated retroactively by three months, back to December 1, 1978.

Alice, you've come a long way, baby. Now you worry more about taxation than about profitability.

Vulcan is launched—I'm the president and CEO of a corporation!

PART II: MATES OF ALL KINDS

1979–1989

CHAPTER 29
THE SONGBIRD

*Surround yourself with the best people you can find,
delegate authority, and don't interfere as long as the
policy you've decided upon is being carried out.*
—Ronald Reagan, 40th President of the United States

I t's been five months since I incorporated, and I realize that even though Mary, who's now a college student, is hardworking and efficient, her assistance isn't enough. When I tell her we'll need another person to help us, she immediately thinks of her girlfriend's mother. Mary says she's tired of being a housewife and has decided to look for an office job. A couple of days later Mary brings in Millie's résumé, and I'm impressed with it. The next day, I interview the forty-three-year-old brunette and then hire her. Millie begins as a part-timer, and I'm delighted with her performance.

Thanks to my friendly garbage men and finally conquering the supermarket labyrinth, my sales grow exponentially. In less than half a year Millie has expanded her hours to become a full-time employee. Vulcan's sales and the pertaining paperwork increase to the point where Mary and Millie can no longer keep up. I realize I need another part-timer. Today I've scheduled two interviews from last week's newspaper ad.

Upon my return after morning appointments, Millie informs me that a lady came in to scout our office before her afternoon interview. Millie says the lady noted my No SMOKING sign, became very angry, and shouted, "Nobody tells me not to smoke—that's my business!" She adds that the lady slammed the door on her way out. I sure hope I like the remaining candidate.

In walks a giggling, plump lady in a print dress. I'm happy to note she smells of perfume, with no hint of cigarettes. She has office work experience and is eager for the job. Her melodious voice charms me. I find this Bev so likeable that I'm glad she has no competition. She says she needs to give only one week's notice at her current job. I'm curious why it isn't the usual two, but I don't ask.

To accommodate a fourth desk, I've removed the closet door and fit the file cabinets tightly inside. Even so, there's hardly any room for the wastebaskets. I purposely go out in the field for Bev's first three days so Mary and Millie can train her to do their overloads. She'll always be answering the phone for them and eventually should be able to help customers like they do.

It's day four now, and even though Mary and Millie are pleased with Bev, I want to observe her firsthand. Things go smoothly for half an hour, but then...

Bev seems to race toward the bathroom as Mary, Millie, and I hurriedly head to the file cabinets. Bev bumps into Mary, and I end up kicking a wastebasket and barely avoid crashing with Millie. We all laugh good-naturedly, but four desks and four people in a hundred square feet isn't working.

But can I afford an office? It's bad enough I've increased my payroll costs. Even though Vulcan's earnings are substantial, I haven't taken out anything but paltry sums, except for what I spent on my gold ring and an upcoming Hawaii family vacation—to be combined with some business visits. As always, greater sales translate to greater payables due before the accompanying receivables are paid. Also, I'll have to come up with sixty to ninety days' worth of rent before moving in. I feel like Sisyphus, but instead of pushing a boulder I push loads of money up a mountain of never-ending bills.

I find only one affordable Dublin office in the papers. After seeing it, I sign a month-to-month lease with the real estate broker who owns it. His first floor is taken up with several agents and himself, but upstairs is a well-lit and air-conditioned attic—no windows, but plenty of room for our four desks, three file cabinets, and a wastebasket each. We share the downstairs bathroom with the real estate people, who let us move in over the weekend.

Now that Vulcan no longer operates out of my house, I feel it's a full-fledged business. Hopefully I'll no longer hear from neighbors and friends, "When are you going to get a job-job?" Or even worse, "a real job?"

There's enough space in this office, but it's stuffy. I notice Mary and Millie still working, but Bev is done for the day. She's got her purse on the desk with her hands folded and is intently looking at the clock. *Not good!* I'm not sure this laughing lady will be permanent. I'll surreptitiously find out tomorrow if Mary and Millie had run out of work for her. If so, I'll see that Bev is assigned specific work instead of merely absorbing overflow.

Damn! Now that we've relocated, I receive a county statement mandating that a Vulcan representative register our relocation. That means a forty-minute round-trip drive and up to an hour standing in line. I've got too much on my plate for this unexpected turn of events. Bev has the least seniority, so I decide to invest two minutes to explain it to her, hoping she can get it done Monday.

"Alice, that should not be my job," Bev tells me indignantly.

"I don't see why not," I retort. "I hired you to lessen my load, and I haven't budgeted the time for this coming Monday. I really need your help." I sigh. "Go home and think about it and the fact that your job is primarily to leave me time to attend to what the rest of you are unable to do."

"That's not what I hired on to do," Bev says, looking me in the eyes, "so it really shouldn't be my responsibility, but I'll think it over this weekend."

It's Monday now, and I tense a little when Bev walks in this morning. Given our last conversation, I don't have high hopes. To my surprise, however, she begins the day with, "Alice, I'm sorry about last Friday. My husband, Bill, owns his business too, and he explained that an owner needs his employees to do whatever they possibly can. He made me see your point of view."

"Great, Bev," I say, thinking, *Bill, I've never met you, but I love you.*

My little family is again in Hawaii—this time with Craig, my hysterectomy-romance sweetie. All four of us have enjoyed each other's company. We've been lulled into relaxation, dazzled by the beauty, the perfumed tropical air, and the bathtub-warm ocean water. I certainly needed this time off!

All but one of our Hawaii days were heavenly, and that day of non-bliss wasn't exactly chopped liver—even though the girls thought so. They begged me to leave them with Craig on the beach rather than make them accompany me on my one business day, but I insisted they come along.

My two customers were highly welcoming, and the two potential customers were cordial and promising. Jeanette and Julie experienced their first business lunch with my biggest Hawaii account. When he greeted us in shorts and an aloha shirt, I was relieved that our non-businesslike attire seemed appropriate. We all wore identically styled sundresses, each a different color. Thankfully, the girls charmed him with their Sunday manners.

Due to last night's late arrival home, my body still attuned to Hawaii's later time, I took it easy this morning and had a late brunch, but now I'll have to be satisfied with Pacific memories and get back to work. I walk in—and immediately begin to sweat. *This office is like a sauna!* With regular clothes on, it's a hellhole. Our so-called air conditioning is a joke!

I can't believe all three ladies can greet me with a smile. Each one, dressed especially nicely, wears the orchid corsage I sent her from Hawaii. I get thanks and compliments for the flowers' freshness and beauty. *What good sports!*

I feel so guilty that I basked in Hawaii's luxury for the past week and then spent this morning asleep at home while my dear, hardworking employees were suffering in a literal sweatshop. I must be grateful all three haven't quit on me. I need to find another place *ASAP!*

Fortunately, Vulcan has successfully survived the recent double whammy of the office rent and hiring Bev. I guess I can afford to pay a bit more for a decent place. I'm afraid tomorrow's priority will be to office hunt rather than to get back to sales.

This is the place! A former Red Carpet Realty office in San Ramon, it's bigger and nicer than we need, but I hope to grow into it. I've discovered that most office leases, including this one, are for three years, so if it were smaller I'd be in a pickle if we outgrew it before 1983. And this office is classy! I'll have my very own back-wall room, which is almost as big as our former guest-bedroom office. The upper half of the wall and door are thick glass, so people will see me when they enter from the outside, and my staff can look in by turning around at their desks. With my enclosure I'll have privacy during phone conversations. I only wish the carpet—a glaring, deep crimson—was a different shade.

The ladies are all very relieved to hear they'll suffer only today and tomorrow in this suffocating hole in the wall. I assure them the next place will be perfectly comfortable.

We've been here in San Ramon for one week now, and we're very content with our new surroundings. The indoor temperature is perfect, and the whole office is bright from the sun shining through the enormous front windows—plus the excellent overhead lighting. I also love being able to walk from my desk to the Brass Door Restaurant in less than two minutes. The food there is always delicious. What a bonus!

Bev has proven to be ultra-valuable, despite her frequent bathroom breaks and her squeals over spiders. She's talkative, but she produces good work, whether on paper or over the phone. I'm sure that her musical voice and personality-plus is a positive influence; it's certainly good for Vulcan's office morale. Above all, people listening to her pleasant, often flirtatious banter can't help but feel her charisma, whether she's attempting a sale or reminding someone that their payment is overdue. I had to stifle laughter the first time I heard her say, in her singsong way, "We have a problem, a tiny little problem. But we need to receive your payment for your late $3,000 bill. We'd be so *happy* if you could get a check in the mail today or tomorrow. Could you do that, please?"

During her school days Bev was never a cheerleader, but I consider her one for Vulcan. When she gets an order, after she hangs up she belts out, "Whoopee, I got an order." Then she stands up and does a little song and dance.

For one Secretary's Day, I decide to take my ladies out in the field to give them some firsthand knowledge of our wire products, balers, and the garbage world. I ask Bayshore Salvage, my former part-time employer and current longstanding customer, if I may show my employees around. We're given a red-carpet tour of the premises. Then they invite us into the boardroom where at least half the board members join us. The room is darkened so we can view a black-and-white movie showing the vehicles and procedures of San Francisco's early garbage days up to the present.

Afterward, the men do a lot of talking in Italian. Unbeknownst to them, Bev speaks and understands Italian very well. She watches them sweetly, with a Madonna-like smile. The rest of us, however, understand nothing, and are bored and restless.

Switching back to English, the men offer us cookies, Cokes, and coffee. We politely decline, thank them for their hospitality, and leave for lunch.

As we drive away, Bev informs us the men were sexually appraising us and calling us fur pies. Perhaps I should be appalled, but I'm mostly amused. *Such naughty boys!*

At lunch, Bev tells us that her husband, Bill, was smitten by her beautiful voice when she was the lead singer in her church choir. After the service he sought out the lady with "the voice." It was truly love at first hearing; he decided before even meeting her that he wanted to be married to the songbird. Then, upon first sight, there was a magnetic attraction between the two. Bev also shares that at one point she planned to pursue an opera career. Since then, I often kid her that she forsook her opera plans for Vulcan.

Our fifth abode was in Pleasanton. It had a large reception area and seven glassed-in, fairly soundproof, individual rooms. Because Vulcan needed only five of them, we'd rented out the sixth and seventh to two attorney brothers. They were moving out, though, and we had an application from a piano teacher.

We weren't sure piano playing could be sufficiently muted by the thick glass, so we decided on an experiment while one attorney and our receptionist were out to lunch. Bev went into the vacant office across from the one attorney (engrossed in paperwork), closed the door, and, as if facing a packed auditorium, belted out an aria.

Up jumped the lawyer with an alarmed look! The four of us burst into laughter as his face reddened. Between guffaws we apologized for the disturbance and decided the piano teacher had better look elsewhere.

When loyal Bev had been with us for nearly seven years, the poor thing had been ill for several weeks. Even with her energy drained, however, she was determined to meet the deadline for her State Board of Equalization task of breaking down portions of the sales taxes into all of the counties. She knew California imposed a deadly late fee, so despite how sick she felt, she came to the office—without makeup, wearing an unglamorous bathrobe and beat-up old house slippers—and quickly gathered some papers to take home.

The following day, dressed as before, she came in and returned the data, along with a perfectly completed form and a lengthy pertaining spreadsheet. Bev's value became set in granite.

CHAPTER 30
MY ORIGINAL SAILS

*If you pick the right people and give them the opportunity
to spread their wings—and put compensation as a carrier
behind it—you almost don't have to manage them.*
—Jack Welch, former CEO of General Electric Co.

S uzie only dabbled at selling and is now so ensconced with her third husband and their mutual activities that she has no time for Vulcan. I love to sell, but it's all I can do to give my many customers the attention they require and keep up with the paperwork I can't delegate. Vulcan's growth is plateauing, which is good for cash flow, but I've just secured a small business loan, so I can afford steep growth and a temporary guaranteed draw for a salesperson.

I advertise in the local papers and get some uninteresting responses. Then a lady named LuLu, from the Los Angeles area, telephones. I agree to meet her in my San Ramon office, assuming that she wants to move to the Bay Area.

When Lulu walks in, I'm surprised to note how short she is. We barely get into our pleasantries when she tells me that she's nearly a legal midget, meaning a person four foot ten or shorter. LuLu is four eleven, and more adorable for her short stature. A born saleswoman, she convinces me that Vulcan would prosper more by developing new territory around her home in Southern California than by filling in the gaps of our growing northern California area.

I tell her, "My only hesitation is the fear that you might quit after I invest in a Southern California warehouse and inventory. That would put me in an impossible situation."

"What do you want from me to assure you I'd be with Vulcan for a long time?" she asks. She rolls up her sleeve. "If you want, I'll prick my skin and sign an affidavit in blood that I'll remain with you for years to come."

I decide to take the risk, which also includes a six-month draw against commission. My only fear now is that LuLu and her husband may decide to start a family. Lulu's only thirty-one, after all, and has no children yet, but I've decided to trust her.

LuLu has impressed me in her nearly six months with Vulcan. Noting that her guaranteed salary draw, which terminates next month, will not negatively affect her, I congratulate myself for taking her on. Then my phone rings.

It's Lulu, with some seriously bad news. Her husband's been offered a job in Chicago, and she's going with him. I beg her not to go.

"But Alice, I have to follow my husband, and this promotion means the world to him."

My head begins to pound. "Last February I explained to you it would be a tremendous investment on my part to train you and set up a warehouse and inventory in Southern California. I even said it would be an unbearable headache if you left a year later—and you haven't even hit your six-month mark yet."

"Alice—"

"Before our agreement," I go on, "you rolled up your sleeve and said if I wanted your blood to prove you would be with Vulcan for the long haul, you'd give it to me."

"I'm really sorry," Lulu says. "When I first hired on I had no idea my husband would get this opportunity in Chicago."

And with that, all my fears about this risk are realized.

It's true that LuLu secured more new customers in L.A. than she could have garnered in northern California, but it'll be a nightmare to acquaint myself with this industrial area of unfamiliar places I've never set foot in, hundreds of miles away from my home.

First, to get to the damn locale, I'll have to either drive five and a half hours each way, or fly and rent a car. Then I'll have to cope with L.A.'s unwieldy freeway system, along with daunting responsibilities: 1) a sizeable amount of warehoused wire inventory; 2) overdue receivables that need personal attention; and 3) customers substantial enough to require visits and lunches.

What a headache!

I leave the girls with my neighbors across the street and take off in my car. L.A. traffic is just as hellish as I expected. I discover that the people here are rougher around the edges than they are up north. They're also slower to pay their bills, but they're bigger accounts, and most are worth the hassle.

I visit a scruffy rag dealer and decide on pleasant chitchat before I demand payment. His heavy body almost puffs up as he brags about fooling the authorities during his last day in jail for a white-collar crime. He describes how he put on a convincing show of remorse until he was irretrievably set free—and then gave them the finger.

I put on a show of being favorably impressed. Then I slip in the fact that his bill is overdue. He has the hubris to ask me to lower the amount. I tell him the best I can do is to deduct the late charges. I don't reveal that I'm Vulcan's owner, which makes it easier to remain inflexible. Upon handing his check to me, he indicates that Vulcan won't receive his business in the future. I don't let on how relieved I am that I'll never see him again.

The workday is over, I've eaten, and it's after nine o'clock. Here I am in Hollywood, driving around in circles looking for lodging—and here, finally, a motel called The Players. How amusing: two lit-up, six-foot-high masks, a white happy-face juxtaposed against a black sad-face. The area is depressing, and there's not even parking nearby, but I'm tired, and beggars can't be choosers.

I've never seen a sign behind the reception desk like this one: No REFUNDS. *Why in the world would anyone want a refund when there's no competition close by?* I just want to complete my day's notes and sleep, but the light in this room is so dim that I can't see well enough to do my reporting. I ask the guy at the reception desk for a brighter bulb. He acts as if I'm requesting a big favor and tells me if I want a different bulb I'll have to buy one. Begrudgingly, I walk toward the small store he directed me to. About ten feet from the motel I notice a tall, flamboyantly dressed black man eyeing me up and down. Creepy!

The damn store doesn't have any light bulbs above forty watts. I return after twenty minutes, and that spooky guy is right where I last saw him. I make brief eye contact, but I feel his eyes bore into me. I think he's a pimp. I hurry into my room and find a phone book. I've always liked Howard Johnson hotels and, with concentration and squinting, I discover there's one at Hollywood and Vine,[22] just a mile away. I wish I'd found it first. Now to ask for my $35 back.

The deskman points to the No Refunds sign. I acknowledge it but argue that I never used the bed and would have remained if they'd had decent lighting. I insist that a person has a right to expect enough light to read and write and shouldn't have to pay when that necessity can't be met.

The man yells, "No refunds!"

I walk away angrily and give the pimp a dirty look.

Now that it's after ten o'clock, I can hardly wait to crash, but when I get to Hollywood and Vine, I find that there's no available parking for two long blocks. I've done all that walking only to find out that this HJ's is a restaurant only. I'm incredulous that there's no lodging. I check the *Yellow Pages* in their booth and conclude that I should go to the Vagabond Inn, also on Vine.

Dejected, I head back to my car. As I walk, a police car with two men in the front seat begins to follow me. They stop by the sidewalk and roll down a window; one officer says, "I like the way you're carrying your purse."

"Thank you," I proudly say. "I read somewhere that's how I should hold it for safekeeping."

"So, where are you going this time of night?" he asks.

I tell the whole story.

"We'll drive you to your car," the officer says. "Hop in the back."

I climb in, grateful for the help.

He cranes around to look at me in the backseat. "To make it easy on you, why don't you follow us to the Vagabond? I'll see to it that you get checked in quickly."

True to his word, he and his partner get me to my hotel and stay while I get checked in. After I get my key, he tells me his shift is nearly over and he'd like to take me to dinner fifteen minutes later. I decline, say I've already had dinner, and thank him. He gives me his card—"In case you change your mind."

I've put on my pajamas and have just begun to write my notes when my room phone rings. It's the officer trying to convince me I need a break and a drink after my long day. I kindly explain that what I really need is to finish my work and get some sleep. He has trouble accepting my third "No. Thank. You." before I nearly hang up on him.

After two months of visits to L.A., I've become better acquainted with lodging options there, and I've figured out which customers to pamper and which sleazebags to eliminate—I just raise their prices ridiculously. I've also decided that it's more time- and cost-effective to fly rather than drive.

With all this determined, I'm finally ready to find and train a new salesperson. I again advertise only in my local papers. I doubt that another Southern California person as enterprising as LuLu will enquire. My intent is to share all of California with my new associate.

This time I'm impressed with a lady named May, who looks like a robust Snow White. May lives even closer to our San Ramon office than I do, and it seems she's very rooted here. She's thirty-nine, with kids about the same age as mine, so I won't have to worry that she'll become a full-time mother. I hire her, and now, one month in, she proves to be a winner. She acquires new customers in both L.A. and the Bay Area at a rapid pace. May is marvelous.

Vulcan is back on track!

CHAPTER 31
MODERNIZING

Don't tell people how to do things, tell them what to
do and let them surprise you with their results.
—George S. Patton, (1885–1945),
General of the United States Army

Even though I don't have any customers in Garden Grove, I'm visiting my parents here on this trip south. The additional one-hour round-trip from where I'd otherwise be lodging is a small price to have an evening and overnight visit with my parents.

Daddy looks awful! Since I saw him last June, he's aged into a little old man, hunched and shuffling, muttering about how "useless" he is. I wonder if he's heard the term *wet leaf*—coined by Japanese wives to describe their retired husbands who were formerly workaholics. Unlike my picture of the typical chauvinistic Japanese man, however, at least Daddy now cleans his three bathrooms and does all the vacuuming.

Only three months ago, Daddy seemed full of vim and vigor. He and Mommy combined a Lake Tahoe trip with a visit to our Dublin home, and Daddy, always happy to be on the road, was pumped up when they arrived. He was probably also still relishing the fresh air and intoxicating aroma of the Tahoe pines, but Mommy, the homebody, was tepid about seeing us. Mostly she seemed to be looking forward to their return, so she could catch up on the soap operas Daddy had set up to be recorded.

For over a year, Mommy had dreaded Daddy's retirement. Sadly, his retirement fantasy lasted for only a month. He was full of detailed plans to drive his brand-new motor home all over the U.S., but Mommy missed home too much. Within two years their trips have been whittled down from three-week excursions spaced two months apart to trips of two weeks' duration spaced at least three months apart.

Last July, shortly after they celebrated their sixty-second and sixty-seventh birthdays—separated by only three days—Mommy told me she had insisted on at least four months between out-of-town excursions, and she wanted them limited to just ten days. I know Daddy had counted on spending at least 50 percent of his retirement years traveling. Now his lifelong dream is deflated like an old birthday balloon.

Less than a year before Daddy's retirement, in preparation for travel, he and Mommy moved out of my childhood home with the exquisite front and backyard landscaping—all lovingly maintained by Daddy on top of his full-time job. They now live in a condo with a postage stamp-size backyard and a front yard maintained by the homeowners' association. Even though Daddy loves gardening, he knew he couldn't travel for extended periods and keep a lawn and plants in good condition, so he's limited his horticultural responsibility to a pair of 2×15-foot strips of soil into which he planted bright, fuchsia-colored bougainvilleas.

Daddy always felt more defined by his jobs than by his non-vocational experiences, his character, or his familial or social ties. I've heard that in the absence of other absorbing interests, it's common for such men to die within a year of retirement. Now, two years out, with him not traveling much, I'm not sure he'll make it to his sixty-eighth birthday. I suggest to Daddy that he find a new job, possibly part time, but he's adamantly against that.

"I'm counting on collecting my Social Security," he says. "If I got a job, I wouldn't get the full amount."

"So what? Why should that matter if it could make you feel more useful, and therefore *happier*?"

"I wouldn't be happy letting Social Security dock the pay I've worked for all these years," he retorts. "I will not let Uncle Sam cheat me."

Since my return home, I've been thinking about how to help my father. I've got it! Daddy always wants to give me advice; why doesn't he work for me—without pay, so his Social Security stays safe—and investigate getting a computer for Vulcan? I've heard they can actually save businesses money in the long run. With my expanding sales I'll eventually have to invest in more clerical hours, so I can cost-justify a computer if it will void the future necessity for an additional employee. I'm weary of interviewing and training, and our records would look so much neater with those automatically printed financial statements.

All morning I've been itching to call Daddy with my idea, but I want to respect Mommy's rule of never calling before 10:00 AM or later than 10:00 PM.

Finally, ten o'clock arrives. I call right away, and happy day—Daddy says he's ready, willing, and able to handle this project. After many hours at Radio Shack, Daddy decides their "turnkey" computer is the best choice for Vulcan. Now he pushes my staff to do their data-entry work as fast as possible, frustrating everyone when he fumes over every small mistake—which with a computer system can end up a big mistake.

He's angry with me because I make the ladies take time off from data entry so they can address, stamp, insert, and seal Vulcan Christmas cards for our approximately 200 customers. Daddy thinks that's foolish; he insists that if the IRS ever visited Vulcan, they'd shut us down. I know that's not true, and I know he knows it's not true. He just wants me to feel bad. Also, he expects me to follow every bit of his advice as if *he* were Vulcan's owner.

Daddy's frustrated that this computer business is taking so long. He says May sells too much and the computer can't keep up with her. I'm incredulous that he wants me to tell her to slow down. He's angry with me for refusing to. At least he's never called me ungrateful for all his work, but he does seem to think I'm being disobedient. When I discuss this with others, they say, "Well, you're the boss." But I could never say, "Daddy, I'm the boss."

May thinks Daddy is jealous of my success—that's why he always unduly criticizes me. Our relationship has gone sour in these months he's worked at Vulcan, a sad outcome, but at least he now stands straight and has regained the spring in his step.

As for the computer saving Vulcan clerical hours, it hasn't happened. My employees and I must still do nearly everything we've always done—plus check on the veracity of the computer's findings. My employees make errors in their data input, which results in obvious glitches on the printouts. When none of them can detect a mistake, I end up investigating. Also, for three months I've had to do some of the work my people have ordinarily done because the damn computer input saps their time.

Now I feel like a hamster getting further behind on my treadmill— but at least when the hamster hops off its treadmill, it can still count on food and shelter. I can't.

CHAPTER 32
MY ORIGINAL FIRST MATE

*The best executive is the one who has sense enough to
pick good men to do what he wants done, and self-
restraint to keep from meddling while they do it.*
　　　　　　　　—Theodore Roosevelt, 26th President of
　　　　　　　　　　　　　　　　　the United States

This computer stuff drives me crazy! Well-meaning people tell me, "Delegate, just delegate." All those people, business-savvy or not, aren't aware of my predicament. True, I've been making more money than I need for subsistence, but I don't make enough to afford another full-time employee, much less one with management and accounting skills. Each of my three clerks is swamped, and they're not interested in working beyond their four or eight-hour shifts.

My youngest yet most senior employee, Mary, now nearly a college graduate, can barely squeeze her daily four hours into her academic schedule. Even though a second twenty-hour-a-week person would be affordable, I abstain for several reasons: 1) part-timers generally aren't as dedicated to their jobs as full-timers; 2) after Mary's graduation, she plans to leave Vulcan for another company to qualify her experience toward a CPA; 3) once Mary's gone, I can cost-justify a forty-hour-a-week person; 4) I'll then invest in an office manager, who'll hopefully allow me more time, but will drain a bulk of Vulcan's otherwise net profit; and 5) in the meantime I'm building up cash reserves for a rainy day. In fact, I'm now able to take advantage of every 2 percent early pay discount.

I want relief from the blizzard of papers on my desk, many of which include employee errors. Time constraints are draining me. In fact, time is my most precious commodity. Analogous to a poor person wishing for more dollars in her pocket, I feel like an affluent person wishing for more hours in the day. Nowadays I could more easily forgive a thief than someone who wastes my time.

I have a backache that won't quit. Because time is money, I decide to bypass Kaiser in Walnut Creek and go to a close-by San Ramon orthopedist today. I'll pay his hefty fee—far above the $2 co-pay Kaiser would demand—but it'll be worthwhile to avoid the two longer drives —one to the general practitioner, the second to the orthopedic surgeon—with possible traffic to fight.

I call fifteen minutes before my appointment today to ask if my doctor is running late—like so many doctors do—and I'm told to just come in as scheduled, so I arrive promptly for a 9:30 appointment. I don't mind waiting till 9:45 to be ushered into a consulting room, but it's now 10:15, and I've been shivering in a thin patient gown for half an hour.

I leave the room to find the nurse and ask when I'll be examined.

"He's running a little late, but he should be available shortly."

To me "shortly" is no more than another fifteen minutes, so I wait that long and then go out again to ask what's taking so long.

"He'll be with you any minute; please be patient."

At 10:45 we have the same conversation.

Now it's 11:00, and I should be back at work, but I'm still wasting time in this cold, clammy place. Once again I go out and confront the nurse, who says the doctor's still busy with an emergency that came up a couple of hours ago.

"Why wasn't this explained to me when I called at 9:15 to ask if you were on schedule? You should have been considerate enough then to reschedule me. Why didn't you just do that?"

She doesn't give a logical answer, just repeats he really should be with me any time.

I'm fuming. At 11:15, I give up and get dressed. Now that I'm tensed up over my lost hours, my back pain is worse. I scowl at their big, stupid note on the wall giving an advance apology in the event the S.O.B. is running late. With my red lipstick I add, "No Respect for Patients" to the sign. Dr. Bastard and his staff might think he's Jesus Christ, but I don't.

I decide not to let that pompous ass get away with his lack of regard for my time, so I invoice him for $100. I've never billed anyone for my time before, but I charge him $80 an hour, which is what I must make to support my overhead and my family. I'm generous: I don't bill him for the first half hour.

I'm glad to have my new debt-collection service, because I expect he'll just ignore the statement, and I don't want to waste my time or my employees' time calling him. I decide that if by two months from the billing date I haven't received my $100, I'll sic that agency on him. He won't be able to ignore that!

As predicted, Dr. Bastard's two months have expired with no payment received. I put my collection service to work, and now, a couple of weeks later, I receive a copy of a page-and-a-half letter from Doctor Bastard. It's addressed to the Bureau of Collection & Investigative Services, State Department of Consumer Affairs, with a "cc" to D. A. Schultz, National Revenue Corporation. There's no mention of me getting a "cc" in this letter, but I got this carbon copy anyway—as well as a copy of my invoice. Some of my favorite phrases in his letter are:

1) "As you can see, the patient's time is quite valuable." (I realize he's being sarcastic, but I don't care.)

2) "This has already caused me some concern in terms of time and worry. It may even cause me some difficulties with credit rating." (All I can say to that is, "Let *him* worry!")

3) He ends the letter with, "I would hope that this matter can be rectified promptly. Obviously, if it is not, I shall have to consult my own attorney." (I gleefully assume he's already called his lawyer and incurred at least a fifteen-minute bill for legal advice.)

4) I love his PS: "I would imagine that the cost of transcribing the dictation of these letters is at least another $20–$40, exclusive of my time." I assume this brouhaha has cost him at least eighty dollars' worth of *his* time.

Well, Dr. Bastard, now we're even!

Mary gives her notice, and I quickly find a jewel of an office manager. Jolynn is an attractive, take-charge thirty-four-year-old. She streamlines our financial records and is also fruitful with her research for an improved warehouse situation. Even better, she becomes an excellent buffer between Daddy and me; thanks to her I never have to investigate the computer errors anymore. With Jolynn's gift of time, I'm enjoying more sleep and more fun with my girls and Craig.

Then the shit hits the fan.

CHAPTER 33
THE EMBEZZLER

He was her man, and he done her wrong.
—Unknown (or Hughie Cannon, © 1904)

Everyone's staring at me. I wonder why. Jolynn approaches, and says she wants to speak privately. We head to the back and walk into my glass-encased room. As I sit behind my desk, Jolynn closes the door and then sits down.

"There's something fishy going on with Craig." She means my fiancé, who now lives with me and is my partner in Vulcan's sideline packaging division—"we had to take over his unsuccessful efforts to get ABC's payment before we put their invoice in for bill collection. ABC insisted they paid the bill three months ago and then faxed us their canceled check. I checked it out, and they're telling the truth. It was endorsed by Craig."

I thank Jolynn and walk out, composed, my head held high. After I get in the car my eyelids act like faulty windshield wipers as I struggle to navigate the car homeward.

Craig is in our home office, and my housekeeper is at her weekly work when I burst in the door and roar, "Get out! Get out this minute, you crook. You thief. You liar. Get out and never let me see you again. You are disgusting. I was a fool to trust you. You, you… you piece of *shit!* Get out! *Now!*"

I collapse on the couch; pound the pillows, and bark "Out. Out. Out!" Craig takes a minute to gather some things and then walks solemnly out the door, not saying a word. As I start upstairs to my bed-room, the cleaning lady offers me a few sympathetic words.

I decide I need to discuss this with a professional listener because I'm too embarrassed to talk to anyone else. If I can't unload my grief and rage, I think I might go crazy. I get an appointment with Kaiser for early evening.

Before the girls return from school, Craig's sweet mother calls to say she's sorry that Craig and I are breaking up.

"I'm sure Craig did something bad, but I don't know what it is, and I don't want to know," she says. "I just want to tell you I'm very, very sorry he hurt you."

My only reply is incessant crying.

She repeats how sorry she is before she ends with, "Goodbye, dear."

I'm sorry, too—that I've wasted three years of my life on this no-good reprobate. What was once a clear spring of promise has now become a headfirst shove into a mud puddle full of thorns and dog shit.

After visiting me in the hospital, Craig, formerly only the Weld-Lock rep, gradually morphed from merely an older, gray haired, red-faced guy with bug-like eyes to a witty, sexy, well-built hunk. We con-tinually held hands, snuggled, and kissed. I'd never seen greener grass or brighter flowers.

The girls and Craig got along famously. Other than me, his loves were animals and children. He owned a water-ski boat and enjoyed sharing it with us. A year into our relationship, he bought me an engage-ment ring and moved in. The girls were happy—not least because Craig took them out for ice-cream cones every day. Two perks for me were his making my bed daily and frequent home-cooked meals—typically barbecued steak, baked potatoes, and salad.

There were some red flags, though. Whenever I overheard Craig's phone calls with his boss, he always said he was in Oakland. When I asked Craig why he wouldn't tell the truth, he said, "He doesn't have to know all my business." The boss had a habit of droning on, to which Craig responded by placing the phone a few inches away from his crotch and quickly moving it up and down. I was amused, but ashamed of my mirth.

It wasn't just his boss who wasn't getting the full story, however; Craig didn't want me in his world either. When he returned from a function I didn't attend and I asked what was discussed, his stock answer was always cryptic. I got tired of hearing, "Oh… things"; "The usual"; "This, that, and the other"; "Not much," etc. I tried to squeeze out a better description by asking questions, but nothing worked.

One afternoon the girls were with Fritz, and I was taking a cookie-and-milk break in the kitchen when I heard the front door open. Craig was back from Oakland after lunch with his mother and sister.

"Hi, Craig. Come in the kitchen and tell me how Nancy and Gloria are doing," I called.

Craig greeted me with a perfunctory kiss. "They're fine."

"So what did you all talk about?"

I got the usual vacuous platitudes.

I looked at a carton of two-dozen tomatoes on the counter. I watched my right arm move toward the tomatoes. Then I watched my hand grab one. I saw a tomato fly at a cupboard. Then some tomatoes hit the walls, the ceiling, the counter, the floor—even the window. In between hurls I heard myself yell in clipped phrases, "I… can't… take this… anymore. I need… conversations. I can't… live with… a… mystery man. Talk… to me, talk to me, *talk to me!*"

Splattered tomatoes layered the floor, the counters were a sea of red pulp, and the ceiling and walls dripped. Craig's bug eyes were more bug-like than ever. I couldn't believe I'd purposely messed up my kitchen like that. We both cleaned up wordlessly. There was no permanent damage, and it sure felt good to vent, but I didn't know how much longer I could tolerate his evasiveness.

Soon after this, Craig quit his job to go into business for himself. He spent half his time manufacturing clear plastic strips for the cold sections in supermarkets. For the other half, he and I developed a fifty-fifty partnership for packaging products—plastic strapping and an exciting goldmine of a new product: stretch-wrap film for securing items on pallets. We sold some major supermarkets on this concept and made bundles of money. Then, one by one, we lost the supermarket stretch-wrap business to the manufacturers. Our mutual venture was no longer lucrative, and Craig's plastic-strip business wasn't as profitable as he'd dreamed it would be.

Somehow, he always had enough money to buy our groceries and daily ice-cream cones for the girls. I inform them that I had to make Craig leave because he stole money from Vulcan. They're sad: no more water skiing and ice-cream runs, and no more adult backup against my discipline. Julie even writes a letter to Craig saying she'll miss him because he was "the most favorite boyfriend Mommy ever had." I give her his mother's address so she can send it to him.

I discover Kaiser has booked me with a psychologist, not a psychiatrist. After he hears my story in brief, the psychologist doesn't want to talk further with me. He escorts me to a psychiatrist who doesn't want to talk to me at all, just hurriedly writes a prescription for tranquilizers.

I pick up the stupid pills, and as I drive home I get angrier than ever. I realize those two awful men who wouldn't talk to me only wasted my time. Goddamn those lazy, do-nothing shrinks!

Back home, I hurry to the bathroom and flush the pills down the toilet. I refuse to become a druggie over this! I've survived worse. I'll make it through this too.

CHAPTER 34
NEW UNIFORMS

*The executive must have an ability to survive and
even appear comfortable in a business suit under
conditions of high heat and humidity.*

—Michael Lipsey, author of
I Thought So, Vol. 2: More Original Epigrams

My friend Pat-Z convinces me to check out the wisdom of a man who was audacious enough to proclaim himself an authority on how businesswomen should dress. I don't record his lecture, but I know I'll remember most of his words, because they upend my preconceived notions.

"Ladies, I'm not here to tell you what's fair or comfortable," John Molloy[23] tells us. "I'm here to tell you what works, and open-toed shoes, whether flat or with three-inch heels, do not work in the business world. I will say it again: You need closed-toe dark-colored pumps, ideally with inch-and-a-half heels—and never higher than two inches."

Everyone groans.

"To be successful in business, comfort and sexiness are not part of the package," he proclaims. "Yes, you need to be attractive, but you also need to be professional. Keep your short skirts and beautiful cleavage out of the office and the sales field. Do not emphasize your femininity with ruffles or lace. Also, pantsuits are best avoided."

I gulp as he continues.

"The perfect outfit is a conservative blouse under a well-tailored suit with a cut somewhat like a man's, something that hides your curves.

Wear subdued colors in only pure fabrics—no polyester—whether for your suit or your blouse. A silk scarf can be very effective if the colors are as conservative as a businessman's necktie. In fact, I highly recommend scarves in patterns similar to male ties."

Ugh. I don't like any of this. I like to feel feminine and sexy. I don't want to dress like a man!

"Do not wear dangly earrings or costume jewelry. If you must wear earrings for your pierced ears, stick to plain gold posts, small hoops, or single pearls. Your watch should look expensive but not flashy. The only acceptable neckwear jewelry is either pearls or a gold coin on a gold chain. The most useful piece of jewelry is a wedding ring—even if you're not married."

No way will I wear a wedding ring!

"Wherever you go, be sure to carry an attaché case. It's best not to carry a handbag, but if you insist on doing so, it should be of leather and high quality. It's okay to hide your purse, or even your lunch, in your attaché case. And remember, businesswomen should have a gold pen available at all times."

How dorky!

"For every significant personal contact, keep a notation of your attire. That will prevent you from wearing the same suit twice in a row. Also, be attuned to the results you achieve with your various clothing choices."

Since his seminar, I've followed Molloy's advice almost religiously. I've never spent so much on apparel in so short a time. It's costly to choose only top-quality items—and it would be more fun to purchase the forbidden clothing and colorful accessories. At least I love my elegant new watch with its delicate, gold-braided strap—which Molloy might consider too feminine, even if it is high-end. I hope he's right that I'll receive a high return on these investments.

In addition to feeling like an imposter, I feel uncomfortably masculine, or at best like a little girl playing dress-up in her daddy's clothes. This all-business outer skin makes me miss my self-image as an alluring woman. Despite my moniker, The Lady with Balls, I do like to feel feminine.

Last night, though, I had an epiphany: I'd give myself a new layer of skin with seductive underwear! That way I could feel more in tune with myself and have the best of both worlds: feel very female, yet dress in Molloy-approved garb—except for the suggested phony wedding ring.

I buy lacy panties, bras, garter belts, and slips in five sets of colors: red, white, powder blue, pink, and black. Abandoning the convenience of pantyhose in favor of the more complicated garters is worth the confidence boost. I love knowing that beneath my exterior of appropriate bland and shapeless clothes there hides a femme fatale. The risible dichotomy helps put me at ease when I wear my no-nonsense armor, which makes the armor feel weightless. I'm no longer a pretender but the real me.

May and I visit Safeway together. She hasn't invested big-time in a new wardrobe as I have, but looks sharp nonetheless, and she's been working on this potential customer for months. We hope that the two of us together will sway the purchase agent's allegiance away from his current vendor and over to Vulcan.

We make our pitch, and… *victory; we get our first Safeway order.* I'll always wonder what would've happened had I worn my slinky, pretty-in-pink dress.

Along with Safeway, May and I secure a number of other new accounts. Vulcan sales are off the charts. As in my early days, I'm strapped for cash right now, but I have a better-than-ever income summary.

For years I've enjoyed October, because by this time of year the maximum double deductions and my Social Security employer- and employee-related requirements are completed. I had marked October as the time when I'd start my Christmas shopping, but with limited cash flow, I recently had to reduce my paycheck to cover just the bare necessities for the girls and me. I hope Jeanette and Julie won't be too disappointed with their paltry Christmas presents.

I get a phone call from a recent ex-boyfriend, Trusting & Trustworthy Tom—Crooked Craig's antithesis. Tom is in the habit of calling me every few weeks. I mention my financial situation, and days later I get a $1,000 check in the mail. Dear Tom attached a note: "Pay me back when you can."

Even though I'm now gaga over my new flame, Teddy Bear, I feel warm fuzzies toward Tom when I receive this gift. My eyes glistened as I called to thank him.

In the few days between Tom's phone call and getting his check, I also met my banker for a line-of-credit request. I'm sure I exuded pride in my black, double-breasted suit as I presented him with a list of receivables—many from well-known corporations—plus a good Dun & Bradstreet credit rating. My bank request was quickly approved.

Now, flush with the available money and Tom's loan, my financial worries feel behind me. I decide to reward myself for jobs well done: I spend the $1,000 and then some on a mink coat, a shimmering, turquoise-sequined dress, and silver-strap high heels for a cotillion at Teddy Bear's country club.

Now home from this shopping extravaganza, I'm exuberant over the irony that I can afford to splurge on ultra-feminine regalia due to my masquerading as a quasi-male. I phone my mother to brag, and look forward to her congratulations.

What I hear is, "Alice Marie, are you on drugs?"

My chest aches at her words; I get off the phone as quickly as possible.

Oh, well, at least Teddy Bear will adore me in this new outfit.

Two weeks after the dance, Teddy Bear breaks my heart: "I need to be in charge," he complains. He was attracted to me while I wore a bikini at a pool party, and maybe he thought of me as a mere trophy—especially because another man in the pool was competing vigorously for my attention, but I think Teddy was taken aback once he got to know me as a strong woman.

My power dressing projects an assertive aura that propels me forward in business but constrains my personal relationships. Now I'm financially prosperous but romantically destitute.

Finding boyfriends is all too easy, but finding Mr. Right seems to be an impossible dream. During my waitressing and college days, the days when I was on food stamps, I assumed that no sensible man would want to marry me. Even Bob didn't ask me to marry him till after my graduation. Upon my change from being a financial liability to a financial asset, however, I've experienced some men wanting me for my money and others feeling threatened by it. I know men are attracted to confident women, but I think too much confidence repels them—like we all need water, but too much of it can sicken or even kill us. I've even been told by a couple of men, "I'm attracted to you physically, but I can't handle your power." It hurts my feelings, but I never let on.

Given all that, I now look back at Fritz's put-downs in a new light. Once I announced my plan to become a lawyer, he tried to put obstacle after obstacle in my way. He said the house wouldn't be kept clean, the meals wouldn't be good, the kids wouldn't get enough of my time; yet even before Herbie came into our lives, Fritz tried to make me feel guilty and lazy for not having a job. When I received my fourth college A in a row, he told me, "You'll never make it through law school because you had to work too hard for those A's." He also occasionally called me Dum-Dum and Lo-Lo—always careful to say it in a saccharine tone. Once, when I told him that a neighbor had visited, he asked if I'd served her coffee and cake. I explained that I hadn't because I was too busy to encourage a longer stay, and he boomed out, "*Miss Hos*-pitality!" over and over, so loudly that I rushed around to close the windows, afraid everyone on our block would hear.

Shortly before he quit his job, I was sitting on our couch in front of the coffee table with my schoolbooks piled high—glad the girls were away at friends' houses so I could prepare for a test the next day. I hoped to finish before Fritz got home from work. He opened the front door as I concentrated on the sentence I was reading. He took three big strides to the coffee table, then bent down and with one arm scattered all my books onto the carpet. "I'm the one who should be going to law school," he spat. "Not you!"

The person I am now would've retorted with recriminations, but the old me was far too complaisant. I almost always tried to pacify Fritz when he got into rages like that. *Stupid me!* I do remember one exception, though.

Our family was seated at the table finishing lunch. Fritz, across from me, made a negative comment about the meal. My anger boiled up, and I snapped my head to the left and gave my right cheek a hard slap with my right hand. "Criticism," I yelled. With my left hand, I slapped my left cheek, propelling my head to the right. "Criticism!" I repeated the yells and slaps several times before I shouted, "I can't take your criticism anymore!" Then I stopped my self-flagellation and took a deep breath, all the while staring at Fritz.

Fritz got up from the table. "Don't ever make a scene like that in front of the girls again," he said. Then he walked away.

This marriage is hopeless.

Have I ever changed from my Edith Bunker days![24] I've become a woman with an impregnable position: I refuse to take shit from any man. This is a fairly recent evolution; even though my dear garbage men deemed me The Lady with Balls after my confrontation with Osgood years ago, they didn't know my well-kept secret: if I hadn't been so desperate for my $5,000, I'd have quietly simmered and slunk away from that wretch. My reaction was instinctual; I felt like an animal that had to choose between fighting and not feeding her children.

When did I make the full transition to the strong woman I am today? I wonder. I imagine it was accomplished in small steps, and the final *me* emerged as I came to feel at ease in my power suits. Nine years ago, when I was fired from Mervyn's, my self-esteem barreled down to its depths—but now I soar beyond our galaxy.

CHAPTER 35
CLEAN AND DIRTY FIRST MATES

Match skills and personality to the task—
that will maximize productivity.
—Alyssa Gregory, entrepreneur, writer,
founder of the Small Business Bonfire

U nfortunately, Jolynn lasts less than sixteen months, at which point she tells me, "I've done everything I can do to organize Vulcan, and now I'm going to set up my own business as a consultant."

Despite my sorrow, I write her a glowing letter of recommendation, thankful that for a glorious year-plus she allowed me enough freedom from Vulcan servitude to get my sanity back.

I decide to find Jolynn's replacement the lazy and more expensive way: through an employment agency. I find one that advertises a thorough vetting of the potential employee's skills and background. I give the agency the same math test Jolynn took before I hired her, and they quickly secure the right person for me. She has an impressive resume and scores 100 percent on the math test.

Nora is professionally dressed, tall, slender, and pretty. Her immediate job is to arrange the details of Vulcan's move from San Ramon to Dublin's Heritage Park. She makes an excessively big production of the task. Either Jolynn or I would've made a few phone calls and conducted no more than two physical overviews of our future office, yet for days on end Nora comes to work late and leaves early, each time with the excuse of arranging the move. Sometimes her lunch hour doubles, allegedly because of the work she's doing to organize our upcoming transition.

Now that we have relocated, however, Nora conjures even worse excuses for being away from the office. She rarely interfaces with her three assistants, each of whom is more proficient than she. Nora is either incompetent or neglectful with her paperwork projects. I come to the realization that she couldn't possibly have attained that perfect score on my math test honestly.

I call her former employers, and every one of them says Nora scammed them one way or another. I've been swindled. First thing this morning, I call Nightmare Nora into my office and fire her.

Red in the face, she yells, "Alice, you have no heart!" She springs out of her seat and rushes outside, ignoring everyone else in the office as she goes.

We all breathe a sigh of relief.

After being hoodwinked by one employment agency, I want nothing to do with another, so I decide to give meek Millie a shot at officer manager. I hope that with the increased pay and status, she'll show more *cojones.*

Wrong!

Millie continues to earn her A+ in bookkeeping, but her management skills rate a D–. I soon discover that whenever she finds someone else's mistake, she silently corrects it. She has always bent over backwards to avoid stepping on toes, and she always will. I'd been foolish to push poor Millie to her Peter Principle. I resolve to never again try to make someone go against her personality.

When Millie gives me her two-weeks' notice, I'm relieved but sad. This lovely lady has been with me for more than five years. She's frustrated me for over a year, but I haven't had the heart to humiliate her with a demotion, and now I'm losing the best bookkeeper I've ever had.

I cast around for what to do and settle on promoting Annie. She's been with Vulcan only five months, but during that time she's made relatively few bookkeeping mistakes, shown herself to have an assertive personality, and displayed good work habits.

I offer Annie the job. Her voice cracking, bordering on tearful, she gives me a mixed message. She fears she has inadequate accounting knowledge, yet she wants the same pay Millie got—and she wants to be salaried, not hourly like Millie was. She justifies this by saying she'll study accounting books at home and probably end up spending more than forty hours a week at Vulcan. I accept her counteroffer.

Annie's work is more flawed than Millie's, but to lessen my yoke of responsibility is more valuable to me than perfection on paper. I'm content to take her occasional contentiousness and resistance to following directions over Millie's obsequiousness, which was so exasperating. *"Whatever you say, Alice. You know what's best."* I don't want a mirror telling me I'm the fairest in all the land; I want another intelligent adult's honest opinion.

I don't, however, ask for anyone's endorsement when, for Valentine's Day, I decide to send out red cards with a heart-shaped cutout that displays a color photo of my five employees and me with the inscription "We Love You."

"That's unprofessional," Annie says disdainfully.

But my mind is made up—and I'm proven right. The valentines garner lots of customer compliments, and now I'm delighted each time I see our heart-encircled photo displayed on the desk of a customer or vendor.

Annie takes excellent charge of hiring people and apportioning work appropriate to their skills; however, she doesn't walk on water like I once thought the perfectly organized Jolynn did.

CHAPTER 36
THE CHARLATAN

Every vocation and hobby has its parasites who infest every gathering to shamelessly promote their products and services.
—Michael Lipsey, author of
The Quotable Stoic – A Book of Original Aphorisms

I've begun to think that perhaps Jolynn doesn't walk on water after all. During her last two weeks with Vulcan, she persuaded me to attend the EST workshops. I now question her judgment regarding her adoration of nutcase guru Werner Erhard.[25] He says we need to get in touch with our *inner asshole.* I've invested sixty hours of my time, four nights at the pricey Claremont hotel in Berkeley, and a $250 fee to listen to this baloney?

At least I won't suffer from hunger or bathroom needs like the 200 others here. Jolynn warned me that an EST session sometimes continues nearly all day without a food, drink, or bathroom break. Some attendees have—almost proudly—announced they've wet their pants. I, however, was careful to stipulate on the signup form that I'm under doctor's orders to empty my bladder before discomfort, and to get nourishment at least every four hours.

A few years ago, Jolynn suffered through this crazy program. She led me to believe I was lucky to be taught by EST founder and master himself, the nationally famous Erhard. Ordinarily, his trainers conduct the seminars, but this time he's leading, supposedly to experiment with some agenda revisions.

Now he expects every attendee to state, "I am an asshole." *Did Jolynn announce that she's an asshole?* I'm astounded that at least fifty people have by now participated in this self-deprecation. I hate that ugly word, and the description certainly doesn't fit me.

Some of the participants balk at first, but with Werner's coaxing, they eventually make the declaration. Does he hypnotize them with his blue-gray eyes and penetrating look? Mind control emanates from his handsome, chiseled face. With his runner's physique and perfect posture, he looks like an Adonis. If he were ugly and chubby, could he hold as much power over all these devotees, or is it just his confidence that makes him so convincing?

Uh-oh. The *Big Man* now faces me. I obediently stand and state my name. The only rebel, I proclaim, "I am a nice person."

A mass intake of breath follows.

Werner's blue eyes laser into mine. "No!" he says resolutely. "You are an asshole, and you need to admit it."

Returning his locked-eye stare without animus, I answer, "That's not true, so I will not say it."

Glaring and increasing his volume, he booms, "Alice! Say, 'I am an asshole.'"

"No!"

He puts a hand on my shoulder and propels me roughly back onto my seat. "Say, 'I am an asshole!'" he thunders.

Another mass inhalation, louder-than-before.

I continue eye contact and say, "You'd better be careful. I have a back injury; that's why I have this cushion."

"We'll talk later," he says quietly. He moves on and asks the next person to stand.

Eventually, Werner succeeds in getting the stupid proclamation from everyone else. Then he has a young pretty lady assistant take charge of the crowd, walks over to me, and requests politely that I follow him.

Glad to interrupt my sitting, I allow myself to be led into a vacant room nearby.

First Werner tells me a little more about himself—the jerk he used to be. Then he asks me some questions about my career and family and what brought me here—nothing too probing. Next he tries to persuade me that I am an asshole because I can't be all lily-white—which, of course, I'm not, but I insist that I can't be an asshole: I lack malevolence, and I feel no shame about my current life and projected future.

When he says we'd better return to the lecture hall, I presume he's run out of energy for further conversion attempts.

The second weekend is doubly crazy. We're instructed to close our eyes and imagine all the scary people who are out to get us. Werner reminds me of an accomplished teller of ghost stories at a preteen girls' slumber party. Suddenly an otherwise quiet blonde screams as if she's about to be murdered. We're all told to keep our eyes closed as we hear the assistant try to calm her while she leads her out of the room.

Werner waits for the door to close and muffle the wails. Then he continues to speak dramatically about frightening villains. "*But,*" he says, increasing his volume, "we have a secret: we know they're afraid of us."

At this point everyone laughs, apparently in genuine relief, but the scenario leaves me cold. For quite some time I've felt that people are afraid of me, and I don't like that, even if it's been financially helpful. Romantically, I've been hurt, most recently by Craig and then Teddy Bear. Also, I've realized some of my employees are intimidated by me. Power can be lonely.

Our last lesson is what I'll call "Getting It." Supposedly, *Getting It* doesn't mean everyone is afraid of us. What in the hell it's supposed to mean is beyond me—yet every attendee but me appears to think they've grasped the wisdom of *Getting It.* And these acolytes seem to pity me for not feeling the same. During our following social time I'm bombarded with, "Alice, do you *get it* yet?"

They may feel sorry for me, but I think they've been brainwashed, with the assistance of peer pressure. They seem like lemmings who can't acknowledge that Emperor Erhard is naked. They don't really *get it* at all.

CHAPTER 37
CLEAN AND DIRTY SAILS

*Lifetimes of hard work, loyalty, and dedication appear
nowhere on corporate balance sheets.*
—Michael Lipsey, author, artist

May was an ultra-valuable saleslady for her first year and a half. Then, at age forty-one, she had an unplanned pregnancy. She continued her excellent work habits till shortly before her baby's birth. It was at least partly understandable when, in the first half year of her daughter's life, she began to rest on her laurels—but for the next two years she treated her job as a sinecure. Her baby seemed to have permanently extinguished that former roaring fire in her belly. I need someone who's eager to pound the pavement, so, with no small amount of sadness, I terminate May's employment and start to look for a new salesperson.

My daughter Julie mentions the job opening to Sarah, one of her babysitting customers. Without even placing an ad in the paper, I hire Sarah. Because of her enthusiasm and intelligence, I have high expectations for this twenty-five-year-old, whose youth is counterbalanced by the advantage of her familiarity with baling wire, learned during a year's employment at Wire-Up. Another plus is that she's a slender, long-legged, head-turning brunette—a competitive edge with men.

For this last year I've been delighted with Sarah, but today, she tells me she needs to speak to me in private.

"Alice, it's not that I'm ungrateful, but I can do better on my own," she tells me. "Instead of a percentage of the gross profit, I prefer earning

100 percent of it. I won't be investing in all those nonessential wom-en doing their unnecessary tasks. Also, I'll get better deals from my distributors than you get. I'm really sorry that I'll be competing with Vulcan, but I have to think about my future."

As I hold my bile down, I ask, "Sarah, don't you remember signing your noncompete agreement?"

Her eyes widen. "What do you mean?"

"Just what I said. You really *don't* remember?"

She's unable to hide a gulp as she responds, "No. May I see a copy?"

"Of course." I open a file drawer. "Give me a minute… Here. You may keep this copy."

"Well, I'll have to show this to my lawyer," she says, sounding much less sure of herself. "But I'm determined to carry through with my plans." She stands. "I have to go now. Bye, Alice."

As she leaves, I stay seated, head spinning. *That double-crossing, ungrateful wench!* I've nurtured Sarah and loved her like a little sister. I thought we had an unbreakable bond, especially since our Pennsylvania convention last October: we shared a room, bicycled amongst the au-tumn leaves, picked juicy apples, and talked about how we were the only businesswomen, let alone Californians, at the entire event. And Sarah received a generous draw and sales commissions here at Vulcan; I'm sure she's never been paid better. To think I imparted all of my company's trade secrets to her! I feel so betrayed.

I immediately inform my employees. They're as stunned as I am.

"You know," Bev tells me, "after our last Christmas party Bill told me, 'Alice had better watch out for that one.'"

I wonder what Bev's husband detected in Sarah. Whatever it was, it went right over my head.

Shortly after I hired Sarah, I was stuck in bed, semi-paralyzed by a herniated fifth lower lumbar disc—probably the result of sitting at my desk or on my car seat for overlong stretches. While I was out of commission, Annie found a replacement for an employee who wasn't working out—a woman I privately referred to as Horrible Harriet.

I graduate from conducting business in my bed, and am now, with the help of painkillers, back in the office. Out of the corner of my eye I observe a twenty-something ebony-haired beauty walking quickly and giggling. In her bold black-and-gold-striped dress, she reminds me of a bumblebee, but only someone as trim as a wasp could look as sexy as she did with those horizontal stripes. She walks with her lower arms raised, hands out, splaying her fingers as if drying her nail polish. When she speaks with other employees, customers, or vendors, she gesticulates more than I'd ever seen anyone do, on or off the phone. Also, I've never heard a woman laugh as loud or as often.

Annie informs me that this dynamo's name is Theresa and that she's a good worker. Annie suggests we hire her in January, once our ninety-day requirement with the temporary agency expires. I shrug my okay.

Since then I've been impressed with Theresa's warmth and joviality on the phone—and her energy. Annie was right: she's a good worker. Over the weekend I decide to give her a shot at replacing Sarah. When I come in this morning I give Theresa the good news, and explain how her income should greatly increase.

Without her usual smile, she answers, "No thanks, Alice. I don't want to be a sex object."

I'm a bit shocked and confused by her response. Then I remember my "been kissed and told" story of a couple months ago.

Nick was finally going to show me the baler that he insisted his garbage company rarely used. I think we'd both gotten tired of my constantly badgering him for a repeat order of his small bale ties. It had been two years since he'd ordered a mere ten bundles, though he frequently ordered large quantities of his other two wire products.

We walked to a far corner of his recyclables shed. It smelled like we were approaching rotting garbage, with an undertone of vomit and fecal matter.

No one seemed to be working in this area. All the rows of paper and cardboard bales muffled the noise of the machines and the trucks from the garbage yard. As we walked, I chattered away about how we'd be better able to predict his wire usage once I counted the remaining bundles. When we reached the baler, alongside stinky flattened boxes, I worked hard not to gag or make a face and continued my small talk.

Midsentence, Nick interrupted me with a tight embrace and a sloppy kiss.

I pushed him away gently but firmly. Attempting a poker face, I finished my sentence and pretended the last few seconds never happened. Nick went along with the charade, and I jotted down the wire count.

"Thanks for letting me see the baler and the wire," I said. "It's time to get back to my office now."

Nick walked me back to my car. We said goodbye and, as usual, shook hands, with no mention of what had just transpired.

Driving back to my office, I smiled as I marveled at this bizarre event—the most *unromantic* place I'd ever been kissed. Then I mused about the other untoward advances I'd suffered over my eleven-year Vulcan career.

I think this was the third one. Statistically, I'll be due another in three and a half years.

I wonder what Theresa would have done if that had happened to her. A lady in the garbage world has to be tough, and to me the short-term discomfort of these little harassments is worth the lifetime laughs. At least Theresa won't fault me for passing her by. Here I thought she had the perfect personality for outside sales, but regrettably she's not interested.

Now to place some newspaper ads.

I've had enough of unproductive searching. I don't know if my dilemma is that I'm too cynical or am so drained that I've lost my insight, but no one I've interviewed has shown me that special spark.

Charisma is a necessity for effective selling, and the people who want to do the job don't have it. The one person who bordered on charisma didn't show enough confidence when she insisted on a salary guarantee beyond my standard six months. I'm exhausted doing 100 percent of the outside sales with no time to scout for new customers. It seems like I huff and puff just to maintain my existing customer rapport, and the innumerable hours I have to spend reading résumés and conducting interviews are dispiriting.

I tell Annie I'm about ready to hire the least lukewarm candidate. She says Theresa has reconsidered being a saleslady and now wants the job.* *If she wants the job, she should tell me herself.* I'm not sure Theresa will be a good salesperson—timidity is no asset in this business. *What the hell!* I need a break from all this; I need some relief, and time to grow the business. I'll give Theresa a chance and pray she succeeds.

Theresa proves to be just what Vulcan needs. Her customers love her, and I hope she hangs on with Vulcan forever.[26]

---

* It wasn't until 2017 when Theresa read an early draft that she found out Annie had spoken up for her. She was shocked and dismayed about that, but in all fairness to Annie, without that intervention, it may have been too late for Theresa's opportunity.

CHAPTER 38
BLINDSIDED

I find that the harder I work, the more luck I seem to have.
—Thomas Jefferson, 3rd President of
the United States

My parents are disgusted with my revolving door of lovers during the past thirteen years. Today, when I speak to her on the phone, Mommy exclaims, "Alice Marie, for once in your life can you try to survive without a man?"

She should talk! I remember when Daddy spent a lot of time helping Vulcan get on computer. Mommy never let more than two hours go by without phoning to ask him trivial questions—how to make the refrigerator colder, what to do with the electricity bill, how to make her soap-opera video eject, etc.

I'll show her: I'll go the next three months with no man in my life. This summer new men probably won't join my ski club, so I can go to the meetings, but besides that, no more mixed-gender parties for me. For home maintenance, I'll just use my helpful neighbor, Dick, or pay a handyman. I'll take an art class and drop out if I see a cute guy. I'll have girlfriend-only dates. Probably I'll see the same old regulars at the gym and my favorite breakfast spot, Bob's Big Boy. I'll have more time for both my kids and my work. I might even sneak in some good books and bathtub soaks.

I'm famished this morning, as I am every workday after a 6:00 AM forty-minute swim. Before beginning my 8:30 grind at the office, I enjoy replenishing the spent calories at Bob's Big Boy. As usual, I heap mounds of food on two dinner-size plates—watermelon slices, orange sections, strawberries, fresh pineapple, and banana rounds on one, and on the other, bacon, sausage, scrambled eggs with onions and chunks of red and green pepper, and yummy hash browns lavishly sprinkled with grated cheddar.

Directly behind me I notice a new male customer, baby-faced but built like a football player and casually but fashionably attired. "Are you actually going to eat everything you've got on those plates?" he asks.

"Of course. I never waste this delicious food," I reply.

He looks at me appraisingly. "Are you one of those once-a-day eaters, then?"

"No, I eat a good lunch and dinner every day too," I say with a laugh.

He raises his eyebrows. "Then how do you keep that slender figure of yours?"

"I swim twenty Olympic laps before I come here."

"Well, I bike twenty miles every day," he says, shaking his head, "but I'd never eat that much food for breakfast."

"This has been working for me for years." I shrug. "I have a high metabolism."

The man follows me to the counter and sits on the barstool next to mine. "You look like you're dressed for work. Where are you going?"

"Home first, then to my office in Pleasanton. Where do you work?"

"I don't have an office. I manage the managers of my apartment buildings in Florida."

"Why are you in California?"

"It's too hot in Florida, and I'm thinking of making investments here. I just got settled last week in my new apartment in Pleasanton, so I haven't yet seriously investigated anything. I'm a new guy on the block."

I notice he doesn't have a wedding ring, so I think he might make a good addition to the Bota Bagger Singles' ski club. He seems to be in his late forties, so I figure he's divorced.

"If you're that new, you might be interested in the local singles' ski club," I tell him. "It meets at Howard Johnson's in Dublin every Thursday at 7:00 PM. They eat dinner, then dance after the meeting."

"Sounds like a good club. I don't know anyone around here yet, and I like to ski."

"If you want, I could introduce you to a lot of the single women."

"I would appreciate that. My name's Bart."

Even if I were hunting right now, Bart wouldn't stir my juices. Though he's tall enough, he isn't my physical type—too thick and brawny, but I appreciate that he's all muscle with no fat. I deduce that his baby face is due to an extremely small nose—incongruous with his large body. Also, his ruddy complexion is a little too pink for my taste, but I'm sure the ski-club women will find him appealing and he'll easily get a date.

For the following three days Bart sits next to me at the breakfast counter, engaging me in idle chitchat. He's childless, but we've both been divorced for over a decade and have had several serious serial romances in the ensuing years. I tell him that despite my enormous breakfasts, the angst I experienced after recently ending a long-term relationship resulted in weight loss.

"That's practical," he says simply. "You thin down to get ready for the next one."

I shake my head. "I don't think I look better now that I'm below my ideal 128 pounds."

"A woman can never be too rich or too thin," he chuckles. "I weigh 220 pounds—slightly hefty for six foot two, but I don't mind since I have such low body fat."

At the Bota Baggers' meeting at Howard Johnson's last night, I introduced Bart to every woman I thought might be a good match for him. I gave him opportunities to linger with these potential love interests, but he followed me everywhere.

Now, this morning, he's again sitting next to me at Bob's breakfast counter.

"Did you especially like any of the women you met last night?" I ask.

"They were all nice, but no one particularly excited me," he says casually.

"I'm sorry to hear that."

"Do you know of any good restaurants around here?" he says, suddenly switching gears. "Would you accompany me to one of them for dinner this evening?"

I don't know what clicked, but I suddenly see Bart in a different light. I get a little chill of excitement. *I might break my three-month vow.*

Dinner last night was delightful. The dancing wasn't quite as wonderful—Bart was somewhat inhibited with the fast dancing and critical of the male dancers who were letting loose and seemed to be having more fun than he was—but he saw me home like a gentleman afterward, and I had a great time.

As agreed, we meet at the buffet this morning for breakfast (an hour later than the workweek grind), and then go cycling together. We bike long enough to work up an appetite, so he treats me to lunch.

As soon as Bart pays the bill, I stand up. "I'm sorry to eat and run," I say, "but I always try to get my weekend office work done on Saturday so I might have a chance of keeping all day Sunday free."

"I understand," Bart says. "But before you go... will you have dinner with me again this week?"

I smile. "Definitely."

Bart and I have become an item. I think he's perfect, a hunk of a knight in shining armor, my *Mr. Wonderful.* He met me in my business clothes and immediately liked what he saw. He can't be attracted to my money, either, because with all his apartment complexes he's better off than I.

Today, six weeks after our first date, on an otherwise beautiful Sunday—Bart changes his colors. He says I'm too bossy; I shouldn't expect him to both pay for our meals and take the least desirable seat; I shouldn't expect him to carry all our store-bought bagged items; I shouldn't expect him to always chauffeur whenever we drive; my casual outfits aren't classy enough; I should wear high heels, not tennis shoes, with my slacks and jeans. I presume he merely woke up on the wrong side of the bed and try to shake off his criticisms.

Now, however, we're at lunch—at McDonald's—my hamburger is only half-eaten when Bart asks, "Hon, would you please get me some more coffee?"

I swallow the bite I'm chewing. "Bart, I'm still eating. You can get your own coffee."

"Geez," he says, looking wounded. "I don't see what's wrong about a guy just wanting another cup of coffee."

"Nothing," I say calmly, "but you can get it yourself."

His brow furrows. "Alice, sometimes you're just not a good girl."

"Well, Bart, if you want a good girl, I suggest you find a nice Mormon lady."

"*Geez!*" He throws up his hands. "All I want is a cup of coffee."

"Then marry a sweet little Mormon lady and forget about *me!*"

"Such a big deal over some coffee! If you ever learn to be a good girl, I'll buy you a mink coat."

I narrow my eyes. "I have a mink coat."

"I'll bet your mink coat isn't white."

"No, it's black."

"I could buy you a white one, and that's a lot more expensive than a black one."

I sigh. "Bart, I'm perfectly happy with my black mink."

He drops it.

Bart is unpredictable. He can be on a sweet streak, then suddenly switch to misogynist mode, railing bitterly against our society of what he calls *female entitlement.*

I look forward to a break from him when I take a seaside Mexican Club Med vacation, a trip I planned before we started dating; however, Bart insists that he should accompany me, so my getaway becomes our first big trip together.

Bart's control issues intensify in Mexico. During the day we argue about the fact that I refuse to serve him coffee. One night he awakens me from a sound slumber, wanting me to kill a noisy cricket that's robbing his sleep. I tell him to stop disturbing *my* sleep and kill it himself. He rationalizes that the racket is coming from my side of the bed. We bicker for an hour while the cricket continues to chirp.

By the end of this torturous vacation, I regret letting Bart accompany me; but during the flight home, he gets nicer and makes me laugh. I shove the cricket and coffee issues to the back of my mind.

When I got home, I was pleased to see that business ran as usual while I was gone. Nonetheless, I knew I'd need to put in extra hours of catch-up work, and I've done just that all week. Now Bart is rankled that I'm not as available as I was before our vacation.

"I used to think that you were really, really smart," he tells me. "Now I know you aren't all that smart. You just work hard."

I raise my arms in surrender and reply, "You're right, Bart. The harder I work the smarter I seem." I think he's disappointed that he didn't arouse my ire. I just can't feel insulted—because the truth doesn't hurt.

It's Valentine's Day. I've been icy toward Bart, so I'm not sure he'll show up. He knows I'll attend the Bota Baggers' party. I hear a gentle knock at the door, and it's Bart, carrying a big heart-shaped box of chocolates—no kiss, card, flowers, or gift, but this will do. I merely say hi and thank you.

I've been assigned to bring hors d'oeuvres. I'm no exemplary cook, but no one makes deviled eggs better than mine. I've just finished stuffing them, sprinkled them with paprika, and carefully placed three dozen beautiful halves amongst lush green sprigs of parsley. The gleaming silver tray frames them beautifully. If I weren't so rushed, I'd take a picture.

"Do you mind driving?" Bart asks. "I've been in my car all day."

I don't mind; in fact, I prefer to use my car rather than his. "No problem," I say. I carefully carry my masterpiece to the car, then ask Bart to hold the eggs, and he does.

We're only half a mile away from home, however, when Bart gets tired of holding the platter. "Can you pull over?" he asks. "I want to put this on the back seat." He gestures to the platter.

"I worked hard on these, Bart," I say. "I don't want any possibility of them getting mangled."

"They'll be fine on the back seat," he insists.

I shake my head. "No, they won't. Please just hold them."

In the loudest voice I've ever heard from him, Bart demands, "*Pull over!*"

I do just that, determined to resolve this disagreement before we go any farther. I park at the curb and turn to him. "Look, Bart, it's unacceptable to put the eggs on the back seat. You either keep the eggs on your lap or you drive the car and I'll hold the eggs on *my* lap. Which do you want to do?"

Bart silently gets out of the car, opens the back door, places the eggs on the back seat, closes the door, returns to the passenger seat, closes the door, and looks straight ahead.

For half a minute there's silence between us as I, too, look straight ahead.

Finally, I burst out, "Bart, you are an, an, an *asshole!* I have never called anyone that in my life, but you are an *asshole!*"

"I won't take that kind of abuse," he says in a dignified tone.

"Then get out of the car and get the hell away from me," I screech. "*Out! Out! Out!*"

Without another word, he exits the car and walks away.

I retrieve the eggs, put them on the passenger seat, and resume driving, my left hand on the steering wheel and my right holding my precious platter in place.

The eggs and I arrive intact.

At the party, a new man with friendly brown eyes cozies up to me right away. Though he's a little too old and his body a little too soft, he still has dark hair and is tall and vaguely handsome.

Al and I have a lot of fun. Before I leave, I agree to give him my phone number. Then I head home, where I notice my message machine blinking. The first message is from Bart. "Alice, I'm sorry I was so obnoxious. I really am. Can we get together tomorrow?"

The second and third messages are repeats of the first, but I'm done with Bart. I've already decided to get to know Al better.

CHAPTER 39
SEARCHING FOR A SOUL MATE

*Identify your problems but give your power
and energy to solutions.*
—Tony Robbins, author, entrepreneur,
philanthropist, life coach

S hortly after Valentine's Day, Al and I become lovers. He's adamant
that he never wants to remarry. Though I eventually do want marriage again, my response is "All I want from you, Al, is a healthy six-
month relationship"—and I sincerely mean it.

Shortly after this conversation, I conclude that I'll want out by then
anyway. Al is a good-time Charlie. He's sweet and fun, but a sloppy
drunk; a dud in bed; lives in too small a world, with no intellectual
interests or travel plans; and lacks the income to match my desired
lifestyle.

I do, however, want to remain with Al for the next several months
while I conduct a self-examination: 1) I jump into relationships too
quickly—with the excuse that all my energy is zapped by Vulcan; 2)
My love life is my escape from that tedium; and 3) When I have a
chance with an emotionally available, nonalcoholic, sensible, educated,
and hardworking man, I miss the fun of the *devil-may-care* element.
I yearn for pizzazz. The few men I've fallen for who weren't bad or
irresponsible were selfish and/or emotionally unavailable. I hope I'm
not yearning for the impossible dream.

When my six months with Al are up, I plan to transfer my Vulcan
energy into finding Mr. Right. Now that I've surpassed my monetary

goal, I can afford to let Vulcan coast for a while. As with my career, I'll do studious research and hone my antennae for useful tips on husband hunting.

I buy books on relationships and how to attract men for marriage. I follow the suggestion to make a list of what I want and what I can offer. Regarding future dates, I decide to: 1) refuse men who obviously aren't qualified, no matter how charming; 2) terminate further dates with anyone who eventually exposes a disqualifying flaw; and 3) invest heavily in the professional advice of a home decorator to make my current, plain-Jane tract home more like a country Victorian dollhouse.

In the meantime, I've realized that to find this elusive man I'll need a source for a wider selection of males than I've previously been exposed to. Having recently stumbled across information about a dating service called Great Expectations (GE), I go to investigate its Walnut Creek office and observe that 700 men and 500 women are profiled in their books. Each applicant fills in both sides of a full page: one side with four photographs and the other with a self-description and specific qualities hoped for in a partner. The price is $1,500[27]—rather steep, but a good deterrent to financial losers. Each person must record his or her first name, town, birth date, height, weight, occupation, education, religion, smoker status, and other key information. When a meeting is desired, per written permission of the selected, the phone number is divulged.

The three open-ended questions are: 1) What I Like to Do; 2) Who I Am; and 3) What I'm Looking For. I answer them all as truthfully as possible. My combined answers illustrate my high physical energy and contradictory nature of extrovert/introvert; daydreamer/mover and shaker; serious/silly; and practical/romantic. I word the most important criterion for my desired one "Fun, but down to earth enough to keep his garden tended."

To activate my membership, I need current photos. I choose an anti-Molloy salmon raw-silk suit with a pale pink silk blouse. To keep my outfit in mint condition, I wrap it in plastic and drive to GE in shorts. Both the photographer and I are early. He looks me over.

"You have nice legs. Before you change, let's take some pictures of you in those shorts." After I change and complete the dressier poses, I get videoed for two minutes.

After half a dozen going-nowhere dates, I finally become smitten with a dashing, suntanned, dark-blond. It's lust at first sight, but I justify latching on to him because he fits my qualifications of income and property ownership. It takes me nearly half a year to realize this man is a money-grubber; even when he became overly frustrated about the fact that my home equity had been reduced via multiple refinancings, I didn't see the situation for what it was.

Neither of us had our profile removed from the books at GE while we were together, and throughout this wasted romance, I continued to receive inquiries and respond to them. Before he left me, pangs of guilt clashed with my jumping heart one day as I gazed at a princely brunet wearing a three-piece suit and a winning smile. I was favorably impressed with his first two paragraphs of *What I Like to Do* and *Who I Am.* I continued to his last paragraph, *What I'm Looking For*—"the 'perfection test': an invitation to visit the south Mendocino coast, have fish 'n' chips at the Point Arena wharf, help cut and load firewood on Signal Ridge, and hike from the lighthouse to the Devil's Punchbowl. Our rooms would be at the Gualala Hotel or the Old Milano Hotel, with a stroll on the beach after dinner."

I let out a big sigh. Those inspiring words are followed by "A sigh at this point means that you're already well on your way to passing the test."

I flush with annoyance. *The arrogant popinjay! Who is he to think I must pass his test? He can go to hell.* As I continue leafing at the other candidates, however, I keep leafing back to this pompous ass's photo, and in the end I write him a gracious note: "Thank you for selecting me. If I weren't already in a committed relationship, I'd look forward to our first date! The only reason I'm still listed in the active member book is that my boyfriend is also in it. I think he enjoys being selected, even though he turns everyone down. If things don't get more serious between us, and if you're still available, you'll hear from me."

Now, two and a half months later, my handsome gold digger leaves me for a woman with more money, and I'm free again.

When I come back to GE after the breakup, I discover that the pompous guy has removed himself from the active member book. I write a second letter: "Last March you selected me, and I wrote you a letter explaining I was involved with another. That's over. Even though you've since gone 'inactive,' I choose to now give you my phone number. You might want to save this note in case you decide to become 'active' again. It happens, you know."

Another two months of go-nowhere dates have come and gone, and I'm again in the GE office. As I thumb through their books, I suddenly see a photo of the arrogant guy with the self-satisfied smile. I'm infuriated that he returned to active status yet didn't contact me.

I swallow my pride and write a third—and last—note. "Do you remember selecting me last 3/31? I wrote you a turndown letter because I was 'involved.' Then on 7/22 I wrote you a 'please ask me out' letter. My number is… Sure hope to hear from you."

The very day after I wrote that note I had a date with Dave, an interesting man who's a lot of fun. Now, after five weeks, I conclude that he meets all my requirements, and he adores me—but too much. If his home base weren't in San Diego, he'd smother me.

Tonight, he tells me he wants to relocate to Dublin to be near me. I tell him I'm not ready to commit to him enough for such a move. He also wants to give me a friendship ring, which is tempting when he describes the various colored jewels, but I tell him it's also too early to accept such a token. I trust this man is marriage material, but he lacks the *wow* factor. *Am I being childish looking for a knight in gleaming armor?*

CHAPTER 40
THE HANDSOME GUY

*You'll never find the right person if you
never let go of the wrong one.*

—Unknown

The phone rings after dinner. I pick up. "Hello?"

"Hi," a man's voice says. "Is this Alice?"

"Yes," I say cautiously. "Who's this?"

"I'm Mike. I just got your last two notes and was wondering if you could go to the 49ers game with me tomorrow noon at Candlestick Park."

"Oh, Mike. Glad to hear from you," I answer, thinking, *How rude of you to call me less than twenty-four hours before a requested date. What an insult!* But he is a handsome dude, and six months ago I missed a chance to meet him. If Dave does move up here and takes up all my weekends, I may never get a third opportunity, so, after a long pause, I say, "Okay. I hope they have hotdogs with sauerkraut like at the Oakland Coliseum."

"Yes, they do. I'll buy you one."

Perhaps I need to discover this handsome guy is a jerk so I can get him out of my system. I wonder if he's that phantom who lurks in the back of my head and prevents me from falling in love with my boyfriend who can't make my heart flutter. It's not fair that the mere picture of this rake has that much power over me. Hopefully his conceitedness will turn me off, or maybe he'll dislike me, or maybe his photo is from long ago, and now he looks fat and dumpy.

I wonder if he'll be disgruntled when he notices that I can't get excited about football. I won't be bored, per se; I love it when the fans yell and go berserk, and I guess the 49ers are a good team. I just can't seem to make myself care if they win or lose. Being such a klutz myself, I've always hated competitive sports; I just like being physically active. Why do people care so much who wins? It's just a game.

Mike is supposed to pick me up in twenty minutes. As I drive home from my swim at the gym, I suffer mixed feelings. I hope this gorgeous hunk finds me attractive, but I also hope he's not as good-looking as his photo image suggests.

I pull up to my house—and he's here already. *Shit!* He looks even sexier than he did in his picture. I give him a little wave as I drive into my garage.

When we're finally up close, I notice the chest hair peeking out of Mike's shirt. *There must be plenty more of that lower down.* I feel ashamed of my horny self as my stomach fills with butterflies. Now I think it would be unbearable if he doesn't like my looks or personality.

He's got a cute little red sports car, just like my old high school flame Rick had. After five minutes on the road I ask him if he chose me for my looks or for what I wrote about myself.

"For your looks," he says. "I have a theory: I know beauty is only skin deep, but ugly goes to the bone."

I laugh. This guy is a cut-up. "Do you prefer to be called Mike or Michael?" I ask.

"All my friends call me Mike, but my wife called me Michael." Instantly, I decide to call him Michael. His video showed his deep sadness about his wife's death, and who knows, I might want to marry him someday. He might as well get used to thinking of me as a future wife.

The game is sort of fun, and the hot dogs are delicious. The excited, cheering fans are a hoot. Now we leave the stadium, and I'm in heaven, because to keep us from being separated in the packed crowd, Michael keeps his hand on the small of my back. Electric shocks run up and down my body. I feel let down when he removes his hand.

Back in the car, I wonder where he plans to take me for dinner—till I realize he's driving me home. The vibes I get are that he's indeed attracted to me. *Is he too cheap to spring for dinner, or is he just ignorant that a football date should end with a dinner out?* I'll give him the benefit of the doubt and hope he's ignorant. After all, he can't be well versed about the adult dating game—his high-school-sweetheart wife died just nine months ago. And I remember that in high school, dinner wasn't exactly protocol following an afternoon date.

When we reach my door, I say, "Would you like to come in for some leftover spaghetti or a TV meal?"

"Spaghetti would be nice," Michael says instantly.

I'm sure glad my spaghetti tastes its best after a day or two. Unfortunately, I didn't heat it enough. Without breaking the flow of our conversation, Michael gets up and puts his plate in the microwave.

Once I became a mother, I learned to tolerate underheated food, but I don't think most men ever learn that. Past boyfriends have either asked me to warm up my offerings or have made strong hints such as "My wife always served her food *piping hot.*" I'm impressed that Michael didn't make a big deal of my deficiency; it's a sign he's good potential husband material.

Michael seems to have liked my spaghetti, and me, too. But damn it, he doesn't ask me out on a second date before he leaves, and neither does he try to kiss me or even hold my hand. I hope it's just that he's the consummate gentleman.

Two days pass without a call from Michael. San Diego Dave is still trying to relocate to Dublin, and I still tell him not to make such a big move. I'm glad I haven't told him about my ski club's upcoming semiformal Snow Flake Ball at the Emeryville Hilton. Now I can invite Michael. I hope he likes dancing. I phone Michael. He's not home, and his son answers. I pray the young man remembers to give Michael the message. If he doesn't call me back, I won't know if he's uninterested or if his kid just didn't tell me I called.

Michael does call, though, and now we have a date in ten days. Dave will be up this weekend. I wonder what Michael will be doing. Even though I can't go out with him, I wish he had asked me.

I'm glad the weekend is over and Dave has gone home. The whole time I couldn't get Michael out of my mind. Vis-à-vis the damn friendship ring and Dave's wish to move to Dublin, I kept saying, "It's too early to get that serious. What's the hurry?"

"To catch you before somebody else does," he always answered.

Now I can hardly wait for next weekend. I feel like I'm going to have a fantasy senior prom date. Even though the dress is sort of old-fashioned—spaghetti straps with a big taffeta skirt, the bold purple and teal colors are modern. When I bought it, I didn't even know about this upcoming ball. I simply fell in love with the party frock—and dreamily imagined wearing it for someone special.

Tonight, Michael is in the same three-piece suit he wore in his picture. God, he's gorgeous!

He finally holds my hand, and we dance well together. One of my ski-club friends asks loudly, "You gettin' any these days, Alice?"

"Wouldn't you like to know," I answer quietly as I steer Michael away from him. *No introductions for* that *joker!*

I'm so glad Michael doesn't drink. On our first date he told me he was a recovering alcoholic. Tonight, we both go through gallons of water to replenish our sweating bodies. Our only fast-dance breaks are for the bathroom. This guy is full of energy—and can he ever dance! Even though I want to be close to him, during the slow numbers I prefer to sit and talk rather than mix our sweat.

Michael remains a gentleman all night; he doesn't even try to kiss me on the cheek, let alone on the lips. As we drive home, I decide that before I walk in my door I'll just give him a perfunctory kiss and hug, like he saw me do with a few of my platonic male friends.

He walks me to my door and... *Oh! My! God!* He's not letting go. This is a schoolgirl's fantasy kiss, except that this time I have no confusion about that hard thing, and he doesn't even try to hide it. It's only when we hear loud steps approach—reminding me of my mother decades ago—that our passion quells. We break our embrace and say goodnight.

I open the door to Julie and wave Michael goodbye.

Michael takes me to his favorite Italian restaurant. I learn that he's proud of his childhood poverty. His parents were hardworking: his father, a lumberjack, and his mother, an in-home beautician and the cleaning lady for the small town's theater and motel. Michael and his brother grew up being kidded about their toes peeking out of their well-worn sneakers. What takes the cake is his story of how the entire family shared the same galvanized steel tub—the brothers bathed in their parents' leftover water.

I learn that Michael and his wife married when she was eighteen and he twenty. To simultaneously afford marriage and college he joined the air force. He hoped to become a pilot, but his poor eyesight disqualified him, and instead he was sent to foreign language school to learn Russian for a code-breaking job in Turkey. He loved the work, and both he and his wife loved their luxurious lifestyle there; American money went far at that time. After the Turkey stint, he was sent to college to learn accounting and ended up with a master's degree in business and later a CPA certificate. Since he never saw combat, he likes to say that he "flew a desk." He developed budgets for bases and did audits. After retirement, his education and experience led him to audit for Lockheed, where he now works.

I compare Michael's marital qualifications to Dave's. Both are retired military, but Dave is better off. Michael retired as a major, Dave as a lieutenant colonel. Michael owns his home; Dave owns several rental homes. Michael is now considering accepting a job in England; if he does, it'll probably end our relationship, as I couldn't run Vulcan from there. Dave, on the other hand, is self-employed and can work anywhere by flying charter planes. The biggest difference between these two is that I'm obsessed with Michael, who has blinded me to other men, including Dave. My daughter Jeanette advises, "Date the handsome guy till you get sick of him, then marry the other guy."

I realize I need to get Michael out of my mind. He's so damn handsome that I'll probably eventually determine that he's a jerk.

We're back at my house now, and we sit on the couch and make out. Michael wants to make love to me, and I to him, but I hold out because weeks ago I bought a ticket to San Diego to combine business with a visit to Dave's. Long ago I learned that dual sexual relationships make me crazy and depressed. If I made love with Michael, I wouldn't be able to let Dave touch me. I could just cancel my plans, but I need to collect a sizeable Vulcan overdue receivable down there. Also, it's time to visit some of my more pleasant San Diego customers. Michael will have to wait.

Being in bed with Dave last weekend was grueling. He kept on asking me what I was thinking. He said he wished he could climb into my mind. I knew that if he could, he'd be heartbroken. I was a coward not to break up with Dave in person. Because I didn't, I now have to phone him. Even if Michael turns out to be a passing fancy, he's the only man who interests me.

Michael drove to Nebraska to have Thanksgiving weekend there with his middle son and daughter-in-law and their newborn baby. He gifted the car he drove there to the young family. Now I'm to pick him up at the Oakland Airport—something I've looked forward to for days.

Wordlessly, we enjoy a long ardent kiss at the terminal. Michael takes up my offer of Thanksgiving leftovers for lunch, and we relish every bite. Without cleaning up, I climb the stairs to my bedroom, Michael behind me. I've never hungered more for a man than I do right now. Before reaching the top of the stairs I lower my jeans, exposing my bare bottom. Then I duck into the bathroom for a minute. Upon opening the bedroom door, I see Michael naked, smiling and as ready as can be.

Alas, in five minutes we're done. *Couldn't he have lasted longer?* I'm still attracted, but this speediness is a letdown. Michael and I talk, kiss, and cuddle—and then slowly enjoy each other. This time, he brings me to ecstasy before he's satisfied a second time.

Nirvana!

I wake up this morning knowing I want to marry Michael. We've dated for just over five weeks, so I'll give him one year from today to propose. If he doesn't, I'll move on.

Michael comes over tonight for a Vulcan office party with my five ladies, each of whom has brought her husband or boyfriend. Michael comes early and bears a dozen long-stemmed red roses. I've made the garbage disposal unusable by overloading, and he wins even more potential husband points by repairing it. The party goes smoothly, and Michael remains after the guests have left. He proposes, and I accept. Because he doesn't know my taste, he wants me to pick out my engagement ring.

Michael suggests I pick out any one-carat diamond ring I want. I choose a pear shape with six marquises over the round part and eight rounds up and down the point, with a ninth below the point. When Michael hears the price, he whispers to me to get a larger center diamond—perhaps two carats. Bursting with excitement and gratitude, I do that.

We decide to get married nine months after our first date, and choose a charming chapel at the San Francisco Presidio.

All those 200 smiling people have come here for us! As I walk slowly down the aisle I look into eyes focused on me and smile back at friends on the right and left. My cream-colored mermaid dress flatters me as if it were custom made.

I have a happy, fluttery feeling as I approach the handsomest groom in the world, who beams at me in his air force dress blues. Up front with Michael are my little niece and Michael's little stepgranddaughter, who have strewn the aisle with rose petals, and look adorable in their lavender-pink, floor-length dresses. My two beautiful daughters and three of my smiling girlfriends, all clad in the same shade of tulle as the little ones, stand behind them. On the other side of my future husband are six good-looking, black-tuxedoed males: Michael's best man, his brother, who's even taller than Michael; my three future stepsons; my brother; and my serious-looking nine-year-old nephew, who holds the rings on a pillow.

The wedding march stops and my heart flutters as I gaze up at my tall, dark, and sexy husband-to-be. Songbird Bev and Jeanette's boyfriend, Dan,[28] sing a duet of *Bridge Over Troubled Waters,* accompanied by Dan on his guitar.

We speak our individually composed vows. After Jeanette and Julie agree to give me away, Michael and I promise to love, honor, and cherish each other till death do us part.

We are man and wife! After we exit the chapel under the swords of Michael's military friends, we separate and hug and shake hands with so many of our well-wishers that we feel like we're campaigning politicians. I'm mobbed and can't get to my unassertive parents till after we're coaxed back into the chapel for a round of group photos.

Having completed the photo shoot, we enter the officers' club reception room to the music of *Going to the Chapel* while the DJ announces each member of the wedding party. Michael and I enter directly behind the three children, who walk in holding hands, my nephew in the middle, towering over the two little girls.

Michael and I begin the dancing to Anne Murray's *Could I Have this Dance for the Rest of My Life?* The only couple on the floor, we reel all over the ballroom as we joyously sing the words and gaze into each other's eyes. On cue, Daddy cuts in and I dance with him for the first time since I was fourteen, when he was my date for a Job's Daughters' dance. Mommy has made it clear that she does not want to dance in front of so many people, so Michael dances with his stepmother instead. Also on cue, my brother, new brother-in-law, and stepsons cut in as Michael dances with other women in the wedding party. I dance with one girl, my niece, her petite body up in my arms; as we whirl, her dress and hair fly around us.

Then the riotous fun begins: The DJ plays our favorite '50s fast-dance songs, and I begin with my nephew, who surprises me with his enthusiasm. He moves like a party animal, and cuts loose in uninhibited synch with the beat.

Finally, Michael and I get to dance together again, and we put all our happy energy into every selection till the DJ decides it's time for speeches and the garter ritual. Someone brings a chair; I loll in it, and lasciviously hike my dress over a foot above my knee to show off my lacy blue-ribboned garter. Michael is on bended knee, as if he's about to propose. That languorous tune *The Stripper* begins to play, and Michael, who no longer looks like a formal gentleman, bites the garter and slowly moves it down a couple inches. He stops and looks at the audience as they howl, after which he resumes biting the garter. Michael eats up the attention; he lowers my garter, then waits for more hoots and catcalls before he returns to his task, using only his mouth, never his hands, till he stands up with the frilly thing firmly clenched in his teeth, like a doggy with a prized bone.

Finally, he takes the garter in hand for the toss. He winds up as if he's about to pitch a baseball—but doesn't release the iconic bachelor-catcher. After doing this several times he finally throws it, and my ex-boyfriend Al catches it.

I'm not as skilled in throwing my bouquet. The first time I hit a rafter. One of Julie's single friends catches my do-over. She's younger than either of Al's daughters, but even so, the winners are paired to lead the bunny hop. A hundred-plus people chain themselves behind the May-December couple, and the fast '50s music resumes.

Later, Michael and I agree that we've never had so much fun at a party!

PART III: TREACHEROUS WATERS

1992—1997

CHAPTER 41
CAPSIZED

The successful warrior is the average man, with laser-like focus.
—Bruce Lee, martial arts professional, film actor

I t's 1992 and Vulcan has been blessed for seventeen years with a handful of insignificant downs and some very steep ups. In the meantime, the girls have finished college and become self-supporting, and I've settled down with my wonderful husband, Michael, on our ranchette in Livermore, just fifteen minutes from my office.

I'm in the middle of congratulating myself on the tranquil life I've built as I note my home fax machine spit out papers. I've taken it easy today—trimmed my eighteen old-fashioned floribunda rose bushes, enjoyed their perfumed scents, basked under the bright sun and clear blue sky, and listened to the occasional bird as the bees droned around me. Now I'm finishing up photo albums from our recent excursion to Denver, where many of Daddy's relatives live.

I'm so fortunate to have struck it rich in love and money. Michael and I, now married three years, are still incredulous that we have each other and share such a fabulous life wherever we are—but especially on our remodeled-to-perfection, five-acre country ranchette. I originally fell in love with its long driveway, lined with pepper trees and gigantic eucalyptuses, which bridges a meandering creek and winds past a barn. When we first saw it, weeds bordered both sides, but I could already envision roses. Next to the grounds of trees and verdant rolling hills, and the glimmering turquoise kidney-shaped pool with its attached hot tub, the residence itself was ugly—an invitation to remodel it to my taste.

Michael and I both have great incomes, so we don't worry about money. My guy surprises me with jewels, and I surprise him with travel plans. We had a fantasy honeymoon in Tahiti, and we've also luxuriated on cruises across the Caribbean and along Mexico, marveled at European castles and museums, and adventured up and down California and to nearby states with stays at cozy B&Bs.

Now to see what news that incredible invention, the fax machine, has brought me.

"*Oh, no!*" I exclaim to the house and the hills beyond. It's a letter from an unfamiliar person at Safeway giving Vulcan sixty-days' notice that they're ending our bale-tie business. There goes 20 percent of Vulcan's gross profit—that's more than twice what Vulcan nets. I thought we would always have Safeway. Throughout our nine-year history, they've never once been displeased with us. The letter acknowledges our excellent service, and then explains that, based on Safeway's high volume, they should deal manufacturer-direct.

Over the years, well-meaning businesspeople have advised me to become a manufacturer, but I haven't because I didn't want to complicate my life. I know nothing about machines, and I dread the idea of hiring and supervising blue-collar workers.

A couple of years ago, my now recently retired Safeway contact, Harry, informed me that a manufacturer was seeking Safeway's business. When I asked the manufacturer's name, Harry, after much hesitation, broke down and told me about World. I remembered being told by a reliable source that the president of World was a convicted felon who had to wear a tracking ankle bracelet. I promised to find out if I could verify the accusation. By way of a helpful librarian's fax, I presented the damning evidence a week later. It looks now like that dear librarian added two carefree years with Safeway to my life.

I also shared with Harry my nine-year-old memory of an encounter with a thug who represented World—the then future spin-off of Wire-Up, one of our major wire suppliers after E. H. Edwards closed. Offering a fire-sale price, the thug tried to intimidate me into selling my business to them, "Or else we'll run you out of town." Before day's end

I faxed an angry letter to Wire-Up in which I threatened to discontinue business with them. Their response was profusely apologetic.

I haven't heard from the thug since, and had almost forgotten about the confrontation. Now it looks like World will run me out of town after all, because with Vulcan's diminished income, our upscale Pleasanton office will no longer be affordable. If their new vendor is World, even if I prove the felony conviction to this Safeway person, I presume he'd still search for another manufacturer rather than stick with Vulcan. It's time for me to face reality and decide how to survive.

If I don't decrease Vulcan's expenses immediately, we'll plunge into bankruptcy. Our biggest expenses are payroll, office space, and warehousing—in that order. I'll have to economize on all three. I'll have to be Scrooge and dole out wage cuts, too, with my salary suffering the deepest cut. Thanks to Michael's higher income, I can afford to lower my salary, but my guy and I will need to put a halt to our extravagant lifestyle—the overseas travel, cruises, five-star dining, and glamorous clothing purchases. The only unpainful cutback will be to the occasional investments we make.

Last month I was so confident of Vulcan's strength that I announced a forthcoming employee stock-ownership plan to my three most stalwart employees. If I'd known how to go about issuing stock, it would've been a done deal by now, but with this bad news, I'm afraid it's a dead issue. My vision of magnanimously awarding valuable stock shares has morphed into bloodletting.

I feel bludgeoned. I need to lie down and think. I guess it was stupid of me to assume Safeway would be Vulcan's eternal customer. If I had thought of Safeway as temporary, I might not have paid everyone so much. Ever since I incorporated, I've given deserving employees annual raises that far exceeded inflation. Tomorrow I'll have to drive to my classy but now-unaffordable office to announce the cuts.

It'll probably be a small comfort to my employees that they're all now paid enough above market that even with a 10 percent wage decrease they'll still be well paid. Otherwise, they might leave me stranded. I don't think I could handle the stress of inept new personnel.

Other than Bev, Annie is the only one to whom I'll hate to break this salary-cut news. I'm glad I don't have any emotional investment in Annie's other two subordinates, but assuming Annie remains with Vulcan, for her sake more than mine, I hope none of her three assistants quit. She's the one who'd have to do most of the replacements' training.

Theresa, paid straight commission, is the only one of us who won't be affected by the loss of the Safeway account. I'm happy for her, and doubly glad she chose to advance from one of Vulcan's hourly clerks to our only full-time outside salesperson. Not long ago she informed me that a customer presented her a supposedly foolproof opportunity to collude against Vulcan. True-blue, Theresa told the scoundrel, "I don't do business that way." I'm thankful that at least *her* wages will remain healthy. Midmorning, I walk out to the main area of the office and draw a deep breath. *How I dread this!*

"Ladies, may I please have your attention. As you probably know by now, we'll be losing Safeway in sixty days. This will result in diminished sales and profits—so much that if Vulcan's expenses aren't cut we'll go bankrupt." I look around the room, my face sober.

"I'm so very sorry, but we must all absorb the pain. Beginning December 1 our wages must shrink—mine by 17 percent and everyone else's by 10 percent. Less painful—we'll have to move to a more affordable office. I'm considering relocation to an industrial area and combining warehouse space with office space. Today I'll begin research on that."

I sigh. "Again, I'm so very sorry about our wage cuts—especially just before Christmas. I wish I could afford to postpone this. Please believe me, I hate to break this news."

Stone-faced, all five employees stare at me. Feeling punched in the gut, I give them a weak smile, shrug, and retreat into my office.

CHAPTER 42
MARITAL PROBLEMS

I promise to be true to you in good times and in bad,
in sickness and in health. I will love you and
honor you all the days of my life.
—Michael and Alice's vows

At a New Year's Eve party the damn hostess cajoled Michael to have *just one* celebratory glass of champagne. For several months after that, he drank only moderately, but now he drinks and behaves like an alcoholic. Among my original attractions to Michael were his abstention, easygoing ways, and gentlemanly speech, but he's lost those charms. When alone with me, he repeatedly spouts the big "F." More than once, after hearing a click and dial tone when he's answered the phone, he's accused me of having an extramarital affair. And now…

"I've been laid off," Michael says as he walks in the door. He forgoes his usual kiss.

Stunned and frightened, I ask, "What happened to the job transfer you were counting on?"

"At the last minute another contender, who's friends with a vice president, got the job. He had more influence than my director friend." Michael takes a deep breath. "My potential future boss tried to fight the switch, but was overruled."

Michael has bragged to me more than once that ever since age twenty, he's always been employed. Now that he's fifty-one, I know he's not as desirable to employers as most of the 3,500 other, considerably younger, people Lockheed had terminated. He sits silently at the kitchen table with the same forlorn expression as Norman Rockwell's baseball-uniformed boy, alone on the bench.

I want to be brave in front of Michael, so I'm outwardly calm and silently ponder our dismal financial situation. Ever since the Safeway loss, World, with its predatory pricing, has gained more ground—and is gradually destroying Vulcan. I've been busier than ever responding to the efforts of World's eager salesmen, who are paid on gross sales, rather than gross profits, as I pay Theresa. Some customers have remained loyal, as long as we've lowered our prices to near World's proffered prices. Others have said *sayonara.* Theresa's commissions and Vulcan's profits have shrunk exponentially.

Despite Michael's Hawaii CPA license and extensive auditing background, months went by without him finding a job in his field. He finally decided to work on straight commission with a company called Business Team (BT), a Walnut Creek-based broker for buying and selling businesses. After hiring on and completing a crash course for the required real estate license, he began work, but it's been ten weeks now, and though he's acquired several listings, he's made no sales—which means no income.

I'm the major breadwinner now, yet for this last half year I haven't allowed myself any clothing purchases other than stockings and pantyhose, and for the first time in twenty-five years, I can't afford a weekly cleaning lady. As much as I love our luxurious country ranchette, I almost regret the purchase with its sizeable mortgage payments. I also resent that while I'm being so frugal, Michael is continuing to waste money on alcohol. I ask him to cut back on this extravagance, and he appears to.

Thanks to a job fair that Lockheed held, Michael now works as a comptroller at a small defense contractor—and makes even more money than he did at Lockheed. I'm happy to resume our luxurious lifestyle.

At home I notice him drinking only a daily beer or two, yet he continues to frequently exhibit unseemly behavior, and he drinks way too much at social events.

We attend a wedding for a friend of the girls today, and as usual Michael drinks too much. At least he shows only his fun side. We walk to the parking lot, and Jeanette accompanies us. As we arrive at our car, she says, "Mommy, you're driving, aren't you?"

"No, I'm driving," Michael says as he pulls out his keys.

"Michael, you've had too much to drink," she says, a worried look on her face. "You need to give Mommy those keys."

"Yes, honey, you need to give me the keys," I confirm.

Michael scowls. "I always drive, and I'm driving now."

"Please, honey, give me the keys," I plead.

"Come on, Michael," Jeannette chimes in. "Give Mommy the keys."

"No!" He sways a little.

Jeannette puts a hand on her hip. "Michael, you're in no shape to drive. Give Mommy the keys."

I keep my tone gentle but firm. "Honey, Jeanette is right. You have to let me drive this time. Come on. Give me the keys."

"Here!" Michael flings them at me.

"Thank you, honey." I step closer to him. "Now let me give you a kiss."

Michael gives me only a sullen look, then turns away.

"Thanks, Michael," Jeanette says as she kisses him.

Without a word, he gets into the passenger seat.

By the time we exit the parking lot, he passes out, his head slumped onto his chest.

The girls arrange for the three of us to meet in San Francisco for a Dutch-treat lunch. I look forward to a relaxed time with them, but I discover they have a weighty agenda. They think Michael has a serious problem, and they want me to do something about it.

"Mommy, if he doesn't stop and go to AA, we'll have to do an intervention," says Jeanette. "You know that he always spikes his iced tea with vodka he hides somewhere in the barn, don't you?"

My eyes widen. "He what?"

"Come on, Mommy," Julie says. "You've got to know that!"

"No. It never entered my mind."

"We always thought you were enabling him," Jeanette says, sounding surprised.

"Never!" I respond as I wonder if he does indeed stash vodka in the barn.

Over the next couple days I observe Michael for evidence of spiking his iced tea in the barn, and I suspect the girls are right. How could I have been so blind? Probably because I'd been focused night and day on Vulcan and other potential business ventures. I should've realized Michael wouldn't act so nutty with only his usual beer and occasional wine, but I never connected the dots. I look in every nook and cranny of the barn today, so it must be in one of the old lockers the former owner's son probably stole from his high school. There's no booze in eleven of them, but a twelfth one is padlocked. I walk back to the house for a flashlight to help me see through its cracks. *Bingo!* I see bottles piled in there.

I form a plan, and... *amazing!* Without an alarm, I awaken at exactly 3:00 AM, just like I told myself to do. I grab my flashlight, slink out of bed, and put on a warm robe. I'm thankful for our wall-to-wall carpet, but fear making a noise when I pick up Michael's keys. *Not a sound!* I'm proud of myself.

I tiptoe through the house, then out the door where I put on my shoes and head down our long dirt driveway to the barn. I find the key that works and open the locker. There are half a dozen empties, one half-empty bottle, and two unopened bottles—all vodka. I leave the empties, pull out the other three, dump the half bottle's contents onto the ground, and place it back with the empties. I close the locker and relock it. For my daughters I hide the sealed vodka in the wheel well of my car—one bottle for each. Then I return to my still-sleeping husband, quietly replace his keys on the dresser, and go back to bed.

When Michael finishes breakfast and heads toward the door, I check the bedroom and notice his keys aren't there. I catch up with him when he's halfway to the barn.

"I know what you're up to, Michael, and you won't find your stash," I say, laying a hand on his arm. "Last night I emptied all the bottles." (A little white lie). "You're drinking too much, and you have to stop. I expect you to go to AA at least a couple of times a week."

He stops short and looks down. "I'll stop drinking, but I don't want to go to AA."

"Michael, you have to. Otherwise you'll probably fall off the wagon again."

"No, I won't," he says obstinately. "I'll never drink again."

"Michael, you *must* go to AA."

He looks me in the eye. "I promise I'll never drink again, but I *don't want to go to AA.*"

"Well, then… will you sign an agreement that if you ever drink again, you *will* go to AA?"

"Yes," he nods.

"Then I'll get it written right now."

We head back into the house, and I compose the promise on a paper. Michael signs and dates it.

When I tell my daughters what's transpired, Jeanette says, "That won't work. We'll need to have an intervention."

I get them to hold off and give Michael a chance. I also buy a breathalyzer.

It's been over a year that Michael's been dry. He no longer spouts profanities or yells while jumping around like a frog. He says quitting cigarettes twenty years ago was harder than abstaining from alcohol, and he never went to a Smokers Anonymous meeting.

He seems to have just as much fun at parties these days. After his lush period, he's remained my energetic, uninhibited, crazy dance partner. Michael and I are such enthusiastic dancers that by midway through the evening we're always soaked with perspiration. Our modus operandi at parties is to fill our wineglasses with water and—so no one takes them away—hide them under the table when we take to the floor. When we occasionally forget to hide our glasses, we're relieved when we find them untouched.

At this evening's affair we're happy to see the table undisturbed and take quick swigs. Michael suddenly puts his glass down with a worried look on his face. "Honey, I want you to know if you smell alcohol on my breath, it was accidental. I thought I was drinking my water, but it was someone else's white wine—and I spit it right back into the glass."

I believe him.

CHAPTER 43
MOMMY'S LIFE (1919–1995)

*The coddled child will learn to depend on others
to rescue him from life's calamities, instead of having
the will and know-how to rescue himself.*
—Myrna Beth Haskell, author, columnist, speaker;
and Alison Hogan, leadership-development coach

Mommy needs surgery to eliminate or untangle some abnormal clusters in her brain. She trusts the "wise" doctor's craniotomy will solve her memory problems. He doesn't think it's Alzheimer's. Mommy often can't remember how to write her name, so she practices for hours till she accomplishes it. Daddy said she was so excited about this operation that she easily signed all the legal forms this morning. Paralysis could be a side effect, but Mommy wants her memory back more than she wants to keep her body under control.

Though Mommy is aware of her memory problems, she's unaware of how strange she is now. In the last couple years she's been swearing like a stevedore, whereas most of her life her speech was ladylike. With me she's overly graphic about sex. She's even initiated sexual discussions with Robby. In the past five years she's been bitter with me because I don't want to confront Daddy about, as Mommy put it, his "trying to make me think I'm going crazy when he hides things."

At my house ten years ago Mommy became infuriated with Daddy for refusing to get up from the couch and look at the clock behind him—neither parent could read their watches without glasses, which they weren't wearing. Even after I told her the time, she continued to nag Daddy. The next day she was angry that he refused another request, this time to get up and find her favorite pen, which she'd misplaced. When I offered her one of mine, she insisted she needed her own.

Fifteen years ago, my parents left my home early as always, but one morning, Mommy couldn't find her bar of Ivory soap. Jeanette often tidied the bathroom, so Mommy suspected she had put it away somewhere. I begged her not to disturb my sleeping teenager and said I'd reimburse her for the missing soap, but Mommy insisted on awakening Jeanette.

"I'm not leaving without my soap!" Mommy said.

Jeanette couldn't find it, and Daddy later told me that on arriving home Mommy found it in her suitcase.

Thirty-five years ago, my girlfriend Patty said she and her mother thought Mommy had no common sense. She's certainly always displayed illogical behavior. When I was in high school, however, she made intelligent corrections to my essays. Nonetheless, Robby and I can't think of a time when she seemed *totally* normal.

As a three-year-old I thought of Mommy as Daddy's big brat. I planned to grow up and marry Daddy so he could have a good wife. As I got older I realized that my mother has always been a peculiar person. In all fairness, she had an unusual childhood: An only child, she was both spoiled and overly controlled. When she tried to stand up in her crib at a slightly earlier age than "normal," her parents, who thought her muscles and bones needed more time to mature, would push her down.

Daddy also told me that after he and Mommy got married—half a year before Mommy graduated from Tulsa University—the two of them lived with her parents, where they shared Mommy's bedroom and enjoyed Grandma's home-cooked dinners. While Grandma cooked and cleaned, Mommy was left alone to study. This arrangement was fine with Daddy, but when he witnessed Grandpa cutting Mommy's meat, he was appalled and demanded that she cut her own. I suspect my grandparents' coddling led to many of Mommy's problems in adulthood.

It's been three hours since the operation should have ended, so I decide to give Mommy a call.

"Help! Help me! Help me!" she screams into her hospital phone.

"Mommy, what's wrong?" I ask, panicked. I'm nearly 400 miles away; there's not much I can do.

"Help me! Help me!" she shrieks even louder.

"Mommy, please tell me what's wrong," I beg.

"Help me! Help me!" she repeats again. This time she follows up with her home phone number, and then begins again: "Help me!"

"I'll see what I can do, Mommy," I say before I hang up. Now I'm the one screaming—"No! No! No!" I'm so afraid for her. I call my girls. Julie breaks away from work to drive over and comfort me. Before she gets here, I speak with the doctor. He tells me that in a day or so Mommy should calm down.

It's twenty-four hours later, and I spend forty-five minutes going through an extensive phone tree. In her even-tempered voice Mommy says, "I'm eating now." *Click.* My feelings are hurt, but no matter. At least she doesn't sound troubled.

I've flown down to Southern California multiple times in the past few months—partly for business, but primarily for family reasons. Mommy is now plainly mentally ill; without supervision, she's a danger to herself and others. We don't know if she'll ever return to the semi-safe state she was in before her surgery, so Daddy and I investigate nursing homes and settle on one close to his condo. Unfortunately, Mommy's behavior at the rest home becomes more extreme and obnoxious than ever. During many nights, in the wee hours, she turns on lights and barges into various bedrooms, insisting the inhabitants stole something of hers. Once she even had a tug-of-war with an orderly over a pair of scissors.

Management tells us to find another place—but then Mommy breaks her hip. Now that she's unable to walk around and bother people, management no longer expects us to relocate her. They figure the attendants are stronger than she is now.

Mommy's not doing well. I think she'll be permanently bedridden. She's no longer lucid enough to know she's lost most of her smarts, she no longer feeds herself, and she likes to be read to sleep—she sleeps a lot these days.

Meanwhile, Daddy isn't getting many home-cooked meals. Friends his age don't do much cooking. He volunteers at a senior-center computer class, and some people there—most of whom are decades younger than he—are so grateful for his guidance that they want to pay him. Daddy always responds, "I don't want money, but I sure would love dinner in your home."

On this trip, I've decided to make Daddy some comfort food. I buy salad fixings, pork chops, a big green apple, raisins, and potatoes. The salad is made; the potatoes are mashed; the apple is sliced; the skillet is heated and coated with pats of yesterday's bacon grease.

I place two pork chops in and they sizzle loudly.

"Alice, don't burn the house down," Daddy yells as he runs from the living room to the kitchen. He reaches for the skillet.

"Daddy, let me be," I implore, my left hand on the long wooden handle and my right against his chest.

"I don't want a fire," he yells, trying to overpower me. We discover the near-equal strength of his eighty-year-old body and my fifty-three-year-old one. "Get that skillet off the burner," he demands hysterically.

"Daddy, leave me alone. I know what I'm doing," I insist, and grip the handle with both hands. "I want to turn the meat now. Please, Daddy, just go away. I promise everything will be fine. I only want to make a delicious meal."

He won't leave. He reminds me of a frightened dog fearing a shot from the vet and refusing to walk into the office. "Won't you at least turn the heat down, please?"

"No, Daddy. I need to get these pork chops *browned.*"

"We don't need them browned. Your mother never insisted on such foolishness. What has gotten into you?"

Luckily, they're seared enough now. I show him the chops. "Look, Daddy, see how nice and brown they are? Now I can lower the heat and throw in the apple and raisins."

We relax and enjoy our dinner. Daddy reluctantly acknowledges that the pork chops aren't burnt, and we have no hint of fire damage. I've come a long way since my early cooking years with Fritz.

The first time I cooked pork chops for Fritz I thought they were great, but Fritz said they should have been browned. Six years earlier, when Mommy was hospitalized for a hysterectomy, I'd cooked them just like she always did. I was sure they were good because Robby—who'd have loved an opportunity to criticize me—hadn't complained.

Oh, well, I thought, *Fritz has some funny ideas about things.*

I bought a pack of blue, yellow, red, and green liquid food color, and planned to mix the red and green to make brown so I'd be able to give Fritz his silly brown pork chops.

But when I was done… oh, dear. Even though it was cooked enough, the meat looked too red. Worried that Fritz would think it was under-cooked, I added a drop of yellow to tone it down. *Yikes!* Now it was bright orangish. I added more green, hoping that would remedy the is-sue. *Shoot!* Now they were almost chartreuse. I put in some more red. *Damn!* They still didn't look really brown, just a dark greenish-brown.

At least I've gotten closer. Uh-oh, Fritz is home. Guess I'll have to settle for this color.

Standing over me next to the stove Fritz said, "Alice, what did you do to the pork chops? They're baby-shit green!"

"Well, you said last week's pork chops weren't brown enough, so I tried to color them brown for you, but I just couldn't do it right."

I've never heard Fritz laugh so loud. Between heaves, he burst out, "You just cook them… ha, ha, ha… ha, ha, ha… till they… ha, ha, ha… *sizzle!*" he yelled. He staggered to the living room couch and fell onto it. He laughed even harder then, tears rolling down his face. When he finally composed himself, he said, "Look, Alice, tomorrow I'll buy a steak and show you how to brown meat."

Sizzle?

When I return from visiting Daddy, the answering machine light is blinking. I press PLAY and hear Daddy's mournful voice say, "Alice, your mother just died."

The death certificate specified cardiac arrest after nine months of brain cancer. Poor Mommy. She never knew what hit her.

Even though she had periods of lucidity in the last few months, not once did she mention her operation. Mommy belonged to the Hemlock Society, but I'll always wonder if she'd have had the courage to end her life before she regressed beyond a certain point. Who knows what that point would've been, though; we've all read books about people with such plans who are unaware when they've gone beyond logical thinking—and Mommy was never logical to begin with.

CHAPTER 44
DESPERATE FOR RELIEF

Success is not final, failure is not fatal:
it is the courage to continue that counts.
—Winston S. Churchill, Prime Minister of the U.K.,
1940–1945 and 1951–1955

Vulcan now leases an office building with a warehouse. We've come down from our prestigious office amongst streets with expensive cars to the industrial area of Hayward, where the streets teem with huge diesel trucks. I paid $100 to my former warehouse owner to locate and approve a used forklift; I know nothing about machinery. We have more warehouse space than needed, so we rent out room to our former Pleasanton tenant for his inventory. There's a railroad spur directly behind us. Now our out-of-state deliveries will be expedited—and less expensive.

Despite the low overhead for office space and warehousing, as well as our wage decreases, our bottom line is still precarious. I decided to expand our product line with LPS, a cleaning agent, a couple of months back, but after much work, I concluded that LPS was more trouble than it was worth.

Because I'm only spinning my wheels at Vulcan, I decide to try to sell the three listings Michael had secured at BT as well as score some of my own. I interview for the job, which is commission-only, and when the owner and his right-hand man express concern that I wouldn't remain long enough to make the training worthwhile, I promise to remain a minimum of two years.

I assumed BT would provide all the clerical assistance that Vulcan does for Theresa, but am dismayed to learn that each salesperson there is responsible for 100 percent of her or his own needs. I'm also disconcerted that Michael's listees demand higher prices than their businesses are worth. I begin to hate this job even more than my Vulcan treadmill. I don't come in as often as expected; I prefer my home office, where no other employees interrupt me.

Today, after four months with BT, I come into their office and receive the news that I'm fired. I'm not upset, but relieved to be set free; however, one of the other employees, an amiable woman, is indignant for me.

I share my euphoria at no longer having to keep my two-year promise, and explain that I have a comfortable—though diminished—income from Vulcan.

"You're the worst kind of business owner, the kind I hate—someone with a business not in desperate straits," she says. "I prefer a business that's in more trouble than yours, likely due to an ailing or deceased spouse or a fresh divorce. You're not desperate enough to sell your business for what it's worth."

Her speech both depresses and uplifts me: I'm depressed to realize I can't sell Vulcan for as much as I'd have expected in the past and am therefore stuck with its headaches, but I'm grateful that my company is still afloat, with all of us healthy and working like dogs to keep it profitable—if only marginally.

My assertive office manager, Annie, insists that I enroll in a Lotus 1-2-3 workshop. "You'll love it," she says.

Doubtful but interested in an acceptable escape from my tedium, I attend two eight-hour classes. Armed with my new knowledge and thankful for my earlier college semester of Symbolic Logic, I conclude that if I program software for Vulcan's inventory predictions, I can save Annie and myself teaching time, and all of us a good amount of annual calculating hours. Lately I've been appalled at the mathematical ignorance of younger people, who can only perform on a rote memory basis with no understanding of the steps involved. I've also been frustrated with the mathematical errors I often come across, which result in some hoop-jumping headaches at the least, and lost profits at the most.

I struggle to develop a software format that can be satisfactorily used by an employee of below-average IQ and/or substandard mathematical skills. With some guidance from Michael and my father, I spend a couple weeks developing a nearly fail-safe inventory prediction system, and then present it to Annie and Theresa. They're skeptical that I can design something effective that requires only two entries: one for the date and the other for the quantity.

Their negativity deflates me, but when I test my program on a few dozen customer histories of at least five years, lo and behold, my invention results in better accuracy than our human-created calculations. Only partially convinced, Annie and Theresa agree, grudgingly, to employ and teach my new system.

It's been almost a year since we implemented my program at Vulcan, and in that time I've received lots of compliments from Annie, Theresa, and Bev. They're impressed—especially by the red-lettered SEE OFFICE MANAGER pop-up, which appears on the screen when Vulcan receives an extraordinarily early order or when an order is overdue. The early orders usually indicate a business pickup, and a missing order indicates either a slowdown or that we've lost someone to World without the customer admitting it. Either way, those red words mean we must sniff around.

As I bask in the glow of my employees' admiration, I'm dismayed to receive a call from one of my L.A.-based suppliers. He wants to expand his non-Vulcan-competing wire products, and is impressed with Theresa's sales ability. "I'm asking you for her hand, because I won't offer her the sales job without your blessing," he says. "I know you'd miss her, but I can give her an opportunity to make more money than she's likely making at Vulcan, and I know you're hurting from competition with World. You could save Theresa's commissions."

I ask him to give me a day or so.

By now it's not only Safeway that we've lost. World offers predatory pricing all over the place, and it's painful. We either have to lower our prices, which are still above World's quotes, and keep our most loyal customers, or say a sad goodbye to the customers who care more about price than loyalty. Therefore Theresa's commissions, along with Vulcan's profits, are dipping. Taking over the majority of Theresa's work in addition to my own could possibly land me in the hospital or the funny farm, but it's doable—and I couldn't look myself in the mirror if I stood in her way.

In the end, I make a counterproposal: I'll retain Theresa at least 10 percent of the time. She'll sell the other guy's products 90 percent of the time and then devote one business day every two weeks to Vulcan's accounts. I also ask for a couple months to prepare for her absence, as well as a gradual yearlong Vulcan withdrawal. I need time to gain rapport with her customers, most of whom have never met me. My vendor friend and I decide that I'll be the first one to approach Theresa, so she'll know that he isn't being sneaky and I won't be bitter about her leaving.

Theresa accepts.

I realize that for this plan to unfold seamlessly I need to designate sales territories. My direction dyslexia has long been my biggest hurdle in effective selling, especially cold calling. Nonetheless, I read maps well, so I get the biggest California map I can find, and mark the locations of each of our 300 California customers. Then I determine efficient visiting areas and color-code the map into seven sections. I buy eight sets of colored plastic folders, the eighth color designated as "out-of-state."

I decide that the first territory I'll take over will include Livermore, my home turf. Then each succeeding month or two, I'll take on another territory.

My year is almost up now, and I'm as overwhelmed and exhausted as I was in Vulcan's early stages. I yearn for the full-time Theresa, or at least another good salesperson, but I have nothing good to offer to someone new. With this diminished market, it wouldn't be wise to take on a new, high-quality salesperson. A possible light at the end of the long tunnel is that World is struggling to pay their bills, and it's rumored they'll fold soon. Can I hold out till that happens?

An in-the-know business friend gives me weekly updates about World. They're awarding commissions to their salespeople over and above the gross profits, and have consequently gotten further and further behind on their bills, even to their employees. Bankruptcy is on the horizon.

I hope World drops before I do. I'm burned out with my ten- to twelve-hour days, which I sometimes work seven days a week. Worse, for the first time since I incorporated, Vulcan might report an annual net loss this year. Also, Michael's high-paid comptroller job ended when his employer went bankrupt, so now he works for less money as an auditor at Kaiser Permanente's Oakland headquarters. I realize that as much as I miss Theresa, it's best for Vulcan, and for my personal finances, that I've taken on most of her former accounts.

I've begun to hate my life, but feel guilty when I admit this to myself, because on the surface I have it made: a wonderful husband, successful daughters, and my magnificent country home. But I don't have enough time to enjoy these blessings.

Since I was canned from BT, I've toyed with the idea of sweat equity; that is, hire a person and give her or him some ownership in Vulcan. It won't be an attractive offer unless or until World folds, but I dream of having a partner or future owner to lighten my load.

My weekly World updates have grown more and more promising, and recently I'm given the name and number of a discontented unpaid salesman. I present my sweat-equity plan to him. He says he'll be in the Bay Area soon, and we agree on a meeting at Vulcan. He stands me up without so much as a courtesy call.

I ask around for the names of other World salespeople—upstanding ones with decent manners—and get a solid recommendation for a man named Mike. I call him today, and we have a lengthy conversation. He still feels loyal to World and insists it's a good company. Despite my contact's saying World should have to liquidate any day, Mike thinks they might be able to have their debts frozen and reorganize. Nonetheless, he's interested to hear what I might offer and accepts my invitation to fly him up here from L.A. I'm excited. He sounds much more impressive than the previous fellow. He has positive energy and a comprehensive understanding of the baler-wire industry. I'm anxious to hear back from him regarding a date for our get-together.

Mike phones back, but it's to graciously decline his interview because he's close to accepting a job at another company. *Damn it!* Then Mike calls again—to tell me World has a temporary inventory problem and has given its salesmen permission to locate and deliver their orders in any way possible. He lists his needs, which Vulcan fortunately has on hand. We agree he'll get commissions under Vulcan's rules. I'm ecstatic over this little business upswing.

Now, three days later, my contact calls to gleefully tell me *the witch is dead*—i.e., World can't regroup and will have to liquidate. I jump up and down joyfully, just like Bev does when she gets an order, and since we have no neighbors within earshot, I yell my lungs out.

"Vulcan will be healthy again!"

After I impart this great news to my employees, I'm too exultant to work. I savor the sunny day as I trim my roses.

Then the phone rings.

PART IV: POSEIDON

1997—2018

CHAPTER 45
AFLOAT

*A very successful business career can turn on
just one great idea, decision, or deal.*
—Michael Lipsey, author, artist

"Hi, Alice. Mike Graffio here. I'm calling to tell you I've reconsidered your job offer and I'd like to accept. I'm the man you need, and I can help build Vulcan up again."

"Mike, that's great. When do you want to start?"

"I'm ready right now."

"Super. I'll write up an agreement and fax it."

"First, though, I need to have some things understood."

Goddamn! The man wants the world from me. He's unaffordable. His demands are merciless: Continue his lease on his top-of-the-line car—far more expensive than the Ford Taurus I have with my future salesperson in mind; health insurance; a guaranteed six-month draw of a whopping $4,000[29] per month, and on top of all that, he wants me to lend him—interest-free—the 7,000 bucks World stiffed him for.

Because Mike insists he can't live on less than $4,000 per month, I think it's only common sense that he not have to begin to repay me till his commissions exceed that minimum. The loan won't be a big deal initially because I have a bigger line of credit than I need, but that loan plus the guaranteed $24,000 over six months, a total of $31,000, is a huge gamble… and I'm not a gambler at heart. This will be the biggest risk of my life. Mike will either help us climb out of the hole we've fallen into or speed Vulcan into bankruptcy.

What the hell? I'll take the chance.

I must be crazy to make this enormous commitment, which means that fifteen years from now Mike will be the primary owner of what it's taken me twenty-two years of blood, sweat, and tears to build. Especially since I haven't even met the man! I think we've spent only two hours, if that, talking to each other—mostly about wire and repetitions of "I'm the right man for the job." As if I haven't heard similar lines—many times over—from the various men in my life. Archie, World's plant manager who recommended him, is respected in the industry, and says Mike's a hard worker, a sharp dresser, likeable, and smart. I don't think Archie has any ulterior motives for saying all that—at least I hope he doesn't. On the bright side, Mike will be able to transfer his World customers to Vulcan. *So what am I afraid of?*

It's almost ten o'clock, and Mike Graffio should be walking in the door any minute. Were we crazy to sign faxes pledging our business marriage? Now I hope we like each other in the flesh.

In he walks.

"Mike, so glad to meet you," I say, shocked that in my two-inch heels I'm almost his height. I'd assumed he would look like the stereotypical Wire-Up and World man. Over the years I've met over half a dozen of them, all well over six feet tall. This guy couldn't be a fraction over five foot ten. His hair is slicked back and displays a high forehead. I'm happy to see that he's as clean-cut as a man can be. Other than his unusual hairstyle, he looks like Mr. Everyman. He's extremely polite and even calls me ma'am—though at only fifteen years older than he, I'm not exactly his senior. I tell him that I'm just Alice, and he never calls me ma'am again.

We have a pleasant and relaxed—at least for me—lunch. Mike thanks me profusely for this business opportunity. I think he has no idea how burned-out and grateful I am that he's decided to invest himself in Vulcan.

I fly down to L.A. to introduce Mike to my customers and explain that he'll take good care of their needs just as I have. *Do they suspect*

I'm silently hoping that'll be true? With one of my favorite customers, a lady with whom I've enjoyed many an intimate lunch, I'm surprised to feel a lump in my throat and a catch in my voice. With most customers, lunches are like rewards to me, even though I pay for them. I'll miss these friends, yet I know our bonds aren't great enough to overcome the 350 miles between us.

At the end of the day, Mike insists that he doesn't need to be introduced to any more of my customers. I'm impressed with his take-charge attitude.

Now that I'm home, I feel a significant portion of my burden has been lifted. Time to do some dirty work; i.e., negotiate wire prices. *Ugh!* I've always hated bargaining, whether over some cheap item in Mexico or twenty-ton truckloads of wire. I need to call Pennsylvania and persuade them that I'm worthy of a better price now than before; after all, with World's demise my buying clout increased overnight.

Proud of the cost reductions I get Pennsylvania to agree to, I hang up. Because Vulcan's sales commission is based on gross profit—not on sales, as World's were—I call Mike to notify him. I expect him to congratulate me.

"You *what?*" he exclaims, his irritation evident. "That's *my* job!"

His job? That's news to me. "I had no idea you expected to negotiate purchase prices for me," I say calmly.

"Of course, I should. You want me to eventually run Vulcan, don't you?"

"Well, yes."

"Then let me do it!" he says in a louder voice than I've ever heard from him.

I have no memory of ever having experienced happiness when someone became annoyed with me—but in this case, I'm delighted to be the target of Mike's anger. "Okay," I say. "If you really want to, you've got the job." Not a lazy bone in *his* body—he's a real work-horse. *I love this guy!* I think I'd have loved him even if he'd called me an ugly name. I see a light at the end of my hellish tunnel: the approach of freedom. With glee, I call all my wire suppliers to explain this turn of events. After I talk to the last vendor, I do a happy dance.

Now that Mike's been with us for six months, I like him more than ever. As far as sales and negotiations go, he's Wonder Man, and he's a genius at networking—my primary weakness. He has a lot to learn about the overall finances—my greatest strength, but he won't be fully in charge for fourteen and a half more years, so I won't worry about that now. Between him and Annie, I can in good conscience semi-retire and travel.

Without Michael's Kaiser income, however, my retirement won't be possible unless we rid ourselves of our jumbo mortgage and move to a less expensive home. Then Michael could retire, *and* we could travel frequently.

We begin house shopping beyond the expensive Bay Area and decide it's worth a try to see if we can garner enough money by selling our house.

CHAPTER 46
LOVING LIFE

As we look ahead into the next century,
leaders will be those who empower others.
—Bill Gates, founder of Microsoft Corp.

Our ranchette is in escrow, so we've secured a cheap rental near Jeanette's Fairfax home. Her baby is due in late September. I've been invited to attend the birth, and afterward will make daily treks to her home for the baby's first six weeks. Jeanette and her husband, Kieran, chose not to be informed of the baby's sex because they want to be surprised.

For the past several months, I've enjoyed accompanying Michael on his out-of-town business trips. This Hawaii one is a real plus. I still keep busy with Vulcan projects, but not unduly so, and I accomplish enough with my handy laptop computer. Our two weeks in Oahu were marvelous; now we've unpacked for a two-week stay in Maui. We've hardly finished putting away our things when Julie calls to say Jeanette is en route to the hospital. *Yikes!* It's a month before she's due, and I'm 2,000 miles away. I phone the airport while Michael throws my belongings into my suitcase. Forty-five minutes later, I run to a plane with the pilot waiting.

When I land at LAX I'm informed that my flight to San Francisco has been changed and I'll have to wait four hours. I begin to hyperventilate, and screech, "My daughter's having a baby. I need to be there. Do something, please."

A good-looking young black man comes over and insists I take some deep breaths before I explain my situation. He's very compassionate, and I calm down as he escorts me here and there; he even butts into a long line to talk to an attendant. He locates my luggage and leads me to the moving line at the terminal. I choke up as I thank this angel.

Now on the plane, I hope the baby hasn't been born yet. I've so looked forward to this birth. I'm relieved that my luggage is handed to me as I disembark. I find my car and simultaneously curse and plead with every slow driver and every red light. At the hospital, I run out of my car, ignore the elevator, and race upstairs to the maternity ward. I'm given a couple of potential room numbers. I run to the first and see a bloody sheet on the bed in the empty room. My heart sinks. Am I too late?

I feel a burst of optimism. Maybe this is the wrong room. I run to the other one—and Jeanette and Kieran greet me. She hasn't yet given birth but is in her last stages of labor. Kieran hands me a video camera and instructs, "No crotch shots." The parents-to-be are big-eyed and gaze at each other lovingly. They seem to be in awe about the miracle soon to erupt. I zoom in on their faces, which are full of amazement. I'm happy that when this baby is older he or she will be able to see Mommy and Daddy's wonderment.

Minutes later, the doctor comes in and says, "Let's get ready." Soon after, the head emerges. Seconds later I whoop, "It's a boy!"

Mike's nine months with Vulcan produces a windfall: We all receive bonuses and get our higher wages reinstated and then some. To our embarrassed hero, we sing, *For He's a Jolly Good Fellow.*

Our escrow closes, and with the proceeds we begin an escrow for an ocean-view home in Gualala, close to Michael's boyhood home in Point Arena. Our current home is Oakland's Marriott Hotel, so Michael can walk to his job at Kaiser. I'm busy planning our European June-through-October bicycle trip and preparing Vulcan to be *Alice-less* for half a year.

Hiring Mike proves to be the best executive decision I've ever made. I'll now readily admit that he wasn't speaking balderdash when he repeatedly stated, "I'm the right man for the job."

Due to tying up loose ends with Vulcan, I've been on a bike for less than two hours during the last two months; swimming has been my only regular exercise. I'm annoyed that Michael, who's in great bicycle shape, got an international driver's license for our trip, thinking that I might not be physically able to bike for the following half year. There's no way I'll be trapped inside a car for a good part of six months! If I were ever told I'd be healthy for one week and then drop dead, I'd rather own a $100 bike than a $100,000 automobile. I'm determined that Michael won't get one second to use that damnable driver's license.

Our first half-day is easy enough as we ease out of Heidelberg. We bike alongside the Necker River till dusk. My stamina isn't challenged till today, our fourth day, when our river route veers into unpopulated high hills. I find the steep climbs grueling. It's dinnertime, and I'm famished, exhausted, and sore.

Ahead of me, Michael casually pumps away as I struggle with every downward pedal, my face contorted with pain. A truck passes, and the driver gives me a look of sympathy. Then he gives Michael a dirty look. I'll bet he thinks Michael has dragged a reluctant me on this extreme climb. I'm reminded of when, in my clumsiness, I gave myself a black eye, and wherever we went together till it healed, strangers always gave Michael disdainful looks.

I see houses and call out, "Let's stop here. I can't go any farther."

"We can't," Michael says. "We have to continue till we get to a real town, somewhere with food and lodging."

I knew that we had no camping gear or any food with us—just sixty pounds each of clothing, rain gear, and books—but I was determined.

"Somehow I'll find a way for us to eat and get overnight shelter. I *have to* eat and rest," I insist. My German comes in handy when I speak with a man in his front yard. He directs us to a guesthouse only four houses up the road.

Now that we've biked for two weeks, I'm in good shape. I had planned our route to be primarily along rivers, thinking we'd rarely deviate from horizontal pathways, but all the castles are at the apexes of the steepest hills, and of course we want to see every nearby castle. With my built-up leg muscles, I can enjoy the arduous climbs, after which I revel in coasting downhill at thirty miles an hour. I haven't felt this carefree since just before I lost Safeway.

After Germany, we have a free flight on an air force medical evacuation plane to England's RAF Mildenhall base. We visit Michael's air force buddy in Walberswick, Suffolk, and stop by the country house Michael and his family rented for four years in the early '70s.

Next a train speeds us to London, where, with our Marriott points, we luxuriate for a week at their expensive Regents Park, but forgo their costly breakfasts in favor of bicycling to eat at the nearby McDonald's. I think our bikes and attire embarrass the management, because they always whisk the bikes into an empty room. All the other hotel guests arrive in upscale cars and taxis.

I'm dismayed by London's TV coverage of the recent Protestants' Orange Order march in Northern Ireland. From early to mid-July this march resulted in great violence against Catholics: buildings, schools, homes, and vehicles were damaged; there were multiple bomb and shooting incidents; and even a couple of deaths. After all the chaos we've seen on TV, I sadly suggest we cancel our plans, but Michael insists we soldier on, since the violence is over.

We've planned Northern Ireland to be one of the highlights of our trip for two reasons: First, that's where my son-in-law, Kieran, grew up and where his parents live. Their town, Keady, is only twenty miles from where the violence occurred. Second, I want to see the Giant's Causeway, a natural seaside creation of 40,000 basalt columns that are 60 million years old; their grandeur has inspired legends.

After a brief time in Oxford and a week at a 200-year-old farmhouse on 420 acres, we train to Liverpool and then ferry to the Isle of Man. We expect tranquility, but are overwhelmed by hundreds of god-awful, noisy motorcycles there for an annual convention. Disappointed, we leave earlier than planned, and now ferry to Northern Ireland, where the Catholics and the Protestants hate each other—even to death.

We're almost there, and I'm still dubious about this part of our journey. In a quiet voice, so no one else can hear, I say, "Michael, to be on the safe side, if we're asked what our religion is, let's say we're Jewish."

He laughs. "Oh, honey, once we open our mouths, they'll know we're Yanks—and all the Irish love us Yanks, whatever religion we are."

I'm not convinced. "Well, if they ask, please say we're Jewish, okay?"

We land in Belfast and a guard asks us a few questions, none of which concerns religion. He smiles when he finds out we're from California and says, "Thanks for bringing your California sunshine with you. We're having the most beautiful summer ever."

On our fourth perfectly sunny day in Northern Ireland, we've just reached the Giant's Causeway. I'm more excited than Michael about climbing to the peak, so he stands below to take my picture.

Exhilarated, I scramble up to the summit and sit down, gaze at the beautiful Irish Sea, take a deep breath, and trumpet, "I've made it to the top of Giant's Causeway. Thank you, God. Now you may strike me dead!"

CHAPTER 47
SEVEN BASIC BUSINESS LESSONS

*I admire the courage and self-reliance it takes to
start your own business and make it succeed.*
—Martha Stewart, American retail executive
businesswoman, writer, TV personality

I didn't plan on this book being instructive, but my early readers and final editor insist that my story cover lessons in how to be an entrepreneur. Though I pride myself on making lemonade out of lemons, I must admit that I created some of those lemons. Due to these blunders, I learned how not to be an entrepreneur. I hope those of you who aspire to create a profitable business can learn from my forty-three years of positive and negative experiences. I'll present these lessons in seven categories.

Lesson One – Money Management

Most businesses fail due to poor money management, and a tight ship is needed in this respect. With my first sale, I discovered that large corporations (and most small industrial businesses) expect to pay no sooner than thirty days after the date of each invoice. With my first wire sale I got around this by begging for immediate payment, and threatened to take the goods back to my supplier if payment wasn't forthcoming. This worked only because my customer was desperate for the wire, but he was displeased and told me that he'd never again accept COD terms from me.

My second wire supplier readily gave me thirty-day terms, but he could have insisted on a credit report. Had he done so, I don't think I'd have passed. My only good credit as an unmarried woman consisted of mortgage and utility payments; additionally, while married, I had good credit records with gasoline credit cards, one $500-limit credit card, and timely car payments. In reality I was a credit risk with a low bank balance, i.e., no working capital. I appeared credible, however, with my pretense as a representative of an established company. Now, in this age of Internet transparency, the best acting job in the world wouldn't work.

A crucial monetary challenge occurs when there's an exponential increase of sales. Without good fiscal management, an apparently thriving business can implode for a couple of reasons: 1) If the entrepreneur's product is derived from purchases acquired previous to her sales, then her income from receivables won't arrive before her payables are due; and 2) even with a hypothetical bottomless pit of money to cover the payables, there may not be the resources in place to handle the paperwork in a timely manner.

From day one, however, I did one thing right, which was to invoice immediately. The earlier the invoice date and the earlier it's received the sooner it's paid. Some entrepreneurs have gone belly-up simply because they took so long to invoice that some of their customers had moved on or run out of funds.

To prevent such problems, one must acquire adequate working capital and have an efficient bookkeeping system in place. I don't recommend that you meet these challenges the way I did. For working capital I risked jail and agreed to live with a man who wasn't right for me or for my daughters. Regarding an efficient monetary system, I didn't overcome my initial sloppiness until I received advice and insults from three retired old men.

One should learn and immediately apply the basic accounting principles of debits and credits. Businesses that don't immediately receive payment and don't immediately pay bills need to use the accrual system in conjunction with constant cash-flow analyses. Therefore the head of this kind of business must be acquainted with accrual versus cash accounting. Today there are excellent software programs designed for every size business. If you're good at accounting and symbolic logic or coding, perhaps you could tailor your own program, but first ask yourself whether that's a productive use of your time.

An organized system is crucial. Sneaky Sarah's parting words, "those nonessential women doing their unnecessary tasks," were prophetic. After her departure I found out that she was careless with our procedures and didn't seem to respect my assistants, who didn't convey their displeasure to me earlier because they knew I was thrilled with Sarah and her bountiful sales.

I did know, however, that Sarah and her family lived hand-to-mouth—not a good background for an entrepreneur. I wasn't shocked when I heard the industry gossip that she'd gone bankrupt. If memory serves, her venture burned out less than a year after she quit Vulcan.

Two unfortunate things sometimes happen with increasing sales, especially with exponential increases. The first misstep can occur when the business's health looks better on paper and in the computer than its cash situation. The entrepreneur might take bigger draws and allow larger expenses than what her otherwise healthy business can afford. A cash-flow analysis can prevent that—if she heeds the analysis.

The second misstep may occur when the business's overdue notes receivable aren't given sufficient attention. You need to budget time—even at the expense of decreased sales or sleep—for reminding errant customers to pay up. When your kindly reminders seem futile, extreme measures are necessary. If you finally acquire full payment, then you need to decide whether to refuse the laggard further credit or dump him for being more trouble than he was worth. One tactful way to dump a customer, rather than refuse him credit, is to raise your price to what it would be worth if you had to repeat your overdue payment collection experience.

After Mike Graffio and his former World customers came into our fold, Vulcan's overwhelmed staff became negligent in both reminder calls and credit restrictions. We celebrated his first year as profitable because on paper it was; however, due to our lax oversight, we later discovered we had a bad $22,000 debt from a bankrupt company. The result was that the year actually ended as a net loss. Fortunately, each successive year more than made up for it.

Bad debts are a fact of business life, and they're more common in a down economy. I wish you such good luck in your early years as I had, but I had it only thanks to a couple of extreme and time-intensive measures. Be aware that an apparently healthy business can surprise you with a sudden bankruptcy. That didn't happen to Vulcan early on, but nearly every mature company, even in a strong economy, experiences bad debts. At a certain growth point, you'll therefore want to budget for a bad-debt allowance. To calculate the amount, consider a percentage of your sales, the industry standard, IRS limitations, etc. Vulcan now readjusts its bad-debt allowance annually.

Inventory control is another important money-managing factor. The less inventory you can maintain without disrupting customers' satisfaction the better. You'll save money due to a reduced need for warehouse space and working capital—which may include interest on borrowed money. The downside to low-inventory purchases, even if enough to keep your customers satisfied, is that you'll lack buying clout, which means the greater the quantity you purchase the lower your unit price (including delivery cost) will be. Here's where the rich get richer because the greater volume of sales justifies a greater volume of inventory purchases.

Bankers will appreciate your business if it's profitable, if you've done everything right for three years or more, and you average a four-figure bank balance or greater. If you average a five-figure balance, bankers will fight for your business, in hopes that you'll not only maintain that sizeable bank balance but will also need to borrow money for larger inventory purchases, new equipment, or new buildings.

Bankers will lose interest, however, if you can't supply the business information they require: An up-to-date list of your accounts receivable, accounts payable, and inventory list. Regarding both your business and personal information, they'll expect balance sheets, income statements, the last three months of bank statements, and the last three years of tax returns, including W-2s and K-1s (only if pertinent to you). They can require the same information of your spouse.

If you buy a building with a mortgage through your bank, the bank will hold you hostage to keep your account with them. They do that by charging a penalty if you pay off your mortgage too soon. When there's wiggle room at certain intervals, those intervals might not coincide with the time when it would otherwise be advantageous to switch banks. That means you're no longer in the driver's seat when you want to negotiate a good interest rate for loans of working capital. Other banks will vie for your business and offer you a better rate, but you'll be stuck. Fortunately, your current bank won't charge you exorbitant interest; their rate just won't be as good as you could otherwise get.

Lesson Two – Product Knowledge

When I discovered that companies needed wire, my first sale was a bust due to lack of product knowledge. If my customer hadn't scrapped that faulty wire and instead demanded his money back, I'm not sure Vulcan Wire would exist today. Perhaps I should believe in a loving guardian angel.

Don't count on getting away with ignorance as I did. Develop thorough knowledge of your product's specifications, which companies manufacture it (worldwide knowledge is needed now), what their prices are for what quantities, how negotiable the prices are, and which companies have the better and lesser qualities, delivery times, and other quantitative factors. Also keep abreast of your competition and any improvements within your industry.

Keep your eyes and ears open to the inner- and inter-company politics, as well as to worldwide politics, because a change in a company's or a country's leadership can make huge changes that might affect your business. Never think you know it all! There might come a day when there's a severe market disruption, or worse, when your product is widely sold at less than your cost or becomes obsolete because of an improvement, fad, or new technology.

Lesson Three – Marketing

All marketing is communication, whether you knock on doors, telephone, use Internet tools, write articles, pay for advertisements, or attend conventions and seminars. You should speak and write well, look good, display appropriate body language, and dress suitably. Today you're expected to have a website too. It's inexpensive to develop one, and with research, you can create a dynamic web presence.

The best invention in the world won't sell if people aren't aware of it. Before the computer age, a near-penniless entrepreneur such as I was had only herself to rely on. Unfortunately, one-person endeavors usually can't afford to pay for radio, TV, or print coverage, but some clever beginning entrepreneurs learn how to attract free media attention. Steven Van Yoder's book, *How to Get Slightly Famous,* gives excellent strategies and examples of how. Van Yoder also explains that these strategies should be continuously repeated, as potential customers often need repetition before they'll actually shell out money for a product.

In addition to you, your product needs to be packaged attractively. Your logo, website, and brochures should be professional and eye-catching. If your product could never win a beauty contest, as Vulcan's wire couldn't, then be sure it's perfectly clean and neat. If it's packaged, have your well-printed logo on the container. You can make an exception if you sell to distributors who don't want to advertise any company other than their own; however, Vulcan's boxed wire does boast, in big red letters, MADE IN AMERICA.

Scout out your customer base, specifically the people with authority to purchase products. Decide on the most effective way to persuade them that they need *your* product. If you're up against competition, be able to succinctly explain the advantages of buying your product rather than the other brands.

Try to find out whether your wannabe customer expects to be wined and dined for a deal to happen. Once you gain a customer, calculate how often you should visit and perhaps fete him or her, whether annual or more frequent gifts are in order, and the appropriate expenditure for such presents.

Keep in mind that some firms have restrictions regarding dining out and gifts. One lady's boss set up a new rule that employees couldn't accept lunches out, She and I already had a pleasant history of quarterly lunches, but after that I began to take her and her husband to dinner.

Lesson Four – Perseverance

Busier than ever these days, people might find your desire to talk to them an intrusion, especially if they've never heard of you. Be prepared for rejection. When someone is curt, it might be that he or she is overly busy or has simply had a bad day. If you're shy, do whatever it takes to overcome that disadvantage. I was fearful during my first sales pitches.

The people in Modesto always lifted my spirits. Often, shortly after I felt burned out from rejection, I visited my friendly contacts there to soak up their warmth, which gave me the strength to get back into the fight. Figure out a way to renew your energy.

Never take no for an answer, unless you get a damn good reason for that no. If I'd accepted it from the inflexible bank clerk and not reached over her head to the manager, I couldn't have run Vulcan efficiently and effectively. If I'd accepted every potential customer's no, Vulcan wouldn't have grown as quickly as it did. Be prepared not only with the energy to persist but with damn good arguments why you and your product should be well received.

Theresa, with her thirty-one years of selling, is now a more experienced salesperson than I. She always considered a prospective customer's refusal a good reason if they said they didn't want to switch to Vulcan because of loyalty to their current supplier. Theresa honored that answer, and told them. "I have loyal customers myself." Then she added, "I'd just like you to keep me in mind." Theresa felt her response gained respect and appreciation, because after a year or two of repeated visits, a good number of these prospects switched and became loyal Vulcan customers.

Remember the old saying "The squeaky wheel gets the grease." Squeak just short of being more trouble than you're worth. This also applies to slow-paying customers and slow-to-produce suppliers. I admit that when I burst into my customer's boardroom, I became more trouble than I was worth to him; however, his dropping me down the stairs harmed his reputation and enhanced mine. Please don't count on your getting away with a similar action, but if you do, I wish you well and would love to hear about it.

I had another difficult customer. He didn't heed my numerous telephoned collection requests, so I drove 150 miles to his business in Fresno with my two little girls. I told him that if I didn't receive immediate payment, the three of us would return the next day with the *60 Minutes* crew. The bluff worked. I was lucky.

The biggest test of my perseverance was during the first five years after we lost the Safeway account, followed by the loss of other valuable businesses. On top of our already diminishing customer list, we had to narrow our profit margins to keep other customers. I worked harder than ever as I cursed my predatory competitor. My staff's paychecks and my own were lower, and consequently our morale was down.

I began again to enjoy the fruits of my labors the day my competitor declared bankruptcy. I acquired their best salesman, who brought his former employer's accounts to Vulcan, later transformed Vulcan into a manufacturer, and reacquired the Safeway account. I'm happy to say that we now have more than ten times the customer base Vulcan had in 1997, so another loss such as that of Safeway wouldn't be catastrophic.

Lesson Five – Integrity

For long-term success you need a reputation as a principled person. In business that means you make no false claims or promises, because your word is your badge of honor. You pay all your bills on time, respond quickly to complaints, never take undue advantage of anyone, respect those above and below yourself, and heed the rules.

When my company was twenty-two years old, I was ready to step aside and let another person lead it. Mike Graffio, who had never met me but knew much about my character, became that person. I'd never met him either, but had heard of his good standing in our industry. Due to both our stellar reputations, we trusted each other enough to sign and fax our agreement sight unseen.

Lesson Six – Delegation

By now you might be ready to delegate. Every productive employee you hire makes your business more secure should you become ill or debilitated. Hopefully, delegation will also allow you to take well-deserved vacations and enjoy the holidays.

To delegate effectively you must be organized enough to make it clear what jobs your assistant must perform. You mustn't hover too closely, but you mustn't leave your assistant to his or her own devices before he or she learns the ropes.

It's fine to pay at least an average wage for the job, but it's preferable to pay over the average. With first hires, however, it's typical that you can afford only a below-market wage, in which case your new employee may be substandard unless he or she is a smart student intern or merely a student whose school hours you must accommodate or a friend or relative helping you out.

Half a year after my first wire sale, I hired a girlfriend who did me a favor by working at minimum wage. She was a godsend till I needed her more than ever during the holiday season. Then she cut her hours. The disadvantage of having a friend or relative work for you as a favor is that the job isn't as important to him or her as to a person who needs the money and can't earn more elsewhere.

Another disadvantage of having friends or relatives work for you is that it might strain the relationship. In 1981, when my dear father left his Southern California home to get Vulcan set up on computer, he wanted no more than free room and board. He became frustrated with me for not heeding his advice to tell my ambitious saleslady to stop selling so much—because the computer couldn't keep up with her—and insisting that my employees prioritize completing our Christmas cards over and above our data input.

My personal cost was that our formerly near-perfect relationship suffered and never reached that status again. My father mistakenly thought I devalued his hard work, which was much more challenging in those days when computers weren't as user-friendly as now. Also, he may have expected me to be a more dutiful and obedient daughter. A friend or relative, especially an elder, might be unable to accept your authority.

I replaced my dear girlfriend with a part-time high school girl for just over minimum wage. After her departure I hired another. Vulcan then graduated by adding two mature and somewhat experienced women who were also part-time hires. These women became valuable employees and increased their hours to full time when their children grew older.

I next delegated sales territory to a relatively inexperienced young woman who was a born salesperson. She quit and was succeeded by a couple of other women before I promoted Theresa to sales. In the meantime, my part-time high-school girl left, and a full-time office manager replaced her. This wonderful take-charge lady resigned fifteen months later, leaving our office systems more efficient than ever.

I then learned an ugly lesson: Investigate the merits of an employment agency before you use it. I hired a second office manager through one agency. After this person caused my other employees and me great grief, I concluded that the agency had given her the answers to the written test I devised. I found that she was both incompetent and dishonest. After I fired her, she sued Vulcan for "unpaid wages," which she and I and all my other employees knew was a scam.

I discovered that the California authorities gave the benefit of the doubt to the "smaller guy" versus a corporation, adding insult to my injury. Keep in mind that California will favor the employee in an unprovable "he-said, she-said" case. Lesson learned: get a time clock.

This state of affairs was costly in both time and money. I requested, but was denied, reimbursement from the agency. They offered to send me another person, but I didn't trust this business and chose not to risk being saddled with another troublemaker.

The awful situation made me leery of employment agencies and outsiders. One of my two mature women was an A+ bookkeeper, but I was dubious about her managerial ability. She was timorous, and I foolishly hoped she could develop leadership. Wrong! I so missed my first office manager's take-charge ways. My diffident office manager corrected employee errors without telling them, perhaps because she feared hurting their feelings or thought they'd consider her a nag. I couldn't bounce ideas off her because she was complaisant. A year and a half after her promotion, my A+ bookkeeper but D– office manager left Vulcan for another job.

My mistake was to think that I could change that lovely lady's nature. Be sure you don't promote a person to the level of his or her Peter Principle, because you may lose an excellent employee. On the other hand, beware of employees who overestimate their worth and abilities, and become bitter when you promote another to their coveted positions.

Three years later, an employment agency was again used, not by me but under the direction of my fourth (and highly assertive) office manager. She favored agencies that gave us temporary workers for an hourly fee and after ninety days allowed us to hire the worker directly, with no additional remuneration to the agency. Her best deal was when she hired Theresa, who initially filled a clerical slot but has since become our stalwart employee of thirty-two years.

For a managerial position, employment agencies generally want a finder's fee. Vulcan hasn't made that sort of agreement since my negative experience of thirty-five years ago. I assume that it's now safer to hire an employee from an agency that charges a sizeable finder's fee, because an unscrupulous agency wouldn't last long due to Internet transparency.

Twenty-six years ago, Vulcan moved to Hayward and rented a combination of office space and warehouse space, which necessitated acquiring a forklift. I'm an ignoramus regarding machines, so I paid $100 to the owner and manager of Vulcan's former warehouse to find us a used forklift and arrange delivery. Over the years, more forklifts were needed, but by then we had warehousemen with forklift-driver certificates who were good judges of these vehicles and able to maintain them.

If your time is valuable in what you know and do best, avoid doing work that another can do for less remuneration than the profits you can bring into your company. Also, don't take the time to struggle to learn what you don't know. I realize, however, that that shouldn't be a blanket rule, because some things will be ongoing that you have a proclivity for and should learn. In one instance, I took a two-day class to learn Lotus 1-2-3. The result was a program I developed to predict when a customer would need more product. The knowledge led to higher efficiency regarding our inventory orders and when to remind the customer that it was reorder time. Later I used this programming skill to simplify corporate income tax planning, stock calculations, and even my personal investments.

Burned out after five years of a predatory competitor's onslaught, I desperately wanted early retirement, or at least semiretirement, so I could travel extensively. I was fortunate to be able to do this at age fifty-six, when my husband and I went on a four-month bike trip in Europe and then began to live three hours north of the Bay Area in the small town of Gualala. This lifelong dream would have been impossible without adequate delegation—this time to the man who's now president and CEO of Vulcan.

Don't think you can't be replaced, but you're right if you don't know how to delegate and choose the right people, even if it takes more than one to replace yourself. Mike couldn't replace my financial savvy, but he more than made up for that with his superb selling, networking, negotiating, and management skills. Four years ago, he'd grown Vulcan to the point that it could pay someone with the ability to replace me as CFO.

So, in your sunset years, dear entrepreneur, remember how I've gradually exited. I'm still employed, but my hours are quite limited. If you're to receive remuneration from the business you founded, you should keep a minimal amount of stock* and try to remain on the board. If you feel too weary, then delegate one of your children or grandchildren or your legal guardian to sit on the board—or at least to study the quarterly financials.

*I suggest you eventually keep less than 20 percent of the stock; otherwise you'll find yourself pestered to gather financial information for the bankers annually or perhaps every other year. Once you maintain only 19 percent, your personal assets cannot be attached for a percentage of your firm's unpaid debts should the corporation collapse; however, you need to maintain a minimal amount of stock for legal access to your corporation's financials. In the event of corporate collapse, if you can prove fiscal irresponsibility on the part of other stockholder(s) who own 20 percent or more, you can legally sue them.

Lesson Seven – Adaptation

My main proactive adaptation was the switch from manual book-keeping to computer software programs—thanks to the help of my brilliant father. I was reactive when I adapted from a bedroom to an attic space, then to nice offices, and finally to a combined office and warehouse.

My secondary proactive move was to attend a seminar in 1982 that taught me to make an organization chart with twenty-four boxes, even though there were only five of us. I was in nine of the boxes. Now, thirty-six years later, I'm in only one box of thirty-three, a box that wasn't in my chart till I began to issue stock in 2000. Over those thirty-six years I gradually removed myself from every box I was originally in. This chart was a tremendous help for delegating.

I must give Mike accolades for being proactive when he did what I should have done years ago: He converted Vulcan from being a mere distributor of wire to become a manufacturer. I had a great fear of the unknown, namely bale-tie machines and blue-collar workers. If I had developed a bale-tie factory, then Vulcan wouldn't have suffered as much during that horrible five-year period.

May you be a braver person than I was. Here's to your success!

REFLECTIONS

One day your life will flash before your eyes.
Make sure it is worth watching.

—Unknown

Loud body-penetrating noises deafen me as Mike escorts me into our newly remodeled building. Machines that until now I didn't know existed add to the clamor of the bale-tie and wire-spooling ones. Chills run over my body. *I started all this, and I don't know shit about machines!*

Today is Vulcan's Christmas party. First, Mike informs everyone about the additional money they'll find in their checking accounts—a larger than ever Christmas bonus and a six-month-retroactive cost of living (COLA) increase. Some exemplary employees also get merit raises on top of the rest. It's a joy to witness all the happy smiles. Also, per my contract, I tender more of my Vulcan stock today, all of which Mike and I transfer to our four deserving high-profile employees, one of whom is Theresa, who returned full-time to Vulcan in 1999.

February 1, 2017, was Mike's twenty-year anniversary with Vulcan. He has so much to show for it, including whopping sales and profits, and significant purchases: two buildings; another business now called Vulcan Packaging; machines to make our bale ties and spooled wire; a wire-welding machine; a wire-chopping machine for better disposal of scrap wire; tools for our machine-repair area, and a repairman. Now, in 2018, we continue to expand.

Mike became Vulcan's president, CEO, and 51 percent owner in 2012. Even though he previously acted like an owner and performed many presidential duties, both he and I felt more powerful when his ultimate leadership became official—him for obvious reasons, and for me, shedding that yoke of responsibility allowed me to stand taller and breathe easier. I was thrilled to have that thirty-seven-year-old weight off my back.

Of course, if I hadn't felt confident about Mike's competence, I wouldn't have experienced those positive emotions, but after I relinquished the reins—thanks to him and my contract, which allots me a comfortable income (COLA adjusted) up to age 110—my paychecks have only grown. Technically, I have no mandatory work responsibilities. Nonetheless, I'd have been irresponsible had I not continued to fulfill most of my previous fiscal duties till 2014. Then, thanks to Theresa's niece, Deena, a very bright young woman, I was able to resign from my CFO position and delegate it to her—but I still enjoy being a board member and Vice President of Stock, and I try to attend as many Vulcan Christmas parties as possible.

I'm thankful God didn't take me literally and strike me dead at the Giant's Causeway. For most of the days since 1998, I've felt on top of the world; I have, however, had two deep downs in those twenty years.

In 2007 I lost my little brother to colon cancer. He was only sixty-one. I'm thankful that I could spend time with him for a good part of his last days, but for months before and after his death, grief gave me a recurring pain in my chest. Even now I can't stop feeling survivor's guilt, because Robby's lifestyle was just as healthy as mine.

In 2014 I lost my father. He was a healthy ninety-eight and a half when he had a freak accident. Before that, we all counted on celebrating his hundredth birthday. Daddy walked well with his cane, drove, did research on his computer, and was a heck of a good bridge player. In fact, the accident happened in the Anaheim Senior Center, where he was supposed to substitute for another card player. He walked too quickly and tripped on a rug, then bounced against a cement bench and broke his neck. He was legally dead before the paramedics revived him to a comatose state. Hours later, he became lucid for a day, then slipped back into a coma before his organs and brain began to shut down. Ultimately, his third wife, my daughters, and I all sadly agreed to pull the plug.

At least Daddy's senior years were full. After he computerized Vulcan, he became the oldest member of a computer club whose other members were a generation or two younger than he. Also, he helped seniors at senior centers learn how to operate their computers; led the Senior Center Volunteer Free Tax Service, and even gave free tax-program assistance to the IRS. He square danced until he had a temporarily debilitating accident at age ninety-three; and after Mommy died, he dated, married wife number two, and after *she* died he dated again till he married wife number three. We called him the Energizer Bunny.

My little Baby Herbie should now have celebrated his forty-eighth birthday. Long ago I found out that his horrid mother once again abandoned him and his younger sister. After a year had passed, she couldn't legally claim her children, which made them eligible for adoption. Rumor has it that a well-off couple in the San Fernando Valley became their new parents. Years later, their biological father, Fritz's brother, committed suicide. I want to believe that the siblings thrived in their new environment.

My daughters live luxurious lives with loving and supportive husbands, and enjoy their smart kids, ages fifteen to twenty-one (all on college tracks), gorgeous homes, and overseas travels. Fritz has turned out to be as great an ex-husband as I could have possibly hoped for.

On my right hand I still wear my Black Hills gold ring, the first unnecessary extravagance after my separation from Fritz. It's a daily reminder that early frugality and continual hard work has served me well. The sparkling wedding ring set on my left hand reminds me of Michael's generosity and the fact that he treasures me.

Michael and I are more happily married than ever. His mother died at age fifty-two, having pickled her liver with alcohol. Now Michael thanks me for saving his life. We've traveled to all seven continents and take turns choosing a location anywhere in the world for an annual one-month trip. In 2016 I chose Cuba, and we treated Jeanette and Julie's families (including my five grandchildren and two sons-in-law) to the trip as well. For 2017 Michael chose a Baja, California, whale-watching cruise on a National Geographic ship. This year I chose Japan.

But there is no place better than our Gualala home in the redwoods. During most of the year we enjoy lunches on our deck while we gaze at the beautiful Pacific Ocean below. One of us invariably sighs, smiles, and says to the other, "It's a wonderful life. Somebody's gotta live it. It might as well be us."

ACKNOWLEDGMENTS

First, thanks to my friend Francoise Kemp. Francoise led me to my dear friend, writing teacher, consultant, and early editor Ida Rae Egli who helped my writing advance from preschool to college-graduate level. My husband, Michael, patiently endured reading and critiquing innumerable drafts. Early readers also included my childhood friends Patty Reidy and Carolyn Wood; community friends Zdena Price (who taught me to think outside the box) and Linda Lambert; and Vulcan friends Steve Brandt, Mike Graffio, and Theresa Rodriquez.

Dear Paula Gordon edited my junior-high-like drafts; next in line came professional editors Ida Egli, Carol Gaskin, April Eberhardt, Krissa Lagos, and Joe Shaw, final editor, who offered fresh ideas and wise counsel. I value the friendship and diligence of proofreaders Mary Alice Bastion, Joel Crockett, Roz Hopenfeld, and Carolyn Wood.

I received invaluable help from four sessions of the Redwood Writers' Conventions and the gifted Lewis Buzbee, Charlotte Gullick, Jessica Sinsheimer, Shirin Bridges, and Elizabeth Rosner, and am grateful to Norma Watkins for guiding me to Cypress House.

I'm delighted with the book cover, for which thanks go to my excellent photographer spouse, the wonderful Facebook friends who voted on the best photo option, and brilliant artist Kiersten Hanna.

Thanks to the entire Cypress House team, led by the patient and whip-smart Cynthia Frank, who orchestrated wrapping up this book with a lovely bow and recommended the savvy Linda Pack's suggestion for the subtitle. I owe the main title to receiving that moniker from those rough-and-ready garbagemen of the '70s.

My home is my castle, but others maintain it: I treasure Mary Thomas' housecleaning, sewing, errand running, delivered homecooked meals, and enthusiastic support. Beyond the windows I gaze through between paragraphs, I relish the blooming greenery kept healthy and gorgeous by green-thumb gardener and fellow plant-lover friend Kathy Bienhoff.

I appreciate the interest and encouragement of my high-school newspaper movie critic and promising-writer grandson Daniel Mone.

Above all, without my darling husband's hugs, dancing and singing entertainment, and loving dedication, this book, as it is, wouldn't exist.

ENDNOTES

[1] Mervyn's was a department store chain founded in 1949 that closed in 2008. In 2004 it had over 200 stores in ten states (Wikipedia).

[2] $5,000 in 1978 is equivalent to $19,639 in 2019 (www.usinflationcalculator.com).

[3] $2.70/hr. in 1974 is equivalent to $14.03 in 2019 per US Inflation Calculator (ww.usinflationcalculator.com).

[4] $2.00 in 1974 was both the federal and California minimum wage (U.S. Dept. of Labor and California Dept. of Industrial Relations).

[5] The OSHA ruling was signed into law 12/29/1970 and effective 8/27/1971 (Osha.gov/history/OSHA_HISTORY).

[6] A New OSHA Assault by Robert W. Lee quoting Senator Clifford Hansen (R-WY) on 6/19/73 (*The New American* 12/28/92).

[7] A New OSHA Assault by Robert W. Lee stating "Congress authorized OSHA compliance officers to conduct searches without warrants or convincing probable cause," and replicating co-author of the OSHA Act, Representative (R-I) William Steiger's declaration in the Congressional Record for January 6, 1977, "Warrantless civil inspections are…absolutely essential to this act's enforcement…" & notation that 5/23/78 U.S. Supreme Court ruling that OSHA's warrantless searches were indeed unconstitutional (*The New American* 12/28/92).

8   In 1975 dollars, $40,000 is equivalent to $190,403 on 2019, per US Inflation Calculator (www.usinflationcalculator.com).

9   Valley State College then was short for San Fernando Valley State College, which in 1972 was renamed California State University, Northridge (Wikipedia).

10   E.H. Edwards Wire Rope was a wire manufacturer from 1916 to 1981 (Wikipedia).

11   Daisy Mae was a blonde cartoon character, the hillbilly Li'l Abner's glamorous girlfriend and eventual wife. The comic strip *Li'l Abner* ran for forty-three years, 1934–1977 (Wikipedia).

12   The Civil Rights Act of 1964 (7/2/64) outlawed discrimination based on race, color, religion, sex, or national origin (Wikipedia).

13   In 1962 dollars, $99 is equivalent to $840 in 2019, per US Inflation Calculator (www.inflationcalculator.com).

14   Today's Recology San Francisco was formerly called Sanitary Landfill Company (recology.com/index.php/recology-history#a-firm-foundation). In 1977 Sanitary Landfill Company was an affiliation of two garbage companies, Golden Gate Disposal and Sunset Scavenger—of which Bayshore Salvage was its recycling division (my memory).

15   By the 1990s, most Italian former senior shareholders had sold out to corporate conglomerates due to the various 1973–84 anti-nepotism legal changes. These included: 1) Out-of-court agreements for affirmative action favoring blacks and Hispanics; 2) U.S. Supreme Court rulings; and 3) A denial of a former ruling review (my observations).

16   What Angelo and I called the pit was the largest garbage transfer station in the world—at least as of 1970 (*GARBAGE,* by Leonard Stefanelli, p. 141).

17   Lenny, formally called Leonard Stefanelli, was the president of Sunset Scavenger from 1965 until leaving in1986. Due to his innovations he

gained an international presence. Later from 2004 to 2012 he was a consultant for the same but expanded and twice renamed company called Norcal and then Recology (*GARBAGE,* by Leonard Stefanelli, pp. 160–181 and 237–239).

18   The Emporium department store on Market Street, San Francisco, was founded in 1896 and operated on and off through 1995. In 2006 it reopened as Westfield San Francisco Centre, featuring a Bloomingdale's department store, a nine-theatre Century Theatres multiplex, and a Bristol Farms specialty foods store (Wikipedia).

19   The Federal Reserve Bank on Sansome Street, San Francisco, was one of the many Federal Reserve Bank locations that shredded more than 5,000 tons of damaged currency annually (FRBSF.org). In 1983 it was relocated to Market Street, San Francisco (Wikipedia).

20    $500 in 1977 is equivalent to $2,113 in 2019 per US Calculator (www.usinflationcalculator.com).

21   The Olympic Club in San Francisco was established in 1860 and closed to women until 1990 (Wikipedia).

22   R.O.C.C. stands for Royal Order of California Can Carriers, meaning garbage men who are either owners, stockholders, or in upper management of the California garbage companies. Associate members were vendors and lobbyists. After the small-business owners could no longer fight the anti-nepotism 12/28/87 U.S. Supreme Court ruling (Martinez v. Oakland Scavenger Co.), they sold out to large corporations. The R.O.C.C. disbanded in the '90s (my memory).

23   Hollywood and Vine area, Hollywood, California: In the '60s it fell into disrepair and disrepute, with many abandoned stores and offices, and visitors looking for Hollywood dreams were often taken aback by the streets themselves, claimed by squatters and panhandlers, a contrast with shinier tourist meccas. It took several decades for redevelopment to take hold (Wikipedia).

24   John T. Molloy wrote the 1977 bestseller *The Women's Dress for Success Book,* based on extensive research. He popularized the concept of "power

dressing." In 1996 he wrote an updated version, *New Women's Dress for Success.*

25   Edith Bunker was the costar of *All in the Family*, an American sitcom broadcast on CBS from 1971 through 1979. She was sweet and understanding and endured her husband, Archie's, insults, which included calling her "dingbat" (Wikipedia).

26   EST is Erhard Seminars Training, founded and run by Werner Erhard between 1971 and 1984, during which time enrollees totaled 700,000.

27   Theresa is now Vulcan's third largest shareholder, and second to me, our most senior employee.

28   In 1987 dollars, $1,500 equals $3,328 in 2019, per US Inflation Calculator (www. usinflationcalculator.com).

29   Dan Vickery later became famous as the lead guitar of the Counting Crows band, formed in 1991.

30   In 1997 dollars, $4,000 is equivalent to $6,383 in 2019, per US Inflation Calculator (www.usinflationcalculator.com).